EMBODIED RELATING

EMBODIED RELATING
The Ground of Psychotherapy

Nick Totton

Routledge
Taylor & Francis Group

LONDON AND NEW YORK

First published 2015 by Karnac Books Ltd.

Published 2018 by Routledge
2 Park Square, Milton Park, Abingdon, Oxon OX14 4RN
711 Third Avenue, New York, NY 10017, USA

Routledge is an imprint of the Taylor & Francis Group, an informa business

British Library Cataloguing in Publication Data

A C.I.P. for this book is available from the British Library

ISBN-13: 9781782202936 (pbk)

Typeset by V Publishing Solutions Pvt Ltd., Chennai, India

For my dear friend and collaborator
Allison Priestman

A Note on Style

I have throughout used "she" and "her" as generic terms for individuals of undefined gender—even though this occasionally leaves room for misreadings of various kinds. "He", "him", and "his" have had a few thousand years of privilege, and we badly need to move on; so until a graceful neutral alternative is established, the best option is to reverse the balance.

CONTENTS

ACKNOWLEDGEMENTS

I have used several previous papers and chapters in writing this book, pulling them apart and combining bits of them with bits of each other and with new material. I list below the main places where I have used each piece, but odd paragraphs may pop up anywhere.

Being, having and becoming bodies. *Body, Movement and Dance in Psychotherapy*, 5(1), 2010: 21–30. Chapter Five.

Body psychotherapy and social theory. *Body, Movement and Dance in Psychotherapy*, 4(3), 2009: 187–200. Chapter Four.

"Each single ego": Telepathy and psychoanalysis. In: N. Totton (Ed.), *Psychoanalysis and the Paranormal: Lands of Darkness* (pp. 187–208). London: Karnac, 2003. Chapters Four, Eight, and Twelve.

Embodied relating. *International Body Psychotherapy Journal*, 13(2), 2014: 88–103. Introduction, Chapters One, Two, Three, Eight, and Nine.

Embodiment and relationship: Two halves of one whole (co-written with Allison Priestman). In: C. Young (Ed.), *About Relational Body Psychotherapy*. Stow, Galashiels, UK: Galashiels Publications, 2012; 35–68. Chapters One, Two, Three, and Eleven.

Embodiment and the social bond. In: K. White (Ed.), *Talking Bodies: How Do We Integrate Working with the Body in Psychotherapy from an*

Attachment and Relational Perspective (pp. 41–64). London: Karnac, 2014. Chapters One, Two, Three, and Twelve.

Foreign bodies: Recovering the history of body psychotherapy. In: T. Staunton (Ed.), *Body Psychotherapy* (pp. 7–26). London: Brunner-Routledge, 2002. Chapter Ten.

Funny you should say that: Paranormality, at the margins and the centre of psychotherapy. *European Journal of Psychotherapy & Counselling,* 9(4), 2007: 389–401. Chapters Four, Eight, and Twelve.

I am grateful to the editors and publishers of all these publications.

ABOUT THE AUTHOR

Nick Totton is a therapist and trainer with over thirty years' experience. Originally a Reichian body therapist, his approach has become broad based and open to the spontaneous and unexpected. Nick has an MA in Psychoanalytic Studies, and has worked with Process-Oriented Psychology and trained as a craniosacral therapist. He has authored or edited fifteen books, mostly on psychotherapy-related topics, including *Body Psychotherapy: An Introduction*; *Psychotherapy and Politics*; *Press When Illuminated: New and Selected Poems*; and *Wild Therapy*.

INTRODUCTION

An opening question

How many kinds of smile are there? A loving smile. A joyful smile. A melancholy smile. A guilty smile. A beaming smile. A tolerant smile. An enquiring smile. A cruel smile. An innocent smile. A chilly smile. A cool smile. A warm smile. An absent-minded smile. A hungry smile. A tentative smile. A jolly smile. A silly smile. A quizzical smile. A triumphant smile. A vengeful smile. A rueful smile. A knowing smile. A naughty smile. A sexy smile. An enigmatic smile. The list is barely started. The category of "smile" has tremendous richness and variety, it is dense with minute and subtle but crucial differences, and there is a correspondingly vast number of words—ordinary English words—available to name these differences. We are experts on the smile without knowing it.

How much work would it take to define and distinguish each of these smiles in terms of objective measurement? And how much of a waste of time would this be, given that the most precise distinctions can usually be made in practice instantly and without analysis? Not that there would be universal agreement on any particular smile, of course: the content of a smile is co-created between the smiler and smilee, so to speak—it is *relational*, my smile is guilty or innocent, absent-minded or intimate, in relation to a particular other. And we do not actually require a reference list of adjectives to check against each particular smile. For many people some of the words may not be part of their vocabulary, for many more they will not in practice come to mind; but each person, if she is neurotypical, will still respond to the quality of a particular smile in a way which is immediate, embodied, and preverbal.

Smiles, then, are a minor example of what this book is about: embodied relating. They demonstrate very concretely that embodied relating is not an esoteric branch of neuroscience, nor an obscure psychotherapeutic theory, but something embedded in our everyday life: we can all "do" embodied relating, though some do it better than others. Like many other important aspects of life, it generally happens of its own accord, but sometimes benefits from the sort of close examination which tends to happen in therapy. However, psychotherapy has a history of keeping embodiment out of its field of awareness, and of preferring language-based relating to all other kinds—indeed, until quite recently, of downplaying here-and-now relationship altogether. All these things are now changing; and this book is intended to be part of the change.

The project

Embodied Relating is a contribution to a collective project which has been under way for some years now: that of developing *a contemporary theory of body psychotherapy*, which dialogues with other contemporary thinking and research, but at the same time asserts its own unique viewpoint through conscious, critical ownership of body psychotherapy's historical positions. A theory which, above all, is founded in lived experience. Many practitioners are involved in this effort; for me personally, the most valuable contributions have come from a group of UK practitioners including Shoshi Asheri, Roz Carroll, Asaf Rolef Ben-Shahar, and Michael Soth, and the training group in Embodied-Relational Therapy of which I am a member together with Allison Priestman, Jayne Johnson, Kamalamani, and Stephen Tame; also from Bill Cornell in the USA; from assimilating the work of certain neuroscientists, notably Stephen Porges, and relational psychoanalysts, notably the late Daniel Stern and the Boston Change Study Group; from the phenomenology of Maurice Merleau-Ponty and the systemic approach of Gregory Bateson; and, of course, from the extraordinarily rich foundational work of Wilhelm Reich, where after over thirty years of reading I continue to find new insights.

Where *Embodied Relating* perhaps enters new territory is in more or less dropping body psychotherapy's long-standing effort to learn from verbal psychotherapy. I suggest that the pay-off from this effort is now exhausted. We body psychotherapists have learnt enough—in some cases, rather too much—and might now usefully focus on *teaching*: teaching verbal therapists that embodiment is central to what they, as well as we, are trying to do.

I hope that among other uses this is a book which body psychotherapists, especially relationally oriented ones, can pass on to their uninformed or sceptical verbal colleagues; and which they can also use to strengthen their own grounding in an updated and revivified version of the core positions of body psychotherapy. So I am speaking in two directions simultaneously, to verbal practitioners and to body-centred ones; which means that at particular moments one group may be struggling to assimilate what I am saying, while the other group may be tapping their fingers and waiting for something interesting. I hope they don't have to wait too long.

I am of course not the first person to write about this topic; and more is being written all the time. However, it seems to me that much of this material has too little commitment to the extraordinarily radical results of taking embodiment really seriously. It reminds me in a small way of negotiations around emancipating some segment of the population—women, say, or people of colour: for a considerable time the hegemonic group often still somehow believes or tries to believe that it can maintain a veto, keep ultimate control of how the newly emancipated group will behave; a transitional illusion which allows privilege gradually to be surrendered. In a parallel way, it is only when the privileging—though not of course the contribution—of the rational and the verbal is finally surrendered, that embodied relationship can be integrated into our work.

Body psychotherapy has rightly been seen to include a very wide range of techniques and phenomena. It ranges from a focus on direct, intimate physical interaction, to an approach in which bodily experience is only observed and discussed across space, as it were; from a project of adjustment and healing, to one of open-endedly following process, to one of narrative construction. There are practitioners offering bodily-inflected versions of many therapeutic modalities—psychodynamic, psychoanalytic, Gestalt, transactional analysis, Jungian, all come to mind—and others working in one or more of a multitude of submodalities which exist under the overall heading of body psychotherapy (for a survey of the field and many examples of both these groups, see Totton, 2003a).

Like most categories, body psychotherapy is best conceived as occupying a circle, with the more richly characteristic examples—"this is *definitely* body psychotherapy"—nearer the centre, and the less typical—"this is *in a way* body psychotherapy"—near the fuzzy edges, while others—"this is certainly *not* body psychotherapy"—are further away still (cf. Lakoff, 1987). However, I will argue that what is or should be at the *centre* of the circle is embodied relating. Body psychotherapy's great contribution to psychotherapy as a whole is its profound sense of how embodied intersubjectivity really is, and equally, how intersubjective embodiment is—and of how a person's style of embodiment therefore defines her style of intersubjectivity, and vice versa.

In what follows I will argue and try to demonstrate that embodiment and relationship are inseparable, both in human existence and in the practice of psychotherapy. If we explore embodiment, we encounter relationship; if we explore relationship, we encounter embodiment. Therapy is more powerful when the practitioner is able to recognise the constant interplay between these two aspects of being human, and to follow and support the shifts of charge from one to the other.

Our embodiment is a relational resource. But to access this resource, and to offer ourselves relationally to our clients, we are challenged to unlearn some of our conditioning and throw off some of our domestication (Totton, 2011). The study of how our developmental environment muffles our native ability to perceive our embodiment—and therefore other people's embodiment—is a central project for therapy, both in working with specific clients and in generating a wider theory. Disconnection from our own embodiment both *protects* and *deepens* our wounds. We are disconnected from relationship because disconnected from our bodies, and vice versa. As body psychotherapists, much of the work we do on ourselves is about freeing our ability to access our current body experience and to process complex somatic states; and this in turn allows us a clearer and deeper perception of relationship.

Touching the ground

When, in the title of this book, I call embodied relating "the ground of psychotherapy", I certainly don't mean that it is the whole of psychotherapy, or even necessarily the most important aspect of it. I am intending a fairly precise claim: that it is the surface on which therapy stands (or falls), the soil in which everything grows (or fails to grow). And like the ground, embodied relating can easily be forgotten or ignored as we hurl great skyscrapers of theory into the stratosphere—theory which in the absence of embodied relating cannot inform effective practice. My claim is that *all relationship is initially between bodies*; and that the capacity to form such embodied relationship is a necessary condition for working as a psychotherapist, psychoanalyst, counsellor, or other psychopractitioner.

Many practitioners do this without realising it, as an instinctive aspect of their reaching-out to clients. But there are several reasons why a conscious awareness of how our work is grounded is helpful. As an important example, it allows us to identify and process the many situations in which relational problems between therapist and client are best understood as issues of embodiment. Like soil, embodied relating is a *medium*: "the Flesh" (Merleau-Ponty, 1968) as it manifests in human relationship. It is the medium through which we assimilate both nurturing and trauma as infants; the medium through which our patterns of creativity and defence are reproduced in the therapy room; and the medium through which, potentially, change can be generated and stuck patterns released. Equally, it is the medium through which stuck patterns can be created and maintained.

It is now widely acknowledged that the somatic response of the therapist can be important in specific situations, often seen as involving particular kinds of "somatising" clients. The theory of projective identification characterises the therapist's somatic response as the effect of an invasion or even attack on the part of the client—an invasion which can be skilfully wrestled into the form of a benign communication (Hinshelwood, 1994, pp. 119–134). I am arguing that somatic resonance is not some special state, but a constant and continuous part of relating, though often outside awareness; so that reactions which are usually experienced in other registers—as feelings, thoughts, or fantasies—are initially founded in bodily response.

The embodied therapeutic relationship is frequently treated as an interesting and somewhat exotic optional extra, relatively marginal to the core themes of verbal therapy: an additional channel through which practitioners—perhaps only unusually sensitive ones, with all the ambiguous implications of "sensitive"—can gain information about their clients' psychological processes. Correspondingly, within body psychotherapy concepts like transference, countertransference, and projection have been adopted and adapted from verbal therapy, and bolted on, often crudely, to our embodied practice.

I will try to show that we should think the other way round, and recognise embodiment as the matrix of human relating. Our theory of the therapeutic relationship needs to be remade from the ground up as a fully embodied account—not just of body psychotherapy, but of *all* psychotherapy. "Embodied countertransference", for example, is not a special subcategory of a wider phenomenon; it is the thing itself. We might more usefully call countertransference which is *not* experienced in the practitioner's body "disembodied countertransference", and ask why and how it has become dissociated. In what follows I will treat transference and countertransference as in effect *a rebranding of embodied relating*; and also argue that embodied relating implies that transference and countertransference are *always* aspects of a reciprocal pair, better conceived as a single phenomenon of reciprocal cross-transference.

Daniel Stern poses a series of questions which are very relevant to the subject of this book:

> Why did psychoanalysis develop as a "one-person psychology", i.e. as having a disproportionately large interest in the intra-psychic, at the expense of the inter-psychic? Why was the therapeutic relationship conceived of as primarily a manifestation of the illness (the "neurosis") of the patient? Why was a sharp cleavage established between talking and acting, and between verbal and non-verbal, and why was the word, the symbolic, given such a remarkably elevated and protected status? And, in the same vein, why were most movement-related therapies split off from the talking therapies for so long, and initially assigned mainly to handicapped or autistic patients as second-class treatments? These questions are all interrelated.

(2010, p. 119)

Stern's questions are, of course, all to do with embodiment and relationship. The "sharp cleavage" between body and mind parallels and reinforces that between client and therapist, and vice versa. It would, though one-sided, not be an absurd exaggeration to say that psychoanalysis came into being as a technique for keeping the body under control, taming the hysterical women who were its first patients. Although psychoanalysis was initially *all about* embodiment (Totton, 1998), since its outset it has obsessively focused on transforming embodiment into words and thoughts. The irreducible rebel element of embodiment was physical sex, and this is in large part why, for therapy, "body" came to mean exclusively "sex", and therefore to be banished from the therapy room.

Reciprocity

One theme which, when I step back, I see running through the whole of the book is reciprocity—more strongly, mutuality. Through the contributions of many disciplines, we are discovering a world where perception is not, as Western thought has always maintained, a one-way process, but a reciprocal one in which our sense impressions create the world just as the world creates our sense impressions. Cognitive science is coming to understand that "[C]ognition is not an event happening inside the system; it is the relational process of sense-making that takes place between the system and its environment" (Thompson & Stapleton, 2008, p. 26); while at the same time phenomenology is telling us that:

> Our bodies are not instruments that put us in contact with already existing determinate things, but rather that which enables things and a world, and which is equally constituted by those things and their world. ... Our bodily organizations—our organs of perception—are reflections of the things that we have been called upon to perceive; and the things as perceived are reflections of our own bodily organs. They are in us, and we in them. There is intertwining.

> (Maclaren, 2013, pp. 3–4)

And in perfect synchrony, relational psychotherapy is realising that transference and countertransference are not two things but only one thing, the two sides of a process of mutual entrainment. Entrainment is the way in which two systems come into synchrony with each other; it seems that humans do this in many ways—for example, according to Guastello, Pincus, and Gunderson (2006), if two people simply talk for twenty minutes their galvanic skin response starts to couple in complex patterns. A famous example is the way that the menstrual cycles of women who live together often begin to coincide (Dorak, 2002). On an infinitely more complex though equally embodied level, through cross-transference client and therapist silently agree to settle on a particular unique form of reciprocal misrecognition as a bridge to relationship with each other—much like two playing children saying "Now you be mummy and I'll be your baby".

The embodied ground of this interaction, however, has been lost sight of over the years, and transference/countertransference has been rebranded as a purely psychological event. This despite the fact that therapists—analysts in particular—constantly talk about their embodied experiences with particular clients, and very much assume that these are indeed *responses* to the client; after all, we do the same thing in everyday life—"He makes my skin crawl", "She's a very warm person", "They're a real headache". Christopher Bollas writes:

> Some analysands enable us to feel somatically rested and receptive, while others precipitate complex body tensions. ... This is not a peculiarity of psychoanalysis, as in all our relations with people, we somatically register our sense of a person; we "carry" their effect on our psyche-soma, and this constitutes a form of somatic knowledge.

> (1987, p. 282)

Embodied relating, in other words, is an open secret, both in therapy and in life; it is not so much denied as discounted. This is made more possible by an underlying assumption, which I will examine in Chapter Nine, that whatever is happening on an embodied level simply cannot be verbalised, so we have no choice but to pass over it in silence—"whereof one cannot speak, thereof one must be silent" (Wittgenstein, 1922, Proposition 7). I hope to demonstrate—if it needs demonstrating—that this assumption, though not Wittgenstein's axiom, is unfounded: that speaking about embodied relating is both possible and valuable.

In the following sections I say something about what I will and won't be discussing in this book.

The question of evidence

Like most other therapy modalities, body psychotherapy is currently very hung up on questions of *evidence*. It seems incumbent upon us to justify our views about good and effective practice, not by our experience of working with many clients over many years, but by some other yardstick which is taken to be more "objective". This is generally either a statistical treatment of a large group of clients who can, at a huge stretch, be regarded as all having the "same" problem and can therefore all be treated in the "same" way—ideally through randomised control trials; or else an application to the therapeutic context of findings from "hard" science, mainly neuroscience.

The quote marks in the previous paragraph represent a condensed critique of this theory of evidence, a critique which it would take up too much space to spell out in full (for treatments of these issues see House and Totton, 2011, and Postle, 2007; see also Totton, 2014). The positivist notion of objectivity which informs the statistical approach is both questionable in itself, and wholly inapplicable to psychotherapy, where meaningful definitions of effectiveness are extremely hard to come by. No two clients have identical issues, and no two courses of therapy, even with the same practitioner, go in identical directions—because no two *relationships* are identical; while the goal by which effectiveness is to be measured is often defined very differently *after* the work than *before*, by both the client and the practitioner, since new narratives and understandings have been produced within the therapy. The whole set of unanswerable questions about "what works" can in practice often be rephrased as "What is the smallest number of sessions with the cheapest practitioner that we can get away with?"

Neuroscience, however, raises more complex issues altogether: ultimately, issues about cultural hegemony, about what overarching narrative controls our culture. What I observe in current writing about both body psychotherapy and psychotherapy in general is an enormous overvaluation of the contribution that neuroscience can make to our work. This in turn stems, I think, from a massive misunderstanding of how neuroscience and psychotherapy relate to each other—which in turn rests on a misunderstanding about how brain, body, environment, and mind relate to each other. The simplistic assignation of psychological processes to brain locations can be addictive.

A good example of this problem is Alan Fogel's recent book, *Body Sense: The Science and Practice of Embodied Self-Awareness* (2009). The book contains a lot of interesting information and ideas; Fogel—both a body-oriented practitioner and a scientific researcher—starts out well, emphasising that:

> There is no omniscient nonbiased scientific observer. All scientists are human, all are shaped by their experiences, and each scientist can make the choice either to reveal those biases or to put on the emperor's new clothes of expert objectivity.

> (p. xiv)

To begin with, Fogel generally treats embodied self-awareness as something which—to adapt a well-known formulation—is done by human beings, not by neurones ("neurones do not think and feel; people and animals do": Thompson & Stapleton, 2008, p. 26). However, he soon descends into a near-phrenological series of identifications between human capacities and neural structures, intended to explain, for example, "how emotion is created in the brain" (Fogel, 2009, p. 56).

Apparently the answer lies in the anterior ungulate cortex, while embodied self-awareness "is associated with" the ventromedial prefrontal cortex or VMPC (Fogel, 2009, p. 53). But just how will it help a practitioner to learn this, and a host of other similar "facts"—when what they are faced with in their practice is a person rather than a brain? Is emotion "created" in the brain, or simply registered there? What is the nature of the "association" Fogel describes—which slides over into a diagram (2009, p. 96) that simply *labels* the VMPC "embodied self-awareness"? The problem with phrenology was not simply that the assignment of qualities to locations was wrong, but that the entire enterprise was misconceived.

Fogel's book, which mixes this sort of reductionism with a good deal of wisdom, is only one example of the widespread confusion in psychotherapy between the embodied human being and the central nervous system. There are probably several causes for this state of affairs. For body psychotherapists, certainly, an important factor in our attraction to neuroscience has been an enormous strengthening of our own status in the psychotherapy world through the almost dreamlike confirmation which it has given to many of our most treasured insights, and which I will discuss further below.

But the central and most obvious cause is clearly the unique status claimed by and widely assigned to science in our culture. Nikolas Rose and Joelle Abi-Rached are very clear about how this status affects our reception of neuroscience's findings:

> Despite the well-known technical problems, assumptions, and limitations of these [scanning] technologies, and the fact that they do not speak for themselves and must be interpreted by experts, the images have undoubted powers of persuasion, and their apparent ability to track mental processes objectively, often processes outside the awareness of the individual themselves, have proved persuasive in areas from neuromarketing to policies on child development.
>
> (2013, p. 13)

We should certainly include psychotherapy and counselling in the list of areas affected by "the belief that we can see the mind in the living brain, can observe the passions and its desires that seemingly underlie normal and pathological beliefs, emotions, and behaviors" (Rose & Abi-Rached, 2013, p. 13). However, Rose and Abi-Rached are equally clear about the damaging effects of an exaggerated focus on the brain and the central nervous system, as if they were separate from the body and from the body's environment:

> We are troubled by the misleading assumption that one can understand neural processes outside those of the bodies that they normally inhabit. ... Stomachs, intestines, lungs, kidneys, and livers—let alone limbs—do these play no part, or merely a peripheral one, in the faculties and functions studied by neuroscience—in memory, in thought, in feelings, in desires? Psychiatric conditions shape and are shaped by mobilizations of feelings and functions across the body. Emotions course through the veins, engage the heart and the lungs, the bowels and the genitals, the muscles, the skin and face. As for cognition, do we not think, literally here, with hands and eyes?
>
> (2013, p. 230)

There are many dissident scientific voices which recognise that "[O]ne cannot simply 'peel away' the body to understand the nervous system's role in adaptive behavior" (Chiel & Beer, 1997, p. 554). As the previous page of their paper makes clear, when the authors write "peel away" they mean this horribly literally, in relation to experiments using "reduced preparations": experimental animals with much of their bodies surgically removed (p. 553). However, "[R]ecent results suggest that adaptive behavior can best be understood within the context of the biomechanics of the body, the structure of an organism's environment, and the continuous feedback between the nervous system, the body and the environment" (p. 553). The animals need to keep their bodies if we are going to learn anything. They need to keep their bodies, full stop.

One might suggest that neuroscientists need to explore this "diverse, interconnected system (a mutuality of moods-objects-neurotransmitters-hormones-cognitions-affects-attachments-tears-glands-images-words-gut)" (Wilson & Foglia, 2011, 280). And indeed some neuroscientists attempt to do so. But really to take Wilson and Foglia's list seriously means accepting the need to move into *a different register of discourse*—one, perhaps, more like the list of smiles with which I began this Introduction, or like the discourse of psychotherapy; although it must be said that therapy itself has a strong habit of ignoring the need to draw from sociological, anthropological, philosophical, and political forms of language.

So part of the project of this book—the project of creating a new model of body psychotherapy—is to find ways of incorporating a plurality of discourses, sufficient to allow us to approach the real complexity of human embodiment. Drawing too heavily on neuroscience alone is reductionist in a very unhelpful way—a bit like a skilled joiner seeking insight into her craft from molecular physics: no doubt there are a few useful bits and pieces to be gathered, but not enough to tell you how to make a better table. In what follows I will make a fair amount of use of the equivalent "useful bits and pieces" which I think body psychotherapy can draw from neuroscience. Most of these, though, are more like fruitful metaphors than anything else—"what if?" nudges that free up our thinking.

I have referred above to neuroscientific work which is based on the cruel mistreatment of animals (even in the absence of any pain, to cut off parts of an animal's body and/or brain is, let's face it, intrinsically cruel). It's not always easy to spot that this is where a particular research finding comes from—it is so casually introduced that one can miss it entirely, and then suddenly come up against the brutal reality, like finding a mangled corpse in one's living room. I have made a choice in principle not to use such research, and would I hope make the same choice even if, as is so easily claimed, the process was "essential" to our understanding—rather than being, as I have already indicated, more likely to mislead: an embodied grasp of the relationship between sentience and the world is surely not likely to emerge from such a disembodied treatment of it, a sort of violent parody of traditional therapeutic detachment. However, I may well have inadvertently referred to some work that involved mistreating animals, and if so I apologise to them, and to you.

Returning to neuroscience in general: my approach in this book has been one of blatant cherry-picking. By this I mean that I am not looking to neuroscience to try to find out what psychotherapy is about or how it should be practised: it makes more sense to me to rely on my experience and the experiences of other practitioners, especially since in any case I do not believe that there is any one way to practise good therapy, any more than there is one good way to paint or write music or indeed to live. I quite unashamedly use neuroscience findings mainly to support what I already believe on the grounds of experience; and also partly to mine them for useful metaphors that suggest new ways of thinking about my experience.

Certain rather solid-looking pieces of neuroscience—for example the social engagement system (Porges, 2011), or mirror neuron theory (Keysers, 2011; but for a critique of the theory see Hickok, 2014)—are of value to body psychotherapy because they support us in trusting what we have already learnt directly: that our organisms have an inherent and skilful tendency to form relationships with others. If neuroscience claimed that this was *not* the case, however, then I would flatly ignore it. I freely admit that this is not a very scientific, or even objective, approach; but therapy is not a scientific or objective undertaking. Nor should it try to be.

Traditionally, therapists lean on one very particular form of evidence to support and illustrate their ideas: the case history, or shorter case vignettes. Several factors complicate this process. All case histories are ultimately necessarily fictional: there is no way that they can "objectively", or even adequately, represent the full complexity of the process that has taken place between a therapist and a client. Not even a complete transcript could do that—not even a video recording: most of what was going on *inside* the two participants would be missing (see Bollas, 2008 for a valuable attempt).

A case study or vignette is therefore more like a novel or short story, as Steven Marcus (2013) observed of Freud's writings which created the genre. It is best in my view to acknowledge this outright, since it takes nothing away from their value—in fact, it adds to it by stripping away extraneous questions of literal accuracy. My own usual process is to start out from two or more actual clients, combine them into one, render them unrecognisable by changing the biographical facts in various ways, and then allow my imagination to create a story about therapy with them which feels valid. That assessment of validity, based on years of clinical experience, is "evidence" of a very different, and in some ways more profound, nature than literal accuracy could provide.

Attachment theory

Some readers may be surprised to find very little reference in what follows to attachment theory, given that it is currently such a fashionable approach, in both body psychotherapy and verbal psychotherapy (I do use attachment theory briefly in Chapter Twelve). To explain fully why I have made this choice would involve an extensive critique of attachment theory, which would be a distraction from what I aim to present here; but as a brief summary, I see it as drastically oversimplified, and tending to substitute arbitrary categories of parent-infant attachment for the adult to adult relationship which is in my view central to effective therapy. As Bowlby says very explicitly, "The therapist's role is analogous to that of a mother who provides her child with a secure base from which to explore the world" (1988, p. 140).

The analogy which Bowlby claims between therapy and parenting is in my view completely false. I accept that many therapists who align themselves with attachment theory would not agree with such a bald statement as the quotation from Bowlby above; but I am afraid that many would—and that even those who wouldn't are influenced in their practice by this model. (In his book *Attachment in Psychotherapy* (2007), David Wallin gives the same quotation a full page to stand alone as the epigraph to his first chapter.) However, our job as therapists is not to replace poor parenting with good parenting, but to help clients become aware (a) of how the parenting they experienced fell short (if it did), and (b) that we are not their parent. I have to admit that I am also influenced by the fact that attachment theory is to some degree founded on Harry Harlow's exceptionally cruel experiments with baby monkeys (Harlow, 1972; Van der Horst, LeRoy, & Van der Veer, 2008).

Easy and difficult writing and reading

I want to thank a few people who have read drafts of some of this book: Hélène Fletcher, Kamalamani, and Allison Priestman, all of whom have made helpful comments (though none of them are responsible for any of my errors or opinions). In discussing it with them, I have come to realise something which has been very illuminating for me: alongside a strong desire to write simply and clearly, I have an equally strong desire to be inexplicit and hard to follow.

I don't think this is pathological, or only to a small degree. I was a poet before I was a prose writer; and in books like this, I am aspiring to poetry, in the sense that poetry works through its *refusal to spell things out*, which corresponds to the real, obscure, clotted density of the world (one writer I much admire is Richard Grossinger (e.g., 1986, 1995, 1998), who is also a poet writing prose, and often on similar topics to my own). As Sir Philip Sidney wrote (1595, p. 153), "Now for the poet, he nothing affirmeth, and therefore never lieth": poetry knows that every assertion is in some ultimate sense a lie, because it oversimplifies complexity. The simpler we make things, the less real they are.

The passages which I like best in this and my other books, therefore, are often those which are darkest and most unclear, demanding several readings. These seem to me potentially closest to reality. I appreciate that this can be very frustrating for readers, who may well feel that such passages are simply dark and unclear—and sometimes this is probably the case! But there it is; no one can be a different writer from the one they are; and at other points in the book I feel I can take pride and pleasure in the simplicity and directness of the writing, because complexity is being held in some different way, for instance through paradox. I simply wanted to say that, although some of the density is a straightforward by-product of the difficult material I am trying to convey, and perhaps at times also of my inadequate digestion of it, some of it is more intentional.

To help readers pick out the wood from the trees, I have included three waymarker sections entitled The Story So Far, summarising what seem to me the most important points I have been trying to make in the preceding few chapters. If, reading one of these sections, you don't recognise what is being said as familiar, then you might want to consider rereading the preceding chapters. But this only applies if you are wanting to study the book in order to assimilate its content: I will be equally happy if you skim the whole thing and then choose to read certain bits more carefully, or if you start anywhere that looks interesting and see where it takes you. In fact, do whatever appeals to you: this is no longer my book, but yours.

CHAPTER ONE

What is embodiment?

> Even as one who encompasses with his mind the mighty ocean
> includes thereby all the rivulets that run into the ocean; just so,
> O monks, whoever develops and cultivates mindfulness directed
> to the body includes thereby all the wholesome states that partake
> of supreme knowledge.
>
> One thing, O monks, if developed and cultivated, leads to
> a strong sense of urgency; to great benefit; to great security
> from bondage; to mindfulness and clear comprehension; to the
> attainment of vision and knowledge; to a pleasant dwelling in this
> very life; to the realisation of the fruit of knowledge and liberation.
> What is that one thing? It is mindfulness directed to the body.
>
> —*Gautama Buddha*, Anguttara Nikaya I:21,
> *Thera & Bodhi, 1970*

I need to warn you right away that it is going to take a little while before there is much direct discussion of therapy in this book. But everything I am going to say before that point is, in my view, required in order to put the necessary ideas in place for us to be able to think usefully about embodied relationship in the therapy room. As you read the next couple of chapters, you will probably find that you are making your own connections with your experience of therapy, both as practitioner and as client; and those connections will, I hope, dovetail with the ones that I gradually begin to make in Chapter Three.

Perhaps the first thing I should say—rather than assuming that, because you are reading the book, we have this as common ground—is that I take embodiment to be central and necessary to our existence, to our being a creature capable of relationship at all. The literary critic Terry Eagleton goes to the heart of the matter: "If something doesn't involve my body, it doesn't involve me" (2013, p. 39). Having a sense of embodied relating depends on having a sense of embodiment itself.

The difficulty here is that many of our habitual assumptions about embodiment are shaped by the fundamentally *dis*embodied attitudes embedded in Western culture—the longstanding assumption that "the real me" is mental and/or spiritual. However, there are a number of new ideas available in contemporary thinking which fit better, I think, with our immediate experience of what it is to be an embodied being. Having said that, it is of course much too simple to give total authority to immediate experience: a constant theme of this book is that our experience is shaped by our "knowledge" just as much as knowledge is shaped by experience, so that we tend to experience what we expect to experience. It would be more accurate, therefore, to say that a number of new ideas are giving us the opportunity to change our experience of embodiment!

Paradoxically, many of these new ideas conflict with our "common sense" notions of how things are; hence they may seem at first sight bizarre and hard to grasp. Although common sense generally claims to be experience-based, it filters that experience through thick layers of received opinion and socially respectable dogma to arrive at an acceptable version. Because our direct embodied experience is obscured by so many assumptions—for example, the mind/body split, the subject/object split, the privileging of reason over emotion, the picture of bodies as separated from each other by space like raisins in a pudding, and the belief that causation flows only in one direction—we cannot rely on it to guide us; we need some sort of body centred practice to support us in identifying and staying congruent with what we perceive somatically (and hopefully this practice will not come with too many built-in assumptions of its own). Alongside such a practice, the new ideas I am going to explore provide a scaffolding for a *phenomenological*—that is, experience-based—reassessment of embodiment. Thus the relationship between experience and theory is entirely dialogical, with each both critiquing and supporting the other.

In order to create a space where we can explore a new interaction of knowledge and experience, I intend to move slowly and carefully, trying to rein in my tendency to leap impatiently ahead. In fact, I need first to take a preparatory detour—actually, two detours, one about the pyramid of rationality and one about mutual causation. Hopefully, the relevance of these discussions will be clear by the time we get to the end of them.

Embodiment and patriarchy

In Western culture, we habitually organise our thinking about embodiment within a hierarchy which is both conceptual and value-based, with mind and rationality at the top, as "'higher functions", descending through capacities like feeling and intuition to the lowly body at the bottom of the pile. This descending pyramid is such a fundamental part of our thinking that it is sometimes hard even to notice it in operation; and the privileging of rational thought as "higher" is so intertwined with the privileging of the masculine over the feminine, culture over nature, "civilised" over "uncivilised", and human over animal that it must be considered an aspect of patriarchal ideology (Rust, 2008; Totton, 2011).

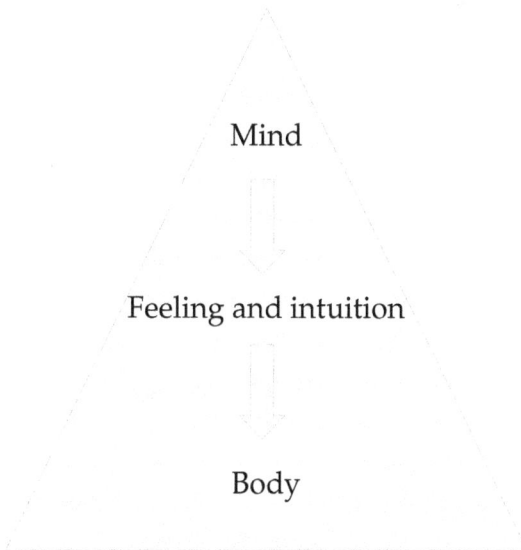

Mind

Feeling and intuition

Body

Figure 1.

The destructive effects of this mindset on both human and other-than-human worlds are of course enormous (Totton, 2011). For immediate purposes, though, I am going to restrict myself to the destructive effect that it has on our ability to comprehend embodiment, encouraging us as it does to think of our bodies as more or less convenient meat trees where our minds temporarily perch before soaring to greater heights.

Because of the role that hierarchy plays in the politics of patriarchal societies, we tend to think of it as representing power and privilege. But there are also *logical* or *ecological* hierarchies (among others), made up of a series of levels where each is dependent on and develops out of—is in a sense a special part or aspect of—the previous one (Wilden, 1987a, 1987b). For example, there is a pyramid we can imagine with the physical world at the bottom, organisms above it, then human beings, then society, then culture: each "higher" stage defines part of the previous one, and depends on the previous one.

However, the reverse is not true—for instance humans could not exist if organisms didn't exist, since they are a particular kind of organism, but organisms in general could exist without humans. This is why the arrows point *up* rather than *down*, and why a narrowing pyramid is

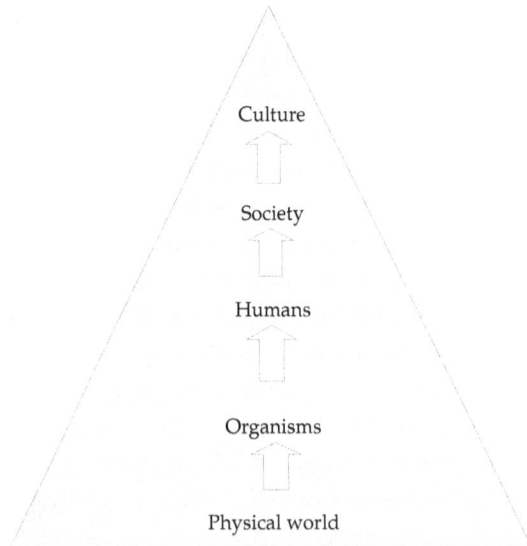

Culture

Society

Humans

Organisms

Physical world

Figure 2.

an appropriate image, although if we included all the higher levels we would have something more like a branching tree. To regard the upper, more dependent levels of the pyramid as superior to the lower, more fundamental ones would make no sense; and in fact this hierarchy does not involve power and status, as the patriarchal one does.

The up-hierarchy of embodiment

John Heron (1992) has taken a useful and clarifying step in coining the term *"up-hierarchy"* for a series like this in which the lower elements sequentially shape and determine the upper ones. Heron's basic up-hierarchy consists of what he suggests are the four fundamental modes of human experience: from the bottom, Affective → Imaginal → Conceptual → Practical. I have adapted this by selecting a different set of moments out of the continuum, starting with the level of our physiology, which most psychologically-oriented systems, including Heron's, leave out of the picture entirely or treat as a separate substrate.

These four levels represent significant moments in what is really a smooth and continuous shift between what we call the *physical* and what we call the *psychological*. Traditionally, Western thought inserts a definitive gap between these two realms—and then puzzles over how

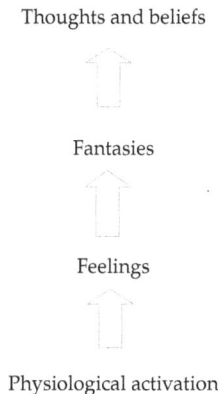

Thoughts and beliefs

Fantasies

Feelings

Physiological activation

Figure 3.

to bridge it (Deutsch, 1959). In some ways the difference between the two is simply a matter of what model is most economical for thinking with. We *could* in principle describe the psyche in terms of atomic interactions, although we would need to know quite a lot more than we do at the moment; but in any case doing so would be unfeasibly longer, clumsier, and more obscure than describing it in terms of thoughts, feelings, memories, attitudes, and so on—a language which has grown up precisely *because* it is useful for describing psychological events, and is also a description from "inside" rather than from "outside" (see the discussion of smiles at the start of the Introduction). It is mainly the shifts of terminology which give the impression of a series of leaps between levels.

Each of these four levels, like the many other intermediate ones which could also be distinguished, takes up and expresses emergent properties of the one below. As Heron says:

> In an up-hierarchy it is not a matter of the higher controlling and ruling the lower, as in a down-hierarchy, but of the higher branching and flowering out of, and bearing the fruit of, the lower.
>
> (1992, p. 20)

Hence there is no sense in which the upper levels of the up-hierarchy are "better" than the lower ones; they are simply more specialised and elaborated developments of aspects of the lower levels' potential. And the image of the psyche "branching and flowering out of, and bearing the fruit of" the body fits very well with the theme of this book, embodied relating as the ground of psychotherapy.

Mutual causation

The up-hierarchy I have illustrated, however, is plainly oversimplified; many levels in many dimensions, and many interpenetrating hierarchies, would be required to come anywhere near an adequate depiction. For example, although in one sense culture clearly emerges from and depends on embodiment—there could be no culture without bodies to create it, while the opposite is not the case (Wilden, 1987, pp. 73ff)—it is undeniable that embodiment is at the same time *socially constructed* (Evans, 2002; Grosz, 1994; Haraway, 1991), emerging from and depending on culture, which gives particular meaning to the concept and shape to the experience. Equally, our thoughts affect our physiological reactions ("The house is on fire!") just as our physiology affects our thoughts.

These are examples—and here begins my second detour—of what Gregory Bateson (e.g., 1971) calls "circular causality", a continuous feedback loop rather than a unidirectional arrow, which is a frequent feature of ecological and other cybernetic systems. Bateson argues that "the organisation of living things depends upon circular and more complex chains of determination" (1980, p. 115). Circular causality is also central to Buddhist thinking, in the form of *paticca samuppada*, "dependent co-arising" (Macy, 1991a, 1991b); and appears in Hinduism as the Net of Indra, an infinite array of jewels each of which reflects all the others within itself.

From a traditional viewpoint, it looks like a trick or an Escher-like optical illusion for causality to loop back on itself: as with quantum mechanics, "common sense" has not yet caught up with what we understand about reality. However, there are actually many examples of circular (or mutual) causality which are familiar to our ordinary experience. For instance, any feedback-based regulatory mechanism—a thermostat, or even a steering wheel—functions through mutual causation, where a change in the setting produces a change in the output which produces a further change in the setting which produces ... and so on. Clearly,

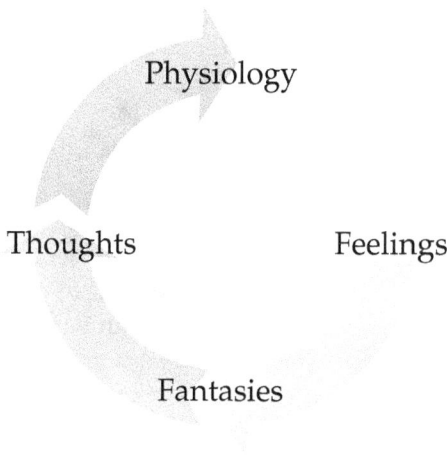

Physiology

Thoughts   Feelings

Fantasies

Figure 4.

where one chooses to locates the "start" of the process—with setting or output, chicken or egg—is arbitrary, and cannot be used to establish a causal arrow of direction. There are also more subtle examples of *teleological* circular causation, where a *goal* affects the process.

The term "cybernetics" derives from a Greek root meaning "to steer", and the science of cybernetics studies mutual causation systems (also known as "autonomous" systems). Our bodies are of course full of systems of this kind, a whole range of physiological thermostats which regulate temperature, heartbeat, and many other vital functions.

> Circular causality involves a perpetual and simultaneous bottom-up and top-down rendering of emergence through self-organization, or in Thompson's [2007] words, both "local-to-global determination (the formation of macrolevel patterns through microlevel interactions) and global-to-local determination (the constraining of microlevel interactions by macrolevel patterns)".
>
> (Witherington, 2011, p. 68, quoting Thompson, 2007, p. 336)

The most immediately relevant aspect of circular or mutual causality for our purposes, however, is its appearance in social and cultural contexts. Ruesch and Bateson give a classic account of this in their book *Communication: The Social Matrix of Psychiatry* (1951), where they argue that organism—or self—and environment exist *only* in relation to each other, and that social values, and reality itself, exist as a function of our belief in them as much as vice versa. This corresponds to my statement above that our embodiment both constructs and is constructed by culture.

We will be looking at some aspects of this in much more detail in Chapters Five and Six; however, perhaps a straightforward example would be helpful in showing that we are considering something of concrete significance, not a rarefied piece of metaphysics. A group of Swedish researchers (Gislén, Warrant, Dacke, & Kröger, 2006) investigated why children of some tribes of sea gypsies in South East Asia are able to see clearly and sharply under water, whereas European children are not. It turned out that this was not simply the effect of a gene, since Swedish children could *learn* to see sharply under water after some practice.

But the sea gypsy children's tribe survives by diving for seashells: the cultural pressure and specialisation of making their living led to the "expression" of a gene enabling adaptation in the muscles that control the lens of the eye—an example of circular causation between biology and culture. The adaptation was not simply a social one, but an actual physical change; however, this would not have taken place without the social context. Note that this is nothing to do with "natural selection" in the ordinary sense—seeing underwater did not literally affect survival and reproduction, but only more general well-being. This phenomenon of selective gene expression is being studied by the field of epigenetics.

Embodiment as a double concept

Equipped with some understanding of up-hierarchies and of mutual causation, we can now return to our main theme. "Embodiment" has two important senses. On the one hand it refers to the *state* of being a self-aware organism, something which all living human beings share: corporeality. On the other hand, it refers to the meta-level *process* of realising and experiencing that we are this self-aware organism, and that there is not really (though there sometimes seems to be) any separate psychological realm divorced from the body, and equally no separate bodily realm divorced from the psyche.

This process of realisation and experience is one in which we are all involved, but which is fulfilled to different degrees in different people at different times—partly conditioned by the social and cultural context, which will be to varying degrees "body-friendly" or "body-hostile". It is not a once and for all achievement, but an ongoing series of advances and retreats. For everyone, there are moments of exaltation or suffering when we *know* ourselves to be unified bodymindspirit, and moments of alienation and dissociation when these aspects of our experience seem to peel apart and even to attack each other. Much of the time we live somewhere between the two.

"Embodiment" in this sense, then, is a name for the moment-by-moment experience of our existence as living bodies, with all the joy and grief, pleasure and pain, power and vulnerability which that involves. This sense of embodiment does not represent a *state*, an either/or proposition, something to be achieved as a finality; but an ongoing *process of becoming embodied*, more and more (or occasionally, perhaps temporarily, less and less) deeply committed to our corporeal experience: an exploration of and dialogue with the organismic aspect of our being, without which we cannot exist but which we always have difficulty fully accepting (Totton, 2008).

This understanding of embodiment challenges us to own and integrate the various woundings we encounter in life, rather than leaving them frozen in patterns of bodily tension and avoidance which create a local numbing in our awareness and sensitivity (see Chapters Seven and Ten). The reality for each individual will always be a set of compromises, as our embodiment finds ways to make the best of its situation, to preserve as much freedom and flexibility as possible while also protecting us from threat; and body psychotherapy tries to help clients explore and re-evaluate these bodily choices (Totton & Priestman, 2012).

When in our culture we refer to "bodies" or "the body", probably the most common usage is to identify the first of the two meanings I have just distinguished, *embodiment without meta-awareness*. Embodiment *with* meta-awareness, the second meaning of the term, is generally referred to as "me", "myself". This is related to the distinction in German between *Körper*, the physical body, and *Leib*, the lived body; which raises the question, "What is it for a physical living body … to be also a lived body?" (Thompson, 2009, p. 80).

Katherine Hayles makes essentially the same distinction between "body" and "embodiment", and brings out some of its deeper, political implications, which I will discuss in Chapters Five and Six:

> Embodiment differs from the concept of the body in that the body is always normative in relation to some set of criteria. … In contrast to the body, embodiment is contextual, enwebbed within the specifics of place, time, physiology and culture that together comprise enactment. Embodiment never coincides exactly with "the body" … Whereas the body is an idealised form … embodiment is the specific instantiation generated from the noise of difference. Relative to the body, embodiment is other and elsewhere, at once excessive and deficient.

> (1993, pp. 154–155)

Several writers on embodiment make similar points, each in their own terminology; for example, Drew Leder writes:

> Times in which the body is most tacit and self-transcending are collected under the rubric of rational "mind". Other experiences

where corporeality comes into strong thematic presence, are collected under the rubric of "body".

(1990, p. 149)

All this suggests, I think, a non-Cartesian way in which we experientially distinguish between mind and body: "mind" corresponds to the self-aware subject, "body" to the involuntary aspect of our somatic experience. This is not the same thing as mind which is aware of its embodiment, of course—sometimes it is the exact opposite, mind which *denies* being embodied. Once again, the polarity of "mind:body" is a falsely symmetrical one: "mind", self-awareness, is an emergent property of "body", just as "culture" is an emergent property of "nature", hence the two exist on different logical levels, and cannot usefully be opposed (Wilden, 1987b, pp. 22–27).

It is, of course, entirely possible to speak in a way which reverses the polarity—"I can't stop my mind chattering on", "My body knows what I really need"—and people often do; but it is in fact still mind which is talking. The body itself, the physical organism, doesn't *tell* us anything (Totton, 2005a). What "the body", embodiment without self-awareness, offers is not *information*, but *expression*—the difference between a groan of pain and someone saying "Ow"—the latter being a piece of phatic language signifying "I hurt". Expression only becomes information when it is interpreted, languaged, either by the subject or by someone else—in either case, by the mind, the self-aware aspect of embodiment, into whose realm interpretation falls.

When I talk about language here, I am not referring only to spoken language: exactly the same applies to intentionally communicative gestures, like a deliberate smile, or expressive dance: both are interpretive, putting a spin on experience. And this act of interpretation transforms the body's expression, translates it into a wholly new register—just as much so when the translation is our own as when it is someone else's. Either way, it is a *social* process, where the body enters into a social world which pre-exists and predetermines its so-called "meanings".

Our lived awareness of being bodies encompasses the bodily process of absorbing and performing social and cultural reality (Thrift & Dewsbury, 2000). From this point of view, embodiment is in part a summation of how the body suffers, accommodates, and transmits an ensemble of social and cultural demands and tensions, which because they have entered our embodiment often therefore appear as simply "the way things are". Pierre Bourdieu calls this ensemble "*habitus*" (see Chapters Six and Seven).

Embodiment in *this* sense can often suppress embodiment in the *other* sense: in a culture largely alienated from embodied experience, there is an ongoing struggle, in which body psychotherapy has always been deeply involved, between *Leib* and *Körper*, lived embodiment and the body as object. As Don Hanlon Johnson says:

> Underlying the various techniques and schools, one finds a desire to regain an intimate connect with bodily processes: breath, movement impulses, balance and sensibility. In that shared impulse, this community is best understood within a much broader movement of resistance to the West's long history of denigrating the value of the human body and the natural environment.

> (1995, p. xvi)

Embodied knowing

Embodiment as process can be understood as the aspiration to achieve a full and practical awareness of the whole up-hierarchy from physiology through feelings and fantasies to thoughts. This aspiration may or may not be ultimately achievable; but in any case, it entails what Varela, Thompson, and Rosch call *enaction*, a coinage from the phrase "embodied action":

> We ... call into question the assumption ... that cognition consists of the representation of a world that is independent of our perceptual and cognitive capacities by a cognitive system that exists independent of the world. We outline instead a view of cognition as *embodied action*.

> (1991, p. xx)

This viewpoint is very much indebted to the work of Merleau-Ponty (1962, 1964, 1968) and other phenomenologists, as well as to the Madhayamika school of Buddhism (Varela, Thompson, & Rosch, 1991, pp. 217–235). It was also anticipated by American pragmatist philosophers like William James and John Dewey (M. Johnson & Rohrer, 2007); Dewey wrote:

> To see the organism *in* nature, the nervous system in the organism, the brain in the nervous system, the cortex in the brain is the answer to the problems which haunt philosophy.
>
> (1925, p. 198, original italics)

However, a whole range of approaches, many of them much more mainstream, now converge on a similar position. The ensemble of such approaches is often known as "embodied cognitive science" (Wilson & Foglia, 2011, n.p.); what they share is a rejection of the traditional view that the body is of little significance to mental processes, and a belief that *cognition is integrally bound up with our embodied nature.* As the entry in the *Stanford Encyclopedia* says:

> Cognition is embodied when it is deeply dependent upon features of the physical body of an agent, that is, when aspects of the agent's body beyond the brain play a significant causal or physically constitutive role in cognitive processing.
>
> In general, dominant views in the philosophy of mind and cognitive science have considered the body as peripheral to understanding the nature of mind and cognition. Proponents of embodied cognitive science view this as a serious mistake.
>
> (Wilson & Foglia, 2011, n.p.)

Among the many strands which make up embodied cognitive science are research and theoretical work around mirror neurons (Oberman & Ramachandran, 2007; Rizzolatti & Craighero, 2004); artificial intelligence and robotics (Clark, 1998); ecological perception (Gibson, 1979; Sewall, 1999); dynamic systems as applied to human development (Thelen & Smith, 1994); and cognitive philosophy (Gallagher, 2005, 2012). All of this material can considerably enrich body psychotherapy's conception of embodiment. Much of it also addresses our embodied cognition of other people, which as we will see in Chapter Three enables, and in some ways actually *constitutes*, embodied relating.

A radical aspect of embodied cognition is that it throws into doubt the whole traditional theory of *mental representation* (as exemplified for instance in Fodor, 1981): the assumption that the mind or brain processes sense data so as to construct a model of the "outside" world—somewhat like a prisoner in a dungeon reconstructing what is going on outside from fragments of light, shadow, and sound. (This is, of course, the famous metaphor of the cave from Plato's *The Republic* (e.g., Lane, 2007, pp. 227ff); except that for Plato it is the physical world which constitutes the cave shutting us off from metaphysical reality.) A further conclusion from the theory of representation is that our ability to understand someone else's feelings and actions is also a kind of modelling, combining sense data, mirror neurons, and analogy with our own internal experience.

Embodied cognition potentially cuts out the representation and modelling (Chemero, 2011), and argues for a *direct connection* between perceiver and perceived—what Merleau-Ponty calls the Flesh:

> Communication is achieved through the reciprocity between my intentions and the other person's gestures, and between my gestures and the intentions which can be read in the other person's behavior. Everything happens as if the other person's intention inhabited my body, or as if my intentions inhabited his body. The gesture I witness sketches out the first signs of an intentional object. This object becomes present and is fully understood when the powers of my body adjust to it and fit over it. The gesture is in front of me like a question, it indicates to me specific sensible points in the world and invites me to join it there. Communication is accomplished when my behavior finds in this pathway its own pathway.
>
> (1962, p. 185)

There is controversy within the embodied cognition community about whether, or how far, representational perspectives should be abandoned. But "radical embodied cognition" approaches (Chemero, 2011) consider our knowing to be an *active* process, rather than a passive representation: we find out what exists by interacting with it, as a body in the world. "Perceiver" and "perceived" are *coupled*: the cognitive unit is brain-body-environment. I say more about this in the next chapter.

CHAPTER TWO

Embodiment and environment

If cognition directly entails embodiment, it also directly entails environment. Just as in Winnicott's famous statement that there is no baby separate from the mother-and-baby system (1947a, p. 88), extended mind theories point out that there is no mind separate from the mind-and-body-and-environment system. This realisation goes back at least as far as Gregory Bateson's work from nearly fifty years ago:

> The total self-corrective system which processes information, or, as I say, "thinks" and "acts" and "decides", is a system whose boundaries do not at all coincide with the boundaries either of the body or of what is popularly called the "self" or "consciousness".
>
> (1971, p. 319)

Bateson goes on to say that not only does mind include "the pathways of all unconscious mentation—both autonomic and repressed, neural and hormonal", but it is also "not bounded by the skin but includes all external pathways along which information can travel" (p. 319).

This was pretty remarkable stuff for its time, and remains pretty remarkable now. The simple example which Bateson gives is of a blind man (Bateson writes "man", "he" and so on) and his stick, which he uses to give him information about the world in much the same way sighted people use vision. So where does his mind end and the world begin? At his hand? Part-way down the stick? At the tip? Or, as seems to make sense, is mind present in the entire interaction between stick and environment? (p. 318).

However, there is a remarkable degree of amnesia about Bateson's frequently prophetic work; hence what is regarded as the modern founding text on the extended mind is Clark and Chalmers' paper "The Extended Mind" (1998), which makes basically very similar points. They argue that:

> Once we recognize the crucial role of the environment in con-straining the evolution and development of cognition, we see that extended cognition is a core cognitive process, not an add-on extra. (p. 12)

Varela, Thompson, and Rosch's enactivist theory goes much further, and, as Thompson and Stapleton (2008) argue, transcends the opposition between "internalist" and "externalist" theories, since in their view organism *cannot be separated from* environment; enactivism, therefore, is neither internalist nor externalist, and in fact it goes beyond externalism, since it denies that cognition is ever actually—as externalists (e.g., Clark & Chalmers, 1998, p. 8) tend to assume it must sometimes or in some ways be—just within the head.

> Cognition is not an event happening inside the system; it is *the relational process of sense-making that takes place between the system and its environment.* ... Cognition belongs to the "relational domain" in which the system as a unity relates to the wider context of its milieu, not to the "operational domain" of the system's internal states (e.g., its brain states). Of course, what goes on inside the system is crucial for enabling the system's cognitive or sense-making relation to its environment, but to call internal processes as such cognitive is to confuse levels of discourse or to make a category mistake (neurons do not think and feel; people and animals do).
>
> (Thompson & Stapleton, 2008, p. 26; my italics)

In other words, cognition is an emergent property of the system—just as Gregory Bateson said long ago (1971)—and cannot be assigned exclusively to isolated elements of the system (like human brains). And Silver Rattasepp (2010) further points out that the concept of extended mind actually rests on an implicit concept of "extended organism": the only possible means, after all, for mind to extend itself into the world is via the whole organism—except that of course "via" is the wrong word: from an embodied enactive point of view, mind is already *in* the world, and *only* in the world. "Cognitive processes emerge from the non-linear and circular causality of continuous sensorimotor interactions involving brain, body, and environment" (Thompson, 2007, p. 11).

For therapists, perhaps one of the most useful discussions of the extended mind/organism comes from Christopher Bollas, who describes in very different language how:

> Without giving it much thought at all we consecrate the world with our own subjectivity, investing people, places, things, and events with a kind of idiomatic significance. As we inhabit this world of ours, we amble about in a field of pregnant objects that contribute to the dense psychic textures that constitute self experience. Very often we select and use objects in ways unconsciously intended to bring up such imprints; indeed, we do this many times each day, sort of thinking ourself out, by evoking constellations of inner experience. At the same time, however, the people, things, and events of our world simply happen to us, and when they do, we are called into differing forms of being by chance. Thus we oscillate between thinking ourself out through the selection of objects that promote inner experience and being thought out, so to speak, by the environment which plays upon the self.
>
> (1993, pp. 4–5)

What Bollas is describing is perhaps most exactly identified as "extended affect", a special but crucially important aspect of embodied extended cognition. This dual process of thinking ourselves out/being thought out through the objects of the world—what in the next chapter I will call "exograms"—is central to our experience and our relationships, and particularly so in therapy, where of course the therapist and the therapy room become highly emotionally charged parts of our world through which we try to "think ourselves out".

As Bollas implies when he speaks of our "being thought out", the concept of extended mind faces in two directions. On the one hand, we "invest" the entities which form our environment with meanings which preserve and illuminate aspects of our self ("invest" is a charged term in psychoanalysis, being the English equivalent of the psychoanalytic term "cathexis", which Bollas must surely be holding somewhere in view). On the other hand, though, we ourselves are at the same time from another point of view "exograms", the product and representative of our environment.

I have written elsewhere, using this ecosystemic perspective, about learning to think of my client as the emissary of a network in trouble—a network which is in the first instance no doubt human, but which may well extend far into other-than-human and more-than human realms (Totton, 2012, pp. 258–259). And I myself as therapist am of course the emissary of my own networks, a product of all the processes and relationships which have formed me, offering to be available as an exogram for my clients, an opportunity for them to think and feel themselves out—just as they become an exogram for me. And ultimately, given the connectedness of everything, their networks and mine join "round the back", so that the therapeutic encounter can be seen as a network folding around in order for one part of it to seek help from another part—a little like a person putting a sore finger in their mouth (Totton, 2012).

Motor imagery

Our embodied extended knowing of the world operates "cross-modally" (Meyer & Damasio, 2009; Stern, 1985): it knits together and translates between the whole range of sensory mechanisms—the well known five senses, but also visceral, proprioceptive, and kinesthetic awareness, our sensing of what is taking place inside our bodies and of how our body is positioned and moving in space, together with interpretive processes like language and visualisation. It is starting to seem likely that, as Daniel Stern suggests, the most fundamental template of knowing is motor imagery, or imagined movement:

> Mental models and neural networks can be reshaped by doing
> something differently, imagining it differently, seeing another doing
> it, or by hearing about it in words. The walls separating different

modes of experiencing are starting to come down as we realize that
it all has to pass by way of imagined movement.

(2010, p. 135)

Stern is drawing here on the neuroscientific research of Gallese and
others, which has led to the conclusion that:

From the very beginning our bodily self-awareness is built upon
the motor potentialities that enable [us] to interact with other bodies and to tune our motor goals and intentions with respect to the
motor goals and intentions of others and vice versa.

(Gallese & Sinigaglia, 2010, p. 754; cf. Fogassi & Gallese, 2004;
Gallese & Lakoff, 2005)

This idea clearly fits very well with an enactive perspective; after all
the term "enaction" itself is a coinage derived from "embodied action"
(Varela, Thompson, & Rosch, 1991, p. xx).

Gallese & Lakoff argue that "[C]ontemporary neuroscience seems to
suggest that concepts of a wide variety make direct use of the sensory-
motor circuitry of the brain" (2005, p. 473). They start out from the fact
that "[I]magining and doing use a shared neural substrate. When one
imagines seeing something, some of the same part of the brain is used
as when one actually sees" (p. 456), and extend this to form a hypothesis that "[T]he same neural substrate used in imagining is used in
understanding" (ibid.). Understanding, imagining and acting are all
grounded in the same neural activity.

When we experience ourselves "grasping" an argument, therefore,
this is more literal than we realise:

The *action* concept of *grasping* is embodied in the sensory-motor
system. ... Arguments of the same form may apply to all other
action concepts, to object concepts, and to abstract concepts with
conceptual content that is metaphorical. ... If all this is correct,
then abstract reasoning in general *exploits* the sensory-motor system. What is the import of our proposal on the nature of human
cognition? We believe that it suggests that rational thought is not
entirely separate from what animals can do, because it directly
uses sensory-motor bodily mechanisms—the same ones used by

nonhuman primates to function in their everyday environments. According to our hypothesis, rational thought is an exploitation of the normal operations of our bodies. As such, it is also largely unconscious.

(Gallese & Lakoff, p. 473)

These ideas dovetail with and extend those of George Lakoff (one of the authors of the paper) and Mark Johnson about the basic bodily metaphors that organise our language (Lakoff & Johnson, 1981, 1999). The expressions, postures, and gesticulations which in most of us accompany the effort to express abstract concepts are not there by chance: they represent and perform the unconscious sensorimotor armature on which concepts, both verbal and preverbal, are shaped and supported in "mental space" (R. M. Young, 1994; see the discussion of Sign in Chapter Nine). And it is motor action which forms "a binding key to multisensory integration" (Fogassi & Gallese, 2004), and hence to an integrated bodily self-awareness.

Gallese & Sinigaglia (2010, p. 748) acknowledge the founding role of Merleau-Ponty in clarifying the relationship between body schema, motor action, and conceptualisation—that the body schema is:

> ... neither the mere copy nor even the global awareness of the existing parts of the body, but its active integration of these latter only *in proportion of their value to the organism's projects*. Psychologists often say that the body schema is dynamic. Brought down to a precise sense, this term means that my body appears to me as an attitude directed towards a certain existing or possible task. And indeed its spatiality is not, like that of external objects or like that of "spatial sensations", a spatiality of position, but a spatiality of situation.

(Merleau-Ponty, 1962, p. 100; my italics)

By "a spatiality of situation", Merleau-Ponty refers to where our body is in relation to what it is engaging with. Phenomenology emphasises how what we engage with in the world *teaches us how to engage with it*. This is clearest in the case of touch: as a simple example, a child stroking a cat for the first time does not simply apply a pre-existing schema of "stroking", but has to learn *how* to do it, in relation to the cat being stroked, and often with the help of an adult: "Gently—feel how soft she is! She likes that, doesn't she? Yes, stroke down from her head—gently, gently!" The meaning of "stroke" is not pre-given, but emerges from interaction, and is distinguished from "press", "rub", or "shove" by the response it gets.

> When I am actively touching, I am also passively following, drawn, as it were, over into the other's bodily intentionality, responsive to it, not the pure agent of my movements. When I am passively being touched, I am also actively shadowing, drawn into a virtual inhabitation of the other's activity, never a pure object of touch. In each case, I am coming to co-exist with the embodied other, to participate with that other body in its movements.
>
> (Maclaren, 2013, p. 6)

This relational way of understanding our engagement with the world will emerge as very important in what follows.

Affordances

Merleau-Ponty's depiction of body schemas as *attitudes directed towards tasks* points to the final piece of the mosaic which we are assembling into a new picture of embodiment in the world. Body schemas integrate parts of the body in proportions and organisations corresponding to what they can contribute to "the organism's projects"—to what we are *doing* in a particular situation. (It actually reminds me of writing this book: integrating a whole range of theories and approaches in proportions and organisations corresponding to how they serve my own project.)

This is part of Varela, Thompson, and Rosch's concept of enaction, or cognition through embodied action:

> Cognition is not the representation of a pregiven world by a pregiven mind but is rather the enaction of a world and a mind on the basis of *a history of the variety of actions* that a being in the world performs.
>
> (1991, p. 9; my italics)

Action in the world creates the "structural coupling" where knowledge arises, as a mutual coming-into-being of world and mind. As part of their argument, Varela and his colleagues offer a lengthy analysis of colour perception, pointing out the problems inherent in an objectivist view of colour as simply "out there":

> The objectivist simply assumes that surface reflectances are to be found in some pregiven world that is independent of our perceptual and cognitive capacities. But how are we to specify what counts as a surface? How are we to specify its edges, boundaries, texture and orientation, if not in relation to some perceiver for whom these distinctions are relevant?

(p. 167)

As well as looking at differences in colour descriptions between human cultures, they point out that while human colour perception is trichromatic—based on three types of photoreceptors each identifying one colour—some animals have dichromatic perception, some tetrachromatic, and some possibly some even pentachromatic (p. 181).

> When people hear of this evidence for tetrachromacy, they respond by asking "What are the other colors that these animals see?"… It must be remembered, though, that a four-dimensional color space is fundamentally different from a three-dimensional one: strictly speaking the two color spaces are incommensurable.

(p. 183)

This question, "What are the other colours?" is a desperate attempt to hold on to the notion of a single objective world "out there". We cannot know these "other colours", because they are not part of our world.

A number of people have addressed this topic from various points of view; for example, the ecologist Jacob von Uexkull, who in the earlier part of the last century coined the term "*Umwelt*" to name the system which comes into being through a particular organism's structural coupling with the world. At the start of his monograph "A Stroll through the Worlds of Animals and Men" (1934), he takes us in imagination to "a flower-strewn meadow" on a sunny day, full of insects and other creatures, and invites us to see that each creature is surrounded by a bubble,

... to represent its own world, filled with the perceptions that it alone knows. When we ourselves then step into one of these bubbles, the familiar meadow is transformed. ... A new world comes into being.

(p. 5)

Von Uexkull is not simply arguing here for species relativism, different perceptions of the same objective world: he describes in great detail how each species modifies its environment to meet its needs, literally *creating* the world of its own project and also literally being created *by* it, in a process of mutual causation which should by now be familiar. As an example, earthworms, to which Von Uexkull refers, have the physiology of marine organisms: by their actions, they succeed in transforming soil into something approximating a liquid, which in turn is the environment best suited for them to "swim" through (J. S. Turner, 2000). Von Uexkull anticipated the concepts of negative feedback and cybernetic loops which are central to so much of the thinking summarised in this chapter. His work is currently being recovered and reappraised; it was a direct influence on Merleau-Ponty (Harney, 2007, pp. 134–135).

Perhaps the most useful version of these concepts for my purposes, though, is James and Eleanor Gibson's theory of ecological perception (E. J. Gibson, 1992; E. J. Gibson & Pick, 2000; J. J. Gibson, 1979, 1982. The theory seems to have been collaboratively developed by Eleanor and James together, though James's name is on the bulk of their writing). Like much of the work reviewed in this chapter, the Gibsons' approach disputes the conventional representational theory of perception which I referred to in Chapter One, and replaces it with direct, immediate perception, with no intervening process of inference or computation. In perceiving the world, we are not performing complex manipulations of sense data in order to reconstruct a 3-D environment from 2-D input. Just as we saw Merleau-Ponty saying in the previous section, we are grasping those elements of our environment *with which we need to interact in order to do things*. We could think of it as "just-in-time" perception, analogous with the way that supermarkets stock up their branches only at the moment and with the products which are about to run out: organisms perceive those parts of the world, and only those parts of the world, which are immediately needed.

The Gibsons refer to the opportunities for action inherent in an organism's environment as *affordances*. These obviously differ radically between organisms—what a mouse can do with a kitchen, say, is quite different from what a cat can do with it, and different again from what a human can do; hence each organism perceives a different kitchen, a different world of affordances, just as Von Uexkull had already argued. (For extensive accounts of affordances, see Chemero, 2011; Shaw, Turvey, & Mace, 1982).

Gibson points out again and again how what we *perceive* reflects what we *are* (a concept sloganised by Mace as "Ask not what's inside your head, but what your head's inside of" (1977, p. 43)). For example, there is information about an organism's height off the ground in both the amount of light available to it (i.e., relative height of the horizon) and the particular surfaces off which that light is reflected.

> The information in light is not just about the things the light bounces off. It is also information about the perceiver and the relation between the perceiver and the environment. Gibson puts this point by saying that proprioception and interoception imply each other.
>
> (Chemero, 2011, p. 109)

But of course the world consists of not just an isolated perceiver, but a whole perceived/perceiving network: we and our bodies "exist along with the environment, they are co-perceived" (Gibson, 1982, p. 418). As a swelling chorus of voices has been saying throughout this chapter and the previous one, the perceiving "subject" at any particular moment is also the perceived "object", defining and defined by the whole network within which each perception is held.

So—what is embodiment?

I have sketched out rather a lot of ideas in this chapter and Chapter One, and it may take more than one reading before they fall into any sort of order. Their underlying unity is, for me, provided by the concept of reciprocity, or even of mutuality. At last, Western thought is overcoming its long, dire habit of *splitting* the experienced world into separate fragments—not just the great supposed dichotomies like mind and body, subject and object, external and internal, observer and observed, but also the conception of each entity as a "windowless monad", with everything ultimately composed of atoms like tiny billiard balls surrounded by space. Piece by piece, the splintered world has been put back together; and most recently, embodiment has emerged as a central aspect of what binds the world into one thing.

Rather than "embodiment", Merleau-Ponty speaks of "the Flesh" (*la Chair*): a term he uses to describe something perhaps not previously conceptualised in Western thought, though it does have analogues in Taoist and Buddhist philosophy. Not surprisingly, this concept is hard to grasp and even harder to summarise. For Merleau-Ponty, exploring the experience of embodiment leads us beyond the traditional Western dichotomy between subject and object, observer and observed. Here is one passage:

> When I find again the actual world such as it is, under my hands, under my eyes, up against my body, I find much more than an object: a Being of which my vision is a part, a visibility older than my operations or my act. But this does not mean that there was a fusion or a coinciding of me with it: on the contrary, this occurs because a sort of dehiscence opens my body in two, and because between my body looked at and my body looking, my body touched and my body touching, there is overlapping or encroachment, so that we must say that things pass into us as well as we into the things.

> (1968, p. 123)

This is not only rather beautiful, but also full of meaning. Merleau-Ponty breaks with the conventional Western model of perception as something which occurs *across distance*, across an unbridgeable chasm between subject and object. As his archetype of perception he takes not vision, but *touch*; and understands vision itself, therefore, as an experience not of distance but of *contact*. When I touch—or see—an object, it is Flesh touching itself. There are strong parallels here with the work of the Gibsons which I have just discussed, and which has been extended into the social world by Alan Costall (2000); and also, of course, with the Reichian and Gestalt tradition of emphasising "eye contact". Using the theories current in his time, John Donne wrote in the sixteenth century of two lovers whose "eye-beams twisted, and did thred/Our eyes, upon one double string" (*The Extasie*).

Flesh is continuous between ourselves and the world; but perception expresses itself through "folds" in the "fabric" of Flesh, creating gaps and spaces in what is otherwise one substance—"dehiscence", which is the term for the opening of a pod to release seeds. The imagery here feels very primal, like an infantile or foetal experience of embodiment; the developing embryo is in fact understood to grow through a series of such foldings, openings, wrappings and unwrappings (Grossinger, 1986; Keleman, 1989), to which the twisting and doubling of the lovers' gaze in Donne's poem seems related. Merleau-Ponty's presentation of perception is not simply embodied, but erotic.

Readers may feel they have been waiting some time for me to make an explicit connection between what I have been saying and psychotherapy. I think we have arrived at that point. If embodiment is so fundamental to our being in the world, to there *being* a world for us at all; if mind is inherently embodied, and if its extension into the world happens through and in embodiment; then therapy must pay serious and deliberate attention to each client's embodied experience, and to the embodied experience of the practitioner—and in particular, to how these two experiences impact upon and relate with each other in the therapy room.

Historically, body psychotherapy has followed the first half of this requirement better than the second half. It has focused on the embodiment of each member of the therapeutic dyad as if they could be held in mind separately, and has taken their interaction to be secondary and controlled by the practitioner's intention. In other words, parallel with traditional verbal therapy, the job of the body psychotherapist has been seen as one of assessing and, if we are honest, *improving* the client's relationship with her embodiment, while treating the therapist's own embodiment mainly as an improving influence on that of the client, and perhaps also as an instrument for perceiving the client's experience.

From the visual to the visceral

In reality, though, the two are far more deeply entangled than that, "upon one double string". Two bodies in the therapy room together are, in Merleau-Ponty's terms, one Flesh; their perception of each other is intimate, immediate.

> Communication is achieved through the reciprocity between
> my intentions and the other person's gestures, and between my

gestures and the intentions which can be read in the other person's behavior. Everything happens as if the other person's intention inhabited my body, or as if my intentions inhabited his body.

(1962, pp. 191–192)

It is through my body that I understand other people.

(1962, p. 186)

Traditionally therapy has relied on the special senses of sight and hearing, the senses that reach out across space. But what we are learning from the sort of work I have looked at in these two chapters is that the space they reach across is in many ways imaginary: that the other is immediately present to me, and that my most effective ways of perceiving her presence are visceral rather than visual, where "things pass into us as well as we into the things" (Merleau-Ponty, 1968, p. 123).

Certainly, much of the work I have been summarising, including Merleau-Ponty, ecological perception, and enactionism, gives great attention to vision. But the function of this attention is to reconceive vision in a way that takes away the sense of objectivity and distance which has long dominated our understanding of it: to understand vision, like the more feeling senses, as a *direct coupling* of perceiver and perceived: not a pure representation of the other, but a co-creation between our embodiment, with all its history, assumptions, and quirks, and hers. Vision itself becomes something more like touch; and touch gains some of the respect previously restricted to vision and hearing.

The most deeply grounded form of touch is the internal self-touching of proprioception and visceral sensation—what we perceive in our bones, muscles, heart, and guts, what shades over ineluctably into feeling and emotion. I become more and more certain that therapy needs to stop positioning the therapist as someone who sits securely in her own subjectivity and looks out across space, across the room, to observe, listen to, and make deductions about the client. Instead we need to let ourselves be reached into and changed by the gravitational pull of the client's presence, to track her effect on us through the deep shifts in our visceral affective state, and from the response that rises up in the deep waters of our bodymind.

This is what I mean by embodied relating; and it is to this that we will now turn.

CHAPTER THREE

Embodied relating

Jeffrey Maitland makes a challenging statement about relating: "Everything that is alive is a relationship" (1995, p. 154). This is perhaps startling, but quite simply true: not only are all living things *in* relationship, they actually *are* relationships.

> Your body is not a complex thing composed of simpler things, but a living relationship of mutually-supporting relationships forming and being formed at every moment. Your body is a relationship in which all relationships are related; fascia is the tissue of that relationship. It is the tissue within which all relationships are relating.
>
> (p. 154)

It follows—and this is the heart of systemic thinking—that the level at which we draw a line around certain relationships of relationships and call them a system, or an organism, is in many ways a matter of convenience. Groups are also relationships of relationships; so are societies. In this chapter and the next three we need to hold this basic fact in mind. In this chapter we will focus on the system formed by dyadic relationships, in and out of the therapy room.

The embodiment matrix

Many practitioners, some of them body psychotherapists and some not (e.g., Athanasiadou & Halewood, 2011; Dosamantes-Beaudry, 1997; Field, 1989; Ross, 2000; Soth, 2005; Stone, 2006; Vulcan, 2009), have observed how processes like transference, countertransference, and projection are frequently experienced in an embodied way by the practitioner. In fact Egan and Carr (2008) have developed a "Body-Centred Countertransference Scale" to measure the intensity of the effect, including sixteen different bodily phenomena. In Booth, Trimble, and Egan's research using this scale on a sample of Irish clinical psychologists (2010), the most commonly reported of these sixteen phenomena were muscle tension, sleepiness, yawning, and tearfulness; the least common, but still significantly represented, were nausea, numbness, sexual arousal, and genital pain. (It is unsurprising that the latter group are less often reported, given the greater likelihood that they will lead to dissociation.)

The position I am putting forward in this book is that the formulation above—that transference and countertransference are sometimes experienced in an embodied way—is actually back to front or upside down: in reality what we are dealing with is an *embodied interaction which is then usually experienced and conceptualised on the level of transference*. I will go on to suggest that the logic of the argument I use to make the case for treating transference and countertransference as fundamentally embodied also implies that we should start to see them as *mutually dependent*, in a further chain of circular causation like the ones we examined in the previous chapters. Transference and countertransference create and shape each other: they are two sides of one phenomenon, cross-transference.

Here is a superbly vivid description of an embodied countertransference, from Susie Orbach:

> For my part, I began to feel rather tiny. Like Alice [In Wonderland] I felt myself grow down and grow in as though I were a miniature. Doreen appeared as a blow-up doll or, perhaps I should more accurately say, an overblown, overgrown, blown-up pretend woman figure such as are sold for sexual purposes on the internet. My diminution was not altogether unpleasant. I went back and forth between feeling teetered over as though I was this little thing underneath her, and then sensing my lungs expand to take a

metaphorical hearty breath as they were poised to shoot forward to prick and deflate her. She was at once substantial and puffed out, carrying too much water to let her feet sit comfortably in her dainty shoes, and yet almost menacingly large and solid.

(2003, p. 4)

We need no context to grasp the *mutuality* of the experience: something is happening both to the therapist and to the client. Or alternatively one could start to distance oneself from this mutuality by re-centring in the therapist's subjectivity, by saying instead "Something is happening to both *the therapist's perception of herself* and *her perception of the client.*" And this distancing does perhaps begin to occur as Orbach interprets her experience:

My body countertransference with Doreen was a visceral rendition of her early experience of bodies around her being too large and yet not sufficiently robust or stable for her to find or develop a body herself from. She *did* feel them teetering over her. She couldn't get them to be in focus, and the volatility of the body size I experienced in the countertransference was a version of the search for a body for herself that could moor itself by finding a place in the physical storm that surrounded her.

(p. 4)

"A visceral rendition", "a version": phrases like these are surely attempts at withdrawal from the "physical storm" in which Orbach was caught up—positioning it as a record or transcription of *something else,* of an experience which was *not* the practitioner's. Embodied countertransference is a micro-enactment, in which the therapist is helplessly acted-upon by the client's presence; and as with full blown enactments, it is neither possible nor desirable to dissociate oneself—in any sense of the phrase—from the intersubjective nexus (Soth, 2005, pp. 49–50). As Orbach makes exquisitely clear, her helplessness is a direct function of Doreen's; it is *necessary* for her to experience it in order to come into relationship with her client. This is similar to what James Hillman says about dreams: that when we interpret them "we wrong the dream, we wrong the soul", because "dreams are the primary givens" (1979, pp. 2, 4). The embodied therapeutic relationship is also a primary given, part of the body's dream; to interpret it can often be to deny it.

My suggestion, then, is that therapists experience an inevitable wish to extricate themselves from most forms of embodied countertransference (sexual desire is sometimes an exception). It makes us feel uncomfortably out of control, and hence both vulnerable and irresponsible. This understandable defensive reaction leads in many cases—though not in Orbach's account—to the preconscious erasure of the most embodied aspects of therapeutic relationship, and the abstraction and intellectualisation of these visceral experiences.

This process—effectively a form of dissociation—allows therapists to stay apparently in command of the situation, safe in their disembodied observer stance; but, just as when we resist full enactments, it limits (without eliminating) the potential for transformative relational experience. I believe that the same factor influences theoretical approaches to the issue. "Embodied countertransference" is nothing but a special case of embodied relating: if we refuse one, then we at least partially refuse the other, and weaken our capacity to connect deeply with our clients. I return to this in Chapter Ten.

The felt sense of the other

Embodied relating, then, is a specialised area of embodied cognition which involves what we might call, drawing on Eugene Gendlin (e.g., 1998), *the felt sense of the other*. I thought briefly and happily that I had coined this expression, but it turns out that it is used by several writers, in particular Akira Ikemi (2005, 2013) who works at the meeting point of person centred therapy and focusing, and writes that "The felt sense is an interaction with the presence of the other" (2005, p. 286). Focusing pays a great deal of attention to the embodied relationship: Gendlin in fact writes that "In therapy the relationship is of first importance, listening comes second, and focusing instructions come only third" (Gendlin, 1998, p. 297).

What especially appeals to me about the phrase, "the felt sense of the other", is its double-sidedness: it names both *my felt sense of the other person*, and *the other's felt sense of me*—surely central to the transference matrix, where transference and countertransference are woven out of the same substance, braided together in a process of mutual co-arising (Totton, 2011; Varela, Thompson, & Rosch, 1991). As Merleau-Ponty says, "Every perception doubled with a counter-perception … is an act with two faces, one no longer knows who speaks and who listens" (1968, pp. 264–265).

This sentence seems to me to sum up and give a context for the whole elaborate therapeutic apparatus of identifications, introjections, projections, transferences and countertransferences, and so on. The medium in which all these transactions circulate is what Merleau-Ponty calls Flesh (*la Chair*):

> The Flesh is the mysterious tissue or matrix that underlies and gives rise to both the perceiver and the perceived as interdependent aspects of its own spontaneous activity. It is the reciprocal presence of the sentient in the sensible and of the sensible in the sentient, a mystery of which we have always, at least tacitly, been aware since we have never been able to affirm one of the phenomena, the perceivable world or the perceiving self, without implicitly affirming the existence of the other.
>
> (Abram, 1997, p. 66)

Merleau-Ponty discovers this reciprocity in the whole of reality (and his thought has been usefully applied to ecopsychology: Cataldi & Hamrick, 2007). He also finds it specifically in human relating, where he names it *intercorporeality* (1968, p. 143), a "carnal intersubjectivity" (p. 173). Through our embodiment, we are immediately and inherently linked in shared understanding: as a symbol of this, no one can touch others without *being* touched by them at the site of physical contact (a reality which is strongly downplayed in body psychotherapy's emphasis on the practitioner touching rather than—more scarily— being touched). "Subjects are joined by their belongingness to a common world. Furthermore … they 'open' onto each other" (Crossley, 1995, p. 57). Embodiment, Flesh, is the matrix for human relationship; and body psychotherapy is perhaps the place where this can be brought most clearly into awareness.

As a phenomenologist, Merleau-Ponty takes our lived experience of embodiment very seriously. He notices, for instance, that:

> Anger, shame, hate and love are not psychic facts hidden at the bottom of another's consciousness. They are … visible from the

outside. They exist *on* this face or *in* these gestures, not hidden behind them.

(1964, pp. 52–53)

Neuroscientists can now interpret this phenomenon in terms of mirror neurons, areas of the brain which fire in response to our perception of someone else's acts or expressions (Aziz-Zadeh, Wilson, Rizzolatti, & Iacoboni, 2006; Schütz-Bosbach, Mancini, Aglioti, & Haggard, 2006); and Merleau-Ponty would no doubt have seized eagerly upon the concept, just as he uses the theory of body schemas, what neuroscience now usually calls "procedural memory", to underpin the notion of inherent bodily knowledge of the world:

> Our body is not in space like things; it inhabits or haunts space. It applies itself to space like a hand to an instrument. And when we wish to move about we do not move the body as an object. ... Through it, we have access to space.
>
> (1962, p. 5)

But mirror neuron theory offers an *external* view ("view" being the crucial word) of embodiment, while Merleau-Ponty strives to articulate an experience from the *inside*:

> I am not in front of my body, I am in it or rather I am it. ... If we can still speak of interpretation in relation to the perception of one's own body, we shall have to say that it interprets itself.
>
> (1962, p. 150)

Merleau-Ponty's ideas cannot really be translated into more ordinary terms: there *are* no ordinary terms for them, until we accept his own terms as ordinary. To translate him into scientific language travesties his project. And yet the experience he describes is not some refined mystical insight; it is at the heart of human life, and at the heart of body psychotherapy in particular. However, body psychotherapists have made surprisingly little attempt to language our deep experience of embodied contact, tending to drape it in bland phrases like "the truth of the body", which really say very little at all (Totton,

2005a). In what follows I shall try to develop a language for embodied relating.

Engrams

Something that emerges strongly from work on embodied cognition is the vital role of implicit or procedural knowledge in human learning. For every repeated activity, from riding a bicycle to forming a relationship, we rely on preconscious or unconscious patterns of activation and behaviour which we developed when first learning the activity (Thelen & Smith, 1994), and which move steadily from foreground to background as we absorb them into our subliminal ways of being in the world, until the experience is of our body doing them "on its own". As sports instructors know very well, it is extremely hard to alter these implicit procedural habits, which have to be brought back into awareness—or, if they are unintentionally acquired "bad habits", brought into awareness for the first time—before they can be changed (Straub & Williams, 1984).

Some of the deepest implicit, embodied patterns we hold seem to be those around relating (Boston Change Process Study Group, 2008). If we apply the above ideas to transference, it becomes clear that it needs to be understood not only as a psychological but also, and fundamentally, as a *bodily* process: a function of implicit procedural memories of childhood relationships, learnt complexes of emotional and physical response situated outside consciousness and in part repressed from consciousness. Our body learns patterns of relating in childhood and infancy, ways of positioning self in relation to the other which become an automatic part of our adult repertoire, encompassing not only embodied speech but also posture, gesture, micro-expressions, pheromone release, and sympathetic/parasympathetic nervous system activation, and extending to our basic metabolism (Eisman, 1985, Ch. 19, pp. 4ff). Each of us has several different patterns of embodied relating available to us, and each of these will be deployed in response to a particular sort of stimulus, taking over our bodymind behaviour and drawing from us particular kinds of accompanying habitual thoughts and attitudes.

As a very simple example, we implicitly "look up to" certain people and "look down on" others, depending on how we assess them according to a complex set of personal/cultural criteria. These relational attitudes will be anchored in *posture*—a shortening and bending of our body in the first case, a lengthening and straightening in the second, accompanied by corresponding differences in how we hold our head and neck and the sort of eye contact we make. Which of these patterns we use will have an involuntary effect on the person we are relating to, a (probably preconscious) *experience* of being looked up to or looked down on. This will stimulate in her a physical/relational postural response which, depending on her habitual attitudes, either colludes with or challenges the attitude we are expressing—either says "Yes, you should look down on/up to me" or "No, you shouldn't". All of these patterns reflect our personal history, and the history of the people who impacted us in our early relationship: they are a re-presentation of the past, when we responded to what other people's patterns told us about ourselves: a sort of possession of our bodymind by early ghosts.

Discussing such implicit patterns, Deane Juhan writes:

> It is the memory and association of things which are *felt* that develop and direct the mind's expression through the musculature, and in this constant feedback between gestures and the feelings that accompany them neither tactile nor emotional feelings can be said to dominate the other.

> (2003, pp. 271–272)

Following and extending Juhan (2003, Chapter Nine), to describe these ghostlike implicit patterns of relating I am going to use the word *engram*: an old fashioned but (before it was enlisted by Scientology) respectable term for the unknown mechanism by which memory complexes are stored and then reactivated by appropriate stimulus (Lashley, 1950). In a neuroscience context, the general assumption is that these memories are stored in the brain; but I am talking about procedural memories effectively stored in the *body*, just as it is our fingers not our brain which perform the physical actions necessary to play the piano (Koch, Fuchs, Summa, & Muller, 2012). Without accepting any of Scientology's belief system, I appreciate its definition of the engram as "a definite and permanent trace left by a stimulus on the protoplasm of a tissue" (Hubbard, 1988, p. 82fn), which feels like something Reich might have written.

The term "engram" literally means something *inscribed within*, which brings out the way that we receive engrams from others before we make them our own. Our embodied relational engrams are formed in our earliest relationships; and we use them, for better or worse, as blueprints in each attempt to negotiate new encounters. They are enormously powerful in shaping our experience, and, equally, other people's experience of us: human bodies constantly respond to and become entrained with each other's relational engrams, and this process in a therapeutic context is traditionally described in the language of transference and projection. The therapist's countertransference is in large part an out-of-awareness reaction to the client's transference engram, and vice versa for the client: joining in the physiological dance (Totton & Priestman, 2012, p. 39).

To illustrate this simply, here is a vignette which I have used elsewhere, but am looking at now in a slightly different way. Early on in therapy with a client, I found my attention drawn to his tight jaw, which I felt expressed an attitude of stubborn defiance. I developed a strong (and unexamined) wish to soften this tightness, and as soon as I felt we had established sufficient trust between us I asked him whether I could press on the muscles in the angle of the jaw while encouraging him to breathe and make a noise. Although he seemed to consent to this process, it didn't go at all well: the client quickly became distressed and asked me to stop, and trust between us was damaged for some while.

After a few months, though, and completely forgetting the previous interaction, I did the same thing, with a similar result—and then again a few months later! Not surprisingly, the effect was worse each time; finally, I grasped that there was something here which needed examination. I was open with the client about my apparent helplessness to avoid repeating the behaviour, and how bad I felt about it. The client started to talk about the intense physical bullying he had experienced as a child from his older brothers, and how he had felt unable to tell his parents: the tight jaw, it seemed, expressed both his inability to speak, his defiance in the face of bullying, and his holding back of sobs—which were now able to be released.

But why had I acted in such a stupid and insensitive way? This enactment, it seems to me, was created by my unconsciously picking up the complex and contradictory messages embedded in my client's tight jaw, and responding to *all of them at once*. My bodymind knew that there was something he needed to tell me; but in trying to access it, I replicated the bullying situation itself, and drove the sobbing deeper within—while at the same time the situation was *showing* me, rather than *telling* me, about the original scenario. I am myself an older brother, and have my own bullying engram which was activated under cover of therapeutic helping. The client's embodied expectation of bullying and resistance cued me to repeat my own childhood behaviour—of which, of course, I am now consciously ashamed—of enjoying physical power over someone weaker.

We are equal partners in the physiological dance referred to earlier: each forward movement of one dancer's limbs implies and elicits, gives meaning to and takes its own meaning from, a backward movement of the other, and vice versa. And listen, they're playing our tune: the dance is a unique synthesis of the two partners' relational engrams, in which each constitutes an exogram for the other. Again we are encountering circular causality, mutual co-arising.

In the model I am offering, transference, countertransference, and projection are all bodily phenomena, based on the activation of procedural engrams which are always implicit—that is, out of awareness—and often also repressed—that is, not available to awareness. The Boston Change Process Study Group refers to this as "implicit relational knowing" (Boston Change Process Study Group, 2008; Lyons-Ruth, 1998). When such engrams are active in the client, any number of channels are available for the therapist to pick them up. As Allen Schore says:

> In monitoring countertransferential responses to the patient's implicit facial, gestural, and prosodic communications, the clinician ... tracks at a preconscious level not only the rhythms and flows of the patient's affective states, but also the clinician's own interoceptive bodily based affective responses to the patient's shifting arousal levels.

> (2005, p. 845)

This tracking can with practice occur consciously.

Among the available channels we can also include, for example, the effect of mirror neurons in creating an echo in ourselves of what we perceive happening in the other. Babette Rothschild (1994) and others have suggested that therapists' tendency to "mirror" in a more ordinary sense—deliberately or otherwise to match clients' posture, breathing, speech rhythms, etc.—renders us particularly open to this sort of echoing; as, of course, does our general position of empathic attunement.

But as I have already emphasised, *all* human beings are impacted on a bodily level by the feeling state of others, whether we recognise it or not, whether we welcome it or not. And the whole message of the relational turn in psychotherapy is that when the therapist is impacted by the client's transference engram, our response is outside our conscious control: our own engrams are activated, and we are swayed deeply by the early experiences which they encode. Both participants are then cast into a maelstrom where we struggle to survive, to self-soothe, and to recognise the actuality of the here-and-now situation and of the other. As Karen Maroda writes, once transference and countertransference appear,

> Each begins to feel misunderstood by the other. They may each feel a myriad of other things, such as unloved, unappreciated, abused, or taken advantage of, by the other. Or they may defend against these negative feelings by being madly in love with each other … emotions run high, crescendoing into overt conflict …
>
> (2002, p. 4)

Melanie Klein has already written in extremely embodied terms about projection, which she describes as an evacuation of rejected body contents into the other, based on an unconscious fantasy of excretion and expulsion (Hinshelwood, 1994; Klein, 1936, 1952). This only needs to be thought about in a slightly more literal way to be wholly compatible with what I am talking about. "Projective identification" (Klein, 1952) describes a particular form of the process by which one person's engram stimulates a corresponding one in the other.

Exograms

There is an even deeper issue here, in fact. What could entitle us to make an absolute distinction between a therapist's internal experiences as traces of the client's material, and a therapist's internal experiences as traces of her own material? What would allow us to assert that what Schore (2005, p. 845) calls our "bodily based affective responses to the patient's shifting arousal levels" *are* "responses", rather than events of which we should acknowledge ownership—indeed, perhaps events to which the client's "shifting arousal levels" are responses?

When two asteroids, for example, are affected by each other's gravitational fields, the difficulty of mathematically treating this mutuality other than by artificially reducing it to two separate equations, one for each celestial body, is the original "two body problem" (Goldstein, 1980) which was later used as an analogy for the relational view of psychotherapy, describing it as replacing a "one-body psychology" with a "two-body psychology" (Balint, 1950). According to two-body psychology, there is a complex, nonlinear interaction between therapist and client which forms a system of its own, irreducible to a series of linear interactions.

The implication of this way of understanding the therapeutic relationship is that we cannot separate out transference and countertransference components and allot linear causality in a straightforward way. We could equally say—as Jacques Lacan does in a provocative early paper (1950)—that it is the therapist's countertransference which elicits the client's transference. Each subject's engram is an "exogram" for the other:

> Other people may (in certain circumstances) form part of our external memory fields, with their own dynamic engrams potentially acting as exograms for us.

> (Sutton, 2008, p. 43)

Sutton is plainly describing a situation of reciprocity, where one person's engram (internal inscription) may become another person's exogram (external inscription), and vice versa. As the German Enlightenment thinker Friedrich Scheiermacher wrote, "Each person contains a minimum of everyone else" (1977, pp. 169–170). This is an omnipresent aspect of human existence, as described in the passage from Christopher Bollas (1993) which I quoted in the previous chapter; and as I suggested at that point, the therapeutic relationship is a peculiarly intense version of it, where the reciprocal entwining of two subjectivities is also the object of their shared attention. I will describe this process from now on as "reciprocal transference" or "cross-transference".

Embodied relating and mutuality

I have already quoted the last sentence of the passage below:

> Faced with an angry or threatening gesture, I have no need, in order to understand it, to recall the feelings which I myself

experienced when I used these gestures on my own account … It is
as if the other person's intentions inhabited my body and mine his
… It is through my body that I understand other people.

(Merleau-Ponty, 1962, pp. 184–185)

Merleau-Ponty is describing the sort of core human experience now
generally framed within the theory of mirror neurons (which had
not been identified when Merleau-Ponty was writing). However, it is
important to realise that mirror neuron theory neither defines the experience it refers to, nor, so far at least, really illuminates it; most of its
effect is simply to *underwrite* the lived experience which we already
have, to license our belief in it by connecting it to physical events in the
brain (cf. Hickok, 2014; see the section of the Introduction entitled "The
question of evidence").

The lived experience of understanding other people's feelings is not
some sort of internal "simulation" of the other's action or expression,
mental modelling based on sense data plus introspection, as is often
claimed by writers on mirror neurons (e.g., Gallese & Goldman, 1998;
Oberman & Ramachandran, 2007), but *a direct and immediate knowing*
(Gallagher, 2005, 2012; De Haan, De Jaegher, Fuchs, & Mayer, 2011).
Wilhelm Reich grasped this long ago when he wrote:

> The patient's expressive movements involuntarily bring about an
> imitation in our own organism. By imitating these movements we
> "sense" and understand the expression in ourselves and, conse-
> quently, in the patient. … The language of facial and bodily expres-
> sions becomes an essential means of communicating with the
> patient.
>
> (1945a, p. 362)

Mirror neuron theory comes to life when incorporated into the wider
field of embodied cognition. Drawing on Shaun Gallagher (2005),
Jessica Lindblom writes:

> Mirror neurons and shared representations are not primarily the
> mediators of simulation but the *enactment* of direct intersubjec-
> tive perception. [Gallagher] exemplifies this view in the imitation
> of facial expression, emphasizing that infants have no need to

simulate the facial gesture internally, as an extra step, since through
actually seeing it, they already simulate it on their own faces. This
means, one's own body is already communicating with the other's
body at unconscious and perceptual levels that are sufficient for
intersubjective interaction to emerge.

(2007, p. 128)

Gallagher and Lindblom are referring to the well established fact that
infants—as early as thirty-five minutes after birth—will, as it appears,
spontaneously try to reproduce adult facial expressions (Meltzoff &
Moore, 1995). There are two interwoven aspects to this process, which
is not really about attempted reproduction: the infant's *response* to
the adult is an involuntary aspect of *receiving* her expressed emotion.
Following Merleau-Ponty, the at-a-distance image of embodied mirroring implied in "reproduction" is better conceived more tactilely, as an
intaglio print, in which the convex and concave, "receiver" and "trans-
mitter" faces of the same image match and coincide. An image is cut
into a metal plate and then inked; a sheet of paper is pressed into the
image with a roller, and this intimate contact produces an embossed
image on the paper. An image (engram) which has been carved into one
surface now stands out from another surface: not simply a reproduction, but a response.

This metaphor of *intaglio* is in a general way inspired by, though quite
distinct from, Jean Laplanche's concept of "embossed" and "hollowed
out" transference (e.g., 1992, pp. 12–13). It returns us to the Merleau-
Ponty passage I quoted earlier: "Every perception doubled with a
counter-perception ... is an act with two faces, one no longer knows
who speaks and who listens" (1968, pp. 264–265). Merleau-Ponty constantly refers back to the experience of touching/being touched by one's
own body; but he applies this reciprocity equally to our relationship
with others and with the world. The example of infant imitation demonstrates very clearly how central embodied enaction is to our experience of relationship. Here is the hinge on which this whole book turns:
the image of embodied relating as "an act with two faces", a combined
engram/exogram, an *intaglio* imprinting which fuses together the experience of two bodyminds.

CHAPTER FOUR

Practising embodied relating

If we accept the ideas laid out in the previous chapter, then the question arises of how we can put them into operation: what do they imply for the practice of psychotherapy? Well, it turns out that a form of clinical practice already exists which is at least halfway to answering the question; this is body psychotherapy, which is uniquely placed to take up and make use of these concepts which match so well with its basic assumptions—though they also challenge it to complement its embodied practice with a theory adequate to the task.

Let me continue, then, with a quotation from Wilhelm Reich, who simultaneously created body psychotherapy as a field and, because of his radical positions, put it for many years out of bounds for mainstream therapists:

> On an elementary level, there is but one desire which issues from
> the biopsychic unity of the person, namely the desire to discharge
> inner tensions ... This is impossible without contact with the outer
> world. Hence, the *first* impulse of *every* creature must be the desire
> to establish contact with the outer world.

> (1945a, p. 271, original italics)

Here in a nutshell is the inherent link between the drive/energy theories of traditional body psychotherapy, and more recent relational approaches. It is our organismic energy which needs and seeks relationship, as its only route to fulfilment: both as a stepping stone towards satisfying needs like hunger, thirst, or sex, and as an end in itself, relationality being a fundamental human need. Relational psychoanalysis has shied away from drive theory mainly because it sees it as identified with a "one-body psychology" (Balint, 1950) as opposed to a relational "two-body psychology". But as Reich's statement shows, there is nothing inherent about this: drives, unless they are blocked, move us into relationship with others and with the world.

The specific contribution of body psychotherapy to the relational approach is to somatise relationship: to *flesh it out*, one might say, as part of our general commitment to supporting clients in fleshing out their whole experience of life. As James Kepner says, speaking of life in general, but in terms applicable to much therapeutic work:

> Most often, our conversation and common contact includes little of our embodied experience in its content, little reference to embodiment in gesture, and little conscious experience of ourselves or the other as embodied beings. Even when we report emotions they are rarely acknowledged as bodily events, located in our bodily self, even though one cannot experience emotion without bodily location. We keep it all very abstract with little bodily referent. It is as if our emotions had no bodily origin or location, but are something we "thought up".
>
> (2003, p. 7)

In contrast, Kepner suggests, "A body therapist must have access to their own deep embodiment and relate to the client in a deeply embodied way" (p. 9): "To be deeply embodied is to have access to one's body experience as *self-experience*" (p. 12, original italics)—in other words, he is talking about the second meaning of embodiment as I described it in Chapter One, embodiment which is self-aware. He is referring to the striking way in which self-aware embodiment can be infectious—or perhaps the right word is *contagious*, since touch is so often a central channel for the communication from therapist to client of what it is to be a lived body.

This communication can only take place within a functioning relationship. To feel someone else's embodied presence is an intimate, intense, demanding experience; if we are dissociated from our own embodiment, or even sometimes if we are not, it can easily feel overwhelmingly frightening. This often leads us to project the experienced threat from within ourselves onto the other person, and to treat them as seductive, intrusive, overpowering—all the more so if there is traumatic experience from the past that can be reawakened. It takes an established relationship of trust to get client and therapist through this crisis; and this depends also on the therapist's ability to manage whatever engrams of seduction or domination arise within herself in resonance with the client's expectations.

The alternative to this anxiety-filled engram is in some ways easier to tolerate, but at the same time harder to shake off: instead of projecting danger onto the therapist, the client projects magical healing powers— instead of handing her the blame, the client hands her the credit, which the therapist may be very ready to take. Things can't really move forward in either case until the client takes back what she is trying to give away, and the therapist gives back what she is trying to take. Of course, very similar things happen around any kind of therapeutic breakthrough.

Embodied-Relational Therapy

My own brand of body psychotherapy, which I practise and teach, is called Embodied-Relational Therapy, or ERT (Totton, 2005b; Totton & Priestman, 2012, on which some parts of this chapter draw). ERT starts out from the perception that we are all embodied and relational beings: two core aspects of what it means to be a human. We need relationships with others in order to survive and thrive both physically and emotionally. As babies and infants we are totally, bodily dependent on our primary caregivers; we are born, therefore, with a hard-wired imperative to form relationships, to actively attract and appeal to adult humans, for example by matching their vocal and facial signals and rhythmically attuning to their behaviour (Hart, 2011; Stern, 1985; Trevarthen & Aitken, 2001; Wilkinson, 2010).

We enter the world as bodies, in other words, primed to seek contact with other bodies. Just as babies can start reproducing the expressions and movements of other people within minutes of birth

(Meltzoff & Moore, 1995, pp. 49–50), within a similar time span they can also recognise the voice of their mother, which they have heard only from within the womb (DeCasper & Fifer, 1980; DeCasper & Spence, 1986). For years after birth our survival depends on our ability to attract and hold the attention of adult carers; and we have evolved many ways of doing so.

But this account is not enough. It is an abstract way of describing what all carers for infants witness: the passionate and skilful delight babies find in creating embodied relationship, and the storms of grief and despair with which they respond to disturbances in that relationship. Long before a baby can form anything describable as a thought, her bodymind is capable of complex and subtly intelligent interactions through gaze, expression, voice, and movement. We arrive in this world eager and expectant to "discharge inner tensions" (Reich, 1945a, p. 271) through forming intense relationships, and with a huge capacity to do so which we hurl recklessly into action like a gambler or a lover staking everything on one throw of the dice. Our bodies tremble and vibrate with urgency to connect, soaring and swooping between peaks of bliss and troughs of agony and despair, visibly expanding and contracting with the responses we receive.

These earliest relationships literally form and shape us and all our future relationships; throughout our lives we can experience the deepest wounding and the deepest healing in relationship. On this topic neuroscience (e.g., Gerhardt, 2004; Marks-Tarlow, 2012a; Schore, 2000a, 2000b) simply confirms the long-held intuitions of body psychotherapy. It seems fair to say, in fact, that babies form relationships before they really have a personal identity, "soft-assembling" relationality out of preprogrammed capacities like the ability to distinguish faces and voices from other features of the environment. So the infant's identity is actually formed as a correlative of her relating to others, a meeting point of innate and acquired skills shaped and conditioned by what carers bring to the relationship: the infant becomes, to some extent, what the carers anticipate in their relating. In developing a theory of (other people's) mind, infants are also developing a theory of their *own* mind, a perspective which allows them to form a concept of self, and to form a self (De Haan, De Jaegher, Fuchs, & Mayer, 2011).

For adults as for infants, when two people meet and come together each continuously affects and conditions the experience of the other. Each relationship is unique, and develops from the conscious and unconscious reactions of both participants. So in therapy, for example, each client responds differently to us, we respond differently to each of our clients, and the quality of the contact formed between us and hence of the work that we do together will to an extent be unique to that dyad. I find from supervision that not all practitioners are aware of *how* different their own experience and behaviour is in the presence of different clients, until their attention is brought to it: there is an unthinking assumption that we act consistently irrespective of who we are with.

But to act the same with everyone would be to deliver manualised techniques; it would render relational work impossible. From a relational viewpoint, consistent behaviour is precisely behaviour that is responsive to context, to how the other affects us; *difference*, not sameness, is information (Bateson, 1971, p. 315). Consistency in the other sense, staying the same, is unresponsive to the other, who will probably become distressed. This is what happens in the well-known experiment where babies are shown video of their mothers' reactions to them, but on a time lapse, so that the reaction no longer corresponds to what the baby is doing now (Murray & Trevarthen, 1985). As Phoebe Caldwell writes:

> What we tell a person when we are out of sync is that we are not listening to them or engaging with them. Intersubjectivity is lost. As far as they are concerned we are treating them as objects since we are not interested in them as potential communication partners.
>
> (2006, p. 277)

These reactions and responses to the unique individual other are not primarily mental events. They are sourced *in our bodily experience*, the physiological activation set in train by the mutual impact and entrainment of two people's embodiment. Much of this happens outside consciousness, and the process is too complex and extensive to track fully either from the inside or from the outside. In the section after this one I will briefly survey some of the many theories that have been developed about the mechanisms through which bodies know other bodies.

Although we don't generally know, and in some cases cannot know, the details of these processes, we certainly can and do become conscious of their final summation in our "intuitive feeling" about the other, our reaction of opening up or closing down, sympathy or suspicion, liking or dislike. A sizeable part of training to be a psychotherapist—though it is quite often implicit learning, not explicitly discussed with trainees—is learning to be aware of and to interrogate these responses in ourselves (Marks-Tarlow, 2012a). For body psychotherapists this is grounded in identifying our *embodied* reactions, before or alongside their translation into an emotional response and then into psychological assessment. Many practitioners who don't see themselves as body psychotherapists make use of this capacity, though, again, they are often not explicitly aware of doing so. I see this capacity consciously to track and make use of one's embodied experience as the central qualification for doing body psychotherapy (see Chapter Eleven).

Relational body psychotherapy takes this a stage further. We can conceptualise it in terms of the distinction already referred to between a "one-body psychology" which situates material within the analysand, and a "two-body psychology", which explores the system formed by analysand and analyst together (Aron, 1990; Balint, 1950). "Body" in this formulation derives from mathematical physics; but for body psychotherapists it obviously has a much more literal significance. In a "one-body body psychotherapy" the practitioner *consults* her own embodied response in order to learn about the client's issues and needs. In a "two-body body psychotherapy", however, as practitioners we *commit to* our embodied response in order to create a living, two-way relationship which forms the crucible of change and growth. Our body bathes in and soaks up the embodied presence of the client; we catch fire from her; we breathe her in and metabolise her; our ground state reverberates to her rhythms, and our own rhythms shift to meet them. Out of this meeting of realities, a third, shared reality is born.

How the body knows things

What I have been saying links up with a strand of my thinking which I have perhaps tended to be shy about, keeping it a little separate from the rest: my work on what is rather unsatisfactorily called the "para-normal" (Totton, 2003b, 2007). Ever since Freud, psychotherapy has had a close but queasy relationship with the paranormal; and rather than seeking to introduce something new and strange into the field, I want to suggest that what we are doing is already much stranger than we care to admit.

Freud wrote, in an often-quoted passage that the analyst:

... must turn his own unconscious like a receptive organ towards the transmitting unconscious of the patient. He must adjust himself to the patient as a telephone receiver is adjusted to the transmitting microphone.

(1912e, pp. 115–116)

Much attention has been paid to the hi-tech (for its time) image of the "receiver"; but it has largely passed without comment that Freud speaks first of a "receptive *organ*". I think this is rather more than a simile: that it is, literally, the organism which "adjusts … to the patient" and comes into resonance with her. The tension between the "organ" which passes without discussion, and the "telephone receiver" which is given detailed attention, signifies a persistent tension between experiential and technical approaches to human interaction—expressed in the way pseudo-technical language can be used in psychotherapy to obscure the real mysteriousness of what happens.

Many, probably most, experienced practitioners have noticed that when something about a client is discussed in supervision, it is common for that client to turn up to the next session and start talking on exactly that theme, often before the therapist opens her mouth; or even for the issue to have been resolved before the session happens (cf. Strean & Nelson, 1962). We generally take this in our stride, without getting very excited about it. But just what sort of mechanism do we think is operating here? Or how do we think it comes about that we find ourselves feeling what the client is feeling, or thinking about whatever is most important to her at that moment? Or, on a slightly different tack, when we suggest to a client who has arrived late that this might represent a resistance to therapy, in what way do we believe that her emotions have controlled the transport system or the weather?

Well, unless our paranoia has swollen beyond useful limits, we don't believe that clients control the weather; but we do seem to believe in a sort of synchronicity that brings various events and feelings into parallel with each other. We believe in a meaningful relationship between what happens in the therapy room, and what Arnold Mindell (1985b) calls the "world channel". We believe, as part of our daily occupation, in things which in other contexts would locate us as well off the edge of the mainstream. But I think that our ways of describing and talking about all these phenomena tend to obscure their essential strangeness, making it seem as though we know what we are talking about.

In analytic settings one might speak of "communicative countertransference"; in humanistic or body psychotherapy contexts, people often tend more to put it in terms of "energy", sensing the quality of the client's energy or the energy between client and therapist; while nowadays pretty much everyone speaks of "parallel process" (for an early discussion see Schlessinger, 1966). Many therapists from all disciplines operate clinically in a sort of mutual "psychic space" where the subjectivities of client and practitioner are experienced as having direct contact with each other (R. M. Young, 1994). Communicative countertransference, metabolising the patient's difficult feelings, parallel process, projective identification, "the energy in the room", and other such ideas are essentially paranormal concepts: they *name* what happens, but without making it the slightest bit less extraordinary. Simply by using the terms repeatedly until they sound familiar, however, we have managed to convince ourselves that they represent a solved problem rather than an open mystery.

What I want to offer here is the suggestion that a good deal—though perhaps not all—of what I am calling "paranormal", in therapy and in everyday life, can be understood in terms of the embodied capacities, in particular relational ones, which I have been describing. Something extra would certainly be required to make sense of situations where, for example, the client shows detailed knowledge of events in the therapist's private life (e.g., Ehrenwald, 1954; Eisenbud, 1946). But there is good reason to think that many paranormal experiences are grounded in officially "normal" channels which allow one unconscious to communicate with another. I have already referred to several of these.

To clarify why I am still wanting to call these sorts of communications "paranormal", it may be helpful to go back to Freud's work on telepathy in psychoanalysis, where he defines the concept of telepathy as the idea that: "[Mental] processes in one person ... can be transferred to another person through empty space *without employing the familiar methods of communication* by means of words and signs" (1933a, p. 39; my italics).

He later makes it clear that "What lies between ... may easily be a physical process" (1933a, p. 55); in other words, the sort of embodied events I have been describing would qualify as telepathy. I think Freud is exactly right on this: telepathy, like other paranormal events, is defined as such not by the *mechanism* involved, but by the *quality of the experience*.

In other words, what is essentially telepathic interaction can take place through the medium of language (Royle, 1991)—though not by language's "familiar means of communication", but rather through involuntary puns, buried associations, what Lacan (1953, p. 56) calls "resonance in the communicating networks of discourse". It can happen through the more phatic elements of language, what Kristeva (1984) calls "the semiotic" (see Chapter Nine), and through subliminal cues of intonation and body language. It can happen through those quietly mysterious phenomena which we call "empathy" and "intuition". It can also happen in ways which appear to us utterly obscure, and demanding paranormal modes of explanation, or at least an extended version of the unconscious: as Derrida says, it is "… difficult to imagine a theory of what they still call the unconscious without a theory of telepathy. They can neither be confused nor dissociated" (1981, p. 14).

My focus here, though, is on the ways in which "telepathy" can happen through extralinguistic phenomena which use unimpeachably physical processes. Among these are micro-expressions and micro-movements which are only noticed subliminally (Ekman, 2003; Pfister, Li, Zhao, & Pietikäinen, 2011); pheromonal stimulation, conveying much information about the other person's sexual and emotional status (Grammer, Fink, & Neave, 2005; Kohl, Atzmueller, Fink, & Grammer, 2001); assessment of the other's threat capacity (Panksepp, 2004, 2006), determining the activity of our autonomic nervous system (ANS) and the relative proportions of sympathetic and parasympathetic activation (Carroll, 2005; Ogden, Minton, & Paine, 2006) and activation of our social engagement system (Porges, 2011); firing of our mirror neurons in response to the other's posture, movements, and verbal behaviour (Keysers, 2011; Pineda, 2010); vitality affect, or vitality forms (Stern, 1985, 2010); subtle physical energy (Oschman, 2000); and much more.

What, then, does identify telepathic communication? Not the mode of operation, but its result: the "unfamiliar", uncanny experience of transparency between subjects. "Uncanny", of course, translates the German word "*unheimlich*". In his essay on "The Uncanny", Freud consults the dictionary, and discovers that "*heimlich*"—the word for what "*unheimlich*" is not—has two linked but opposed meanings: first of all, "belonging to the house, not strange, familiar, tame, intimate, friendly, etc."; but then also "concealed, kept from sight, so that others do not get to know of or about it, withheld from others" (1919h, pp. 222–223). What is "*unheimlich*", then, is "not secret"—revealed, laid bare, out in the open. It is a skeleton out of the closet: something which we would rather keep in the family, familiar, but which by its exposure is made strange and frightening. Things which we all know go on, but which polite people don't talk about. Even to themselves.

Jan Ehrenwald's little-known book on telepathy in psychoanalysis, *New Dimensions of Deep Analysis*, published in 1954, "uncannily" antici- pates much of my argument. He is writing about what might now be called entrainment or embodied resonance: the "actual sharing" of another person's "motor, vasomotor or glandular processes" (p. 144). He calls this "enkinesis":

> One could say empathy is projection guided by perception; enkine- sis is introjected action guided by empathy. ... We must not forget that empathy and enkinesis are, nevertheless, nothing but the sen- sory and motor aspects of the identical process of social interaction.
>
> (p. 144)

Ehrenwald concludes, as I do, that "... there is no sharp demarcation line between the two marginal functions of the ego discussed here [i.e., empathy and enkinesis] and *psi* processes in the stricter sense [i.e., para- normality]" (p. 144). I will return to these issues in Chapters Eight and Twelve.

The obvious question

I am beginning to ask and answer the question: if even part of what I have written in this chapter is true, why are human beings not—as we certainly appear not to be—transparent to each other, why are we not of one flesh? Why is human life suffused with experiences of misunder- standing, of loneliness and isolation, and also with attempts to avoid close contact—what Freud (1908a, p. 153) described as "the feeling of repulsion in us which is undoubtedly connected with the barriers that arise between each single ego and the others"? This feeling is one of the central problems in human life which therapy tries to address; it is also, of course, something from which therapists themselves suffer, often in quite subtle ways—for instance the tendency which I identified in Chapter Three to downplay and dissociate from embodied relating in the therapy room.

On one level the question about human alienation is an unanswerable meta-theoretical question about the nature of existence; or rather, a question with only two answers, between which there is no way to choose except by following our own temperamental preference. These alternative answers can be briefly summed up as "innate imperfection" and "contingent circumstances", with Freud for example preferring the former and Reich for example the latter. (See Freud, 1930a; Reich, 1945b. For a speculative narrative of possible contingent circumstances, see Chapter Twelve below.) There is no clear way to choose between these explanations except through personal preference; but Freud and Reich certainly both agree that the arrangements which we call "civilisation" have a great deal to do with it. However, my question was how we explain alienation *if what I have written in this chapter is at least partly true*; and I think that what I have written is incompatible with the explanation based in innate imperfection. I am going to save a full attempt at an answer until Chapter Twelve.

Staying closer to the immediate situation, though, there is a lot we can say about how this alienation, once established, is transmitted through the generations. We can think of an infant experiencing the *intaglio* imprint of an adult's early wounding, as it has been preserved and maintained in the adult's character structure (see Chapter Seven); and then of how the infant in turn struggles to survive and assimilate the invasion of this "foreign body" (Laplanche, 1976; Totton, 2002), helplessly imprinted by it just as she can be temporarily imprinted by a facial expression. As Martin Stanton summarises the thinking of Jean Laplanche:

> The first intake of messages from the other is neither naturally assimilated, nor greeted with projective elaboration, but experienced as an intrusion of the other. The affective processing of the inside of the body is therefore also primarily marked out as "other"—the inner body is therefore an "inner foreign body" (*corps etranger interne*).
>
> (1997, p. 38)

In other words, because some of what we as babies take into our bodies from our carers feels like an intrusion of painful and incomprehensible material which we have no way to assimilate, our bodies themselves become identified with that intrusion and are experienced as alien—as if the expression a baby takes on from an adult were to become irremovably fixed to her face. Laplanche, like Freud, sees this as part of the human condition; I feel it makes more sense to see it, like Reich, as a product of the social environment—some messages of the other cannot be assimilated not because this is intrinsically impossible, but because they are messages about intolerable wounds, damaged attachments. Either way, this is the condition we are currently born into, by being born into embodied relating in this culture. As Sandra Bloom writes:

> The human stress response is an evolutionarily designed survival strategy that is extraordinarily effective under the conditions for which it was originally designed. The tragedy is that human beings are no longer particularly well suited to the environments we have created for ourselves, environments within which our most dangerous enemies are frequently members of our own families, while the institutions we have created to sustain and protect us often turn out to be the engines of our own destruction.
>
> (2006, pp. 21–22)

We will look at this again in Chapter Twelve.

Pattern recognition

In his last book, *Forms of Vitality* (2010), Daniel Stern gives an excellent example of how relational engrams work:

> A mother and her 9-month old son were sitting side by side on the floor playing with a cardboard jigsaw puzzle.
> The boy picked up a piece of puzzle and brought it to his mouth.
> His mother said in a normal voice "No, it's not to eat, it's a leaf" (of the puzzle). She stopped his movement with her hand.
> The boy answered "Ugh." Then he tried again to get the piece to his mouth.
> She repeated, in a firmer voice this time, "No!"
> His response was "Uuggh!"
> She escalated even higher and said, "NO, IT'S NOT TO EAT!!!"
> He escalated even further, "UUGGHH!!"

She then leaned forward toward him, lowered her eyebrows, and said in a flat voice with no melody and much vocal tension (as in anger), "DON'T YOU YELL AT YOUR MOTHER. I SAID NO!"
He then over-escalated her, yet again, and said "*UUUGGGHHH!!!*"
At this point she gave up and conceded the victory to him. She sat back, her face softened and broke into a slightly seductive smile. She said, with a melodic voice, "Does that taste good?"
He then put the puzzle piece in his mouth.
She then made him pay for his victory. With a disgusted wrinkling of her nose and a slightly contemptuous voice she said, "It's only cardboard, does that taste good?"

(pp. 146–147)

This interaction creates a relational engram which no amount of verbal therapy would be likely fully to unearth. Stern suggests that:

> The whole scene … was a lesson in how to negotiate with a woman. … The infant … was already learning non-verbally about the negotiation of the authenticity of desire. He will spend the rest of his life expanding his knowledge of how to do this. In addition, it will come into play in the consulting room.

(p. 148)

Stern also emphasises that embodied dynamic patterns—"vitality forms", persistent structurings which in earlier work (e.g., Stern, 1985) he calls "vitality affects"—are central in constructing and maintaining this engram.

When as a client we come to meet a therapist, we deploy an ensemble of embodied-relational engrams developed through previous interactions, against which we measure and test our interaction with the therapist to see where it best fits. We have an inbuilt preference for using an existing engram rather than developing a new one, because the latter process is emotionally and energetically expensive: it requires a melting-down and recasting of our armouring, so to speak (and only if and when this melting-down does take place can the therapy be transformative). So locking our interaction into a familiar pattern is parsimonious, in some senses even skilful: as with all human activity, our first resource is pattern recognition.

The shortcoming of pattern recognition, of course, is that it opens the door to misrecognition, a "best fit" that actually doesn't fit: as Freud was warned long ago by his friend Wilhelm Fliess, "The reader of thoughts merely reads his own thoughts into other people" (letter from Fliess to Freud in Masson, 1985, p. 447). And because relationship is always a co-creation, always *between* the entities relating, how we as therapists are approached by the client influences our own experience of the situation, as we in turn parsimoniously try to fit it into our ensemble of previously experienced situations. We often find ourselves, without consciously willing it, giving embodied assurances that in fact we *are* like the client's mother, father, etc. And in fact it makes equal sense to see the client as responding to the engram with which we present her, rather than vice versa. In the first meeting we can imagine both parties riffling speedily through their range of familiar engrams until there is a click of (mis)recognition between one belonging to the therapist and one belonging to the client, which then lock into place like an Enigma machine.

What we as therapists can try to do, therefore, is to surrender *with awareness* to this process of engram-matching. If we don't surrender to it, nothing useful happens, no relationship is formed, no information is gained; if we surrender totally and lose awareness, nothing useful happens, no relationship is formed, no information is gained. Like The Fool in the Tarot pack, we dance precariously on an edge between these two attractors (see Chapter Ten). We play.

Before we look at therapy as play (in Chapter Eight), however, quite a lot more needs to be said about some other factors which feed into the embodied therapeutic relationship. Embodiment, and embodied relating, are not just a personal experience, although individual genetic inheritance no doubt influences them. They are also profoundly shaped by other sorts of inheritance: from our family's culture, and from the wider, nested social cultures which contain us. Not only are the extent and focus of our embodiment socially constructed; what we understand embodiment to be, and the value or otherwise which we place on it, are equally a function of our identification with or rebellion against our cultural milieu. I will explore these issues in the next chapters.

THE STORY SO FAR, 1

It may be helpful at this stage to have a brief summary of the key points of my argument. I will offer a summary every few chapters as we go along.

1. Embodiment is both a *state* (corporeality) and a *process* (becoming aware of and identified with myself as corporeal).
2. When we speak of "the body", we usually mean "embodiment without self-awareness". When we speak of "the self", we usually mean—though without necessarily realising it—"embodiment with self-awareness"—since embodiment is a necessary though not a sufficient condition for self-awareness.
3. Mind emerges from continuous, non-linear sensorimotor inter-actions involving circular causality between brain, body, and environment.
4. Hence mind is both embodied and extended.
5. This involves a reciprocal relationship: mind extends into its environment, which means that the environment also extends into mind. Mind is an aspect or expression of its environment, a representative/representation of the systems of which it is part.

6. This approach leads to a reconceptualising of vision, which loses its privileged status and its connotations of distance, separation, and objectivity. Correspondingly, there emerges a revaluation of touch and visceral/proprioceptive perception as central forms of knowledge about the world and other people.

7. Embodiment is fundamental to human relationships, as a conscious or unconscious substrate which shapes, and is shaped by, verbal and mental interactions and responses. The reciprocal impact of one embodiment upon another can be seen as an *intaglio*-like process, whereby through the pressure of contact an "incised" pattern in one surface creates an "embossed" copy in the other.

8. The embodied relational substrate generates *engrams*: complex, stubbornly persistent patterns of activation formed in early life relationships and applied to current ones. Engrams are parsimonious: they would always rather repeat than innovate, although innovation does happen when there is no alternative.

9. In relationship, engrams operating in each person activate the most relevant—often complementary—engrams in the other, via a process of coupling: an embodied resonance and entrainment in which each becomes an "exogram" for the other—each uses the other as an opportunity to replay powerful life themes.

10. As with many other involuntary experiences, we are adept at discovering justifications for our engram-defined responses in the perceived behaviour of the other. At the same time, however, our engrams *are* in fact activated, though not created, by subtle cues in the other's embodied behaviour.

11. In psychotherapy just as in life, therapists are drawn through contact with each client into an unconscious reactivation of embodied relational engrams. Their task is not to avoid this inevitable process, but to find ways of bringing it to awareness, both for themselves and for their clients.

CHAPTER FIVE

Embodied relating in its social context

In Chapters One and Two I focused on individual embodiment; in Chapters Three and Four, on embodied relating, emphasising that embodiment is always embedded in and at the same time in fact *creates* a relational context. But this context is wider than individual, one-to-one relationships; and in this chapter and the next one we will explore how embodiment both forms and is formed by the wider contexts of family, culture, and society. As we will see, some of our social embodiment is conscious, some is preconscious, and some is unconscious. The unconscious aspects are repressed because they embody *conflicts*—between social requirements and individual desires, or between different social forces. As Wilhelm Reich established, both the preconscious and the unconscious aspects are tightly associated with—effectively, embodied in—patterns of muscular tension, which as we will see in Chapter Seven are also patterns of psychological character:

> Muscular attitudes and character attitudes have the same function in the psychic mechanism: they can replace one another and be replaced by one another. Basically, they cannot be separated. They are identical in their function.
>
> (1942, pp. 270–271)

I have already mentioned in previous chapters that many theorists of embodied cognition think human social interaction is facilitated by our ability to *simulate* the experience of others, to use mirror neurons and other capacities to create an internal model of someone else's internal state. Merleau-Ponty provides a more fully embodied conception of fleshly intersubjectivity or intercorporeality, which we can summarise as saying that "[T]he body and its sensorimotor processes function as a social resonance mechanism" (Lindblom, 2007, p. 144).

However, while our embodiment is the *ground of* social relations, it is also constructed *through* social relations—one of the chains of mutual or circular causation discussed in previous chapters. Our relationships with others, especially in childhood, shape our embodiment in profound ways; and through these individual relationships, social norms and demands are transmitted, below the threshold of awareness, into our own bodies. Katharine Young writes eloquently of how:

> This haunting of our own bodies by the bodies of others is constant, a persistent familiar in our ordinary lives. ... The body is the flesh of memory.
>
> (2002, p. 45)

In this chapter I will explore this process of transmission, and suggest that it is never a simple transcription, but always a negotiation between power and freedom (Foucault, 1997, p. 292).

Social embodiment

Shaun Gallagher has recently widened the concept of the "extended mind" which I discussed in Chapter Two (Clark & Chalmers, 1998, and previously Bateson, 1971) to apply not only to the body and the physical world but also to the social world:

> Just as a notebook or a hand-held piece of technology may be viewed as affording a way to enhance or extend our mental possibilities, so our encounters with others, especially in the context of various institutional procedures and social practices may offer structures that support and extend our cognitive abilities.
>
> (2013, p. 4)

In other words, we are all continuously using each other and our environment as "exograms" (Sutton, 2008), extensions of our minds. But since we are also being used in the same way *by* others, the concept of "our" minds, like "our" bodies, is thrown into question, exposed as to some degree illusory: rather, there are collective projects flowing through and between us, expressing themselves and becoming concretised in different ways at different moments in different bodyminds. As Todd May writes:

> Social practices are the sedimentation of history at the level of the body. When I teach, when I write this article, when I run a race or teach one of my children how to ride a bicycle, my body is oriented in particular ways, conforming to or rejecting particular norms, responding to the constraints and restraints of those practices as they have evolved in interaction with other practices over time. Through its engagement in these practices, my body has taken on a history that is not of my making but is nevertheless part of my inheritance.

> (2005, p. 524)

"Mind" cannot be separated from "body": it is the knowing continuum of Flesh which underlies and gives meaning to our social world. As has often been said, language would be an inadequate tool for communication if we didn't already know what each other means.

The linguist Edward Sapir says something similar about gesture:

> We respond to gestures with an extreme alertness and, one might almost say, in accordance with an elaborate and secret code that is written nowhere, known to none and understood by all. ... Like everything else in human conduct, gesture roots in the reactive necessities of the organism, but the laws of gesture, the unwritten code of gestured messages and responses, is the anonymous work of an elaborate social tradition.

> (1949, p. 556)

Embodiment, as Sapir writes in the case of gesture, "roots in the reactive necessities of the organism"; but what we conceive these necessities to be is itself socially constructed. Our embodied cognition enacts our world; but the world, including the social world, sets the conditions of our embodied cognition.

Embodiment, in the sense of consciously self-aware corporeality, is inherently languaged (Merleau-Ponty, 1968, p. 155; see also Chapter Nine); and language, equally, is inherently embodied—"discourse itself is a fleshy process … It is produced through the work of the body" (Crossley, 1995, pp. 50–51). Cutting the circle of causation at any point, privileging either disembodied language and society or the unlanguaged, unsocialised organism, is fundamentally unhelpful and untrue to our experience: disembodied language and unlanguaged body are, in ordinary circumstances, equally imaginary entities.

What is constructed as our embodied subjectivity combines traumatic and nurturing elements, often in the same engram, and inherited through generations as well as new-minted (Totton, 2010; for more on trauma see Chapter Ten). Both trauma and nurture are what we *take in* from the world into which we are born. They are the stuff out of which we are made, out of which we make our selves. But unless the self we construct is an open system, open to the world and to others in both inward and outward directions (since we find the world and others within as well as outside ourselves), it is both illusory and deadly. In the play of therapy, it is sometimes possible to expose and explore our deadly defences against openness without destructive effect; but only when the therapist is prepared to join in the serious game (see Chapter Eight).

The somatic society

In some of this chapter, I will be explicitly addressing fellow body psychotherapists, though hopefully what I have to say will also be of interest to others. Body psychotherapists, I suggest, have so far paid remarkably little attention to social and philosophical studies of embodiment. Neuroscience, we might say, operates on one edge of the field of body psychotherapy, that which looks to the biological organism. The social sciences exist on the opposite edge, where individual experience is placed in the context of society and culture. Balancing ourselves between these two edges can perhaps help us to grasp more clearly what is unique and important about our own role as body psychotherapists, specialists in embodied relationship, where the social and the biological interact.

The consensus of social science writers is that in current Western society, more even than in human society generally, the body plays a unique and central role. We live in a "somatic society ... within which our major political and moral problems are expressed through the conduit of the human body" (B. Turner, 1996, p. 6), and where the body has become "the principal field of political and cultural activity" (ibid., p. 162), as seen in issues ranging from genetic modification and cloning, through abortion, contraception, transplants, euthanasia, assisted suicide and life support termination, to anorexia, vaccination, Alzheimer's, organic food, plastic surgery, and MRA. Turner in fact suggests that:

> A sociology of the body is the study of the problem of social order, and it can be organised around four issues. These are the reproduction and regulation of populations in time and space, and the restraint and representation of the body as a vehicle of the self. These four issues presuppose the existence in Western society of an opposition between the desires and reason.

> (1996, p. 68)

Paralleling this somatisation of social relations, in the social sciences— sociology, anthropology, social psychology, geography etc.—and also in the philosophical theories which underpin them, over the last three decades there has been a massive "turn to the body" (Csordas, 1994, p. xi; cf. Hancock et al., 2000, pp. 10–11; Lyon & Barbalet, 1994, p. 51; Sampson, 1998, pp. 42–43) which has generated much rich material. As well as numerous general works of theory such as Benthall and Polhemus (1975); Burkitt (1999); Grosz (1994); Lakoff and Johnson (1999); B. Turner (1996); and Williams and Bendelow (1998), there have been a vast number of contributions on specific topics, too numerous to mention, many of them appearing in the scholarly journal *Body and Society*.

To get some sense of the sort of material I am talking about, the most recent tranche of the Online First section of *Body and Society*'s website on February 1, 2015 contained the following titles: "From disfigurement to facial transplant: Identity insights" (Le Breton, 2014); "Intense embodiment: Senses of heat in women's running and boxing" (Allen-Collison & Owton, 2014); "Disability and Deleuze: An exploration of becoming and embodiment in children's everyday environments" (Stephens,

Ruddick, & McKeever, 2014); "Trends in the turn to affect: A social psychological critique" (Wetherell, 2014); "Material feminism, obesity science and the limits of discursive critique" (Warin, 2014); "Informal surrogacy in China: Embodiment and biopower" (Yang, 2014); "Rapid home HIV testing: Risk and the moral imperatives of biological citizenship" (Banda, 2014); and "The biopolitics of transnational adoption in South Korea: Preemption and the governance of single birthmothers" (Kim, 2014). For a different and even longer list of articles and chapters see Totton, 2008, pp. 188–189.

My first purpose, then, is simply to point out the existence of this enormous range and quantity of work, a fair amount of it directly relevant to the practice of body psychotherapy. One might well ask why on earth body psychotherapists don't make more use of it. At least some of the answer, apart perhaps from general ignorance and lack of time, is that social scientists employ a theoretical apparatus with which most body psychotherapists (like psychotherapists in general) are unfamiliar, and which tends to put off our habitually untheoretical modality. Much social science work is conceptually underpinned by the writings of Michel Foucault (1976, 1977a, 1977b, 1984a, 1984b); another important philosophical reference point is Maurice Merleau-Ponty (1962, 1964, 1968), on whose work I have already drawn. A third significant source is the work of Pierre Bourdieu (1977, 1990), himself a sociologist, who tries to theorise the means by which social regulations and beliefs are transmitted through the body. I will try to indicate the main themes of these theoretical positions, and some of their potential applications to body psychotherapy and to psychotherapy in general.

What is a body?

The first thing that becomes apparent when trying to get one's bearings in this terrain is that social theorists are working from fundamentally different assumptions to most body psychotherapists (and probably most therapists in general). We tend strongly to assume the objective reality of the body as our starting point. In the context of social theory, this position is called "foundationalism", or (if one wants to be insulting) "essentialism"; it is one of several competing positions, and by no means the most fashionable. Much more popular are the several varieties ("strong", "weak", etc.) of "social constructionism", which take "the body", along with all other elements of human experience, to be an artefact of culture rather than a product of nature: "As the point of overlap between the physical, the symbolic and the sociological, the body is a dynamic, mutable frontier" (McNay, 1999, p. 98).

Whatever may exist "out there" in the world, social constructionism argues that everything we can *know* about it is the product of human interpretation; and this applies to embodiment as much as to every-thing else. It is widely agreed in the social sciences that various features of postmodern society—for example the development of plastic sur-gery and other technologies for bodily alteration, and the development of "identity politics" positions which critique normative attitudes to the body—highlight this fact.

> With an increasing awareness of the negotiable and changeable possibilities of the body comes an increased recognition that it is impossible to speak about the "nature" of the body or take for granted the body as a fixed category.
>
> (Evans, 2002, p. 1)

If you are not familiar with this way of thinking it may appear abstract and solipsistic, and certainly it can be carried to extremes, as Katharine Hayles points out:

> One contemporary belief likely to stupefy future generations is the postmodern orthodoxy that the body is primarily, if not entirely, a linguistic construction.
>
> (1999, p. 192)

It is hard, though, to argue with the view that our understanding of even the basic categories of existence is deeply affected by cultural assumptions, often unconscious ones at that. What after all *is* a human body? For an orthodox Christian or Muslim or Hindu, it is a mortal vessel for an immortal soul. For a Western medical practitioner, it is a complex piece of biological machinery. For a shaman, it is perhaps an assemblage of magical quartz crystals. Are these all the "same" body? Is there any means of deciding which is the "real" body out of these and dozens of other versions? Any method of investigation inevitably assumes the truth of one or another version of the body, and hence begs the question. Louise McNay takes a middle way:

> The body is the threshold through which the subject's lived experience of the world is incorporated and realised and, as such, is neither pure object nor pure subject. It is neither pure object since it is the place of one's engagement with the world. Nor is it pure subject in that there is always a material residue that resists incorporation into dominant symbolic schema.
>
> (1999, p. 98)

This encourages us to ask a slightly different question: *whose* body is the "real" body? It is now widely recognised that our cultural habit is to treat the bodies of women, gays, people of colour, people with disabilities, children, old people, and so on as, in Elizabeth Grosz's words, "modifications or variations of the (implicitly white, male, youthful, heterosexual, middle class) human body" (Grosz, 1994, p. 188). With embodiment, as with many other significant aspects of existence, the mainstream (white, male, etc.) version becomes the neutral norm, understood to have no specificity of its own, but to be the yardstick against which all other versions are measured.

It is no accident that the first theorists who applied social constructionist ideas to the body were mostly feminists. Women have been at the sharp end of the dominant construction of the body in Western culture, a construction which opposes "body" to "mind", and aligns a whole set of other categories along the axis thus created, so that, as Fraser and Greco put it, we are faced with "the frequent feminisation and racialisation of any notion of the body *at all*" (2005, p. 7); in other words, categories like "embodied", "female", "non-white", "emotional", "natural", "primitive", are often placed in alignment with each other. Feminists have generally rejected this conflation of the somatic and the feminine, and the mind-body split on which it rests, which identifies "self" with "mind" and makes it "possible to claim for the liberal subject its notorious universality, a claim that depends on erasing markers of bodily difference, including sex, race, and ethnicity" (Hayles, 1999, pp. 4–5). "The body" is modelled on white male heterosexual able bodies; yet simultaneously and deeply paradoxically "the body" is also inherently feminine and non-white.

So there is already one lesson, I suggest, that we as body psychotherapists can learn from social theory: to be wary of claims to universality. There is a strong, usually inexplicit tendency within our discipline to treat "the body" as a fundamental substrate of human existence, with absolute and inherent qualities. This is of course just a form of body-mind dualism, projecting onto bodies various traits and attributes—notably authenticity—which are constructed within culture and have meaning only within culture. The body as wise and noble savage, in fact! And this brings us back to the alignment I mentioned above between "bodily" and "primitive". It can be given a negative valence, as it commonly is in our culture: body=primitive=bad; but historically, body psychotherapy, influenced by 1960s counter culture, has tended simply to reverse the valence to positive without questioning the alignment itself: body=primitive=good.

Producing the body

Michel Foucault and his followers employ a very useful formulation: they talk of bodies, along with other apparently objective phenomena, as being *produced by discourse*. While bodies in a general sense can perhaps be agreed to be "there" rather than "not there"—more like tables than unicorns—any particular understanding and perception of bodies has been created in response to particular social requirements: created through a certain way of thinking and talking about bodies and their attributes. (This is plainly also true of tables, by the way: what we agree to define as "a table" is a matter of social convention.) As Donna Haraway puts it, "Neither our personal bodies nor our social bodies may be seen as natural, in the sense of existing outside the self-creating process known as human labour" (1991, p. 10). But Marx, on whose discourse Haraway is drawing, showed how human labour is itself subject to alienation through external domination, for example by capital. Foucault treats the body as a crucial site of conflict between various forms of power and resistance to power—like a contested territory, repeatedly fought over by outside forces and local guerrillas.

Foucault deliberately avoids creating a systematic theory (Kolodny, 1996), but two concepts in particular from his work seem related to the concerns of body psychotherapy. These are "technologies of the self", and "disciplines of the body". Foucault defines technologies of the self, slightly sarcastically, as forms of knowledge "which permit individuals to effect ... operations on their own bodies or souls, thoughts, conduct, and way of being, in order to attain a certain state of happiness, purity, wisdom, perfection, or immortality" (Foucault, 1997, p. 225). This formulation brings together a wide range of processes and behaviours which might at first sight seem very different from each other: for example, positive thinking, plastic surgery, gym training, prayer, recreational drugs, psychotherapy, diets, meditation, botox, yoga, colonic irrigation. It certainly intersects with body psychotherapy, although there are of course other ways of conceptualising this activity.

Technologies of the bodily self—a subset of the general approach which Foucault terms "care of the self"—also intersect with *disciplines* of the body, by which Foucault denotes methods of forcing the body to behave and shape itself according to externally defined requirements. He connects this approach with eighteenth-century shifts in modes of social domination, and shows how it operates in environments like prisons, madhouses, schools, and families (Foucault, 1973, 1977a). Here Foucault's work links up with that of Wilhelm Reich, whose book *The Mass Psychology of Fascism* (1945b)—little read, I am afraid, by body psychotherapists—tries to show how the authoritarian family in particular operates to produce an embodied character structure suitable for the working environment of capitalist society: an issue to which we shall return towards the end of the next chapter, and again in Chapter Seven.

We can therefore think of *technologies* of the body and *disciplines* of the body as polarised but intersecting. Take the example of diet and exercise: from one point of view, a project of self-care aimed at increasing health and fitness, but from another point of view—and often simultaneously—a culturally imposed punitive discipline under which the individual tries to shape herself according to an impossible norm; and from yet a third point of view, a vehicle for addictive forms of psychological disorder, which may themselves be construed as acts of rebellion against repressive family structures. Or take the example of body psychotherapy itself: from one point of view, body psychotherapy is a project of self-care, where the therapist facilitates the client in achieving greater ease, relaxation, self-esteem, happiness, and so on. At the same time, though, body psychotherapy can easily operate as the transmission belt for a whole array of social demands on the individual, some of which we perhaps first encounter at primary school: Stand up straight! Breathe! Speak up! Work hard! Relate well to others! Feel good about yourself!

There is a third way in which body psychotherapy can function, again not wholly distinct from the other two but intertwined with them. This third way is sometimes defined as a project of "liberation", a term to which Foucault takes exception as falsely absolute, and for which he substitutes the concept of "freedom" (one can be free to different degrees, rather than wholly free or wholly unfree). As he says,

> In human relationships, whether they involve verbal communication … or amorous, institutional, or economic relationship, power is always present. I mean a relationship in which one person tries to control the conduct of the other. So I am speaking of relations that exist at different levels, in different forms; these power relations are mobile, they can be modified, they are not fixed once and for all … In power relations there is necessarily the possibility of resistance … If there are power relations in every social field that is because there is freedom everywhere.
>
> (1997, p. 292)

We can usefully apply this to the therapeutic relationship in general, shot through with power relations but also with freedom (Totton, 2006). And it applies in particular ways to body psychotherapy, where the relationship is conducted partly through the medium of the body, the medium in which as children we first experience domination, and where it continues to exercise itself most directly: the ultimate threat behind all domination is physical violence of some kind.

> Of course, states of domination do indeed exist. In a great many cases, power relations are fixed in such a way that they are perpetually asymmetrical and allow an extremely limited margin of freedom.
>
> (Foucault, 1997, p. 292)

One such case is the power of adults over children, which is truly, in Foucault's famous phrase (1977b, p. 148), "inscribed" on the body through its physical manipulation and disciplining.

In her powerful paper "Fleshing out gender: Crafting gender identity on women's bodies", Valerie Fournier argues that "… gender identity is performed … through inscriptions on the body" and that "[T]hese inscriptions do their work of gendering by inflicting pain" (2002, p. 58). She relates this to Foucault's goal of showing "how the relations of power are able to pass materially into the very density of bodies *without even having to be relayed by the representations of subjects*" (Morris & Patton, 1979, pp. 69–70; my italics): in other words, how power is incorporated into and shapes our bodies wholly outside our awareness.

Theory alone seems unlikely to achieve the goal of showing this; some sort of *practice*, some sort of embodied activity, is surely required to materialise the unconscious power relations of the body. But isn't this precisely what body psychotherapy can do? Are there not times when we can literally feel *in our hands* the power relations which have entered "the very density" of our clients', and our own, bodies? Power relations which are usually in the first instance Oedipal or infantile, but ultimately drawn from the structures of power which shape the social order (again, there is more on this in the next chapter). However, our practice in this area is, I suggest, under-theorised, experienced more than understood; and here we can perhaps usefully draw on social theory.

As I have said, Foucault's ideas have come to dominate the social sciences. Some of the many hundreds of "Foucauldian papers" can be slavishly regurgitative, and even silly (a personal favourite is "The au pair body: Sex object, sister or student?" (Cox, 2007)). But it is for good reasons that the model has become so widely used. It offers uniquely powerful tools for analysing issues around embodiment in specific situations. Foucault's approach always situates bodies within a set of specific cultural discourses/practices, and tries to show *what sort of body*, what sort of bodily experience, these produce, and what contradictions are thrown up by this process.

A significant example is the contemporary emphasis on shaping and controlling one's body and its surfaces as a way of constructing and maintaining a viable and acceptable identity. While some aspects of this programme are syntonic with both social norms and individual identity, many other aspects are seriously dystonic, throwing up symptoms and behaviours which frequently bring people into conflict with their sense of self and/or with social norms: body dysmorphia, eating disorders, plastic surgery, delicate cutting, exercise addiction, substance abuse, and more. Any of these problems can bring people to body psychotherapy. But is it enough to model the problem in purely individual terms, as therapists habitually do, without considering its social significance, the demands on their embodiment which individuals suffer?

Beyond social constructionism?

Social constructionism (for which, in general and in the psychotherapy context, Kenneth Gergen (e.g., 1999, 2001) is perhaps the best advocate) is a bracing corrective to the simplistic realism still prevalent in body psychotherapy circles as in much of psychotherapy as a whole. However, there are some serious problems with constructionism, both globally and in relation specifically to the body. It can be and has been criticised (e.g., Cromby & Nightingale, 1999) for taking an external, mental view of human experience, including the experience of embodiment: privileging thought and language to such an extent as to ignore what it is actually like to *be* a body.

Note that Foucault's key term "inscription", which we saw used by Fournier in the passage quoted above, is a metaphor drawn from the realm of language. Social constructionists tend to love Kafka's story *In the Penal Colony*, where a machine tortures prisoners by literally inscribing their crimes upon their bodies (Kafka, 1995; cf. Butler, 1989; Grosz, 1994, pp. 134ff). But language, though it impacts enormously on embodiment, is not *prior* to embodiment either historically or logically (Burkitt, 2003); and one theorist who fully recognises this is Maurice Merleau-Ponty (1962, 1964, 1968).

While Merleau-Ponty recognises the inseparability of embodiment and language, he sees this as emphatically not a question of inscription. Rather than embodiment being languaged, we may say that language is itself *embodied*:

> An intertwining of sensible-sentient bodies (speaker and listener, writer and reader), an intercorporeality. ... always tied to praxis, and thus, at the very least, to the situation of the speaker, *qua* embodied being. ... Discourse itself is a fleshy process for Merleau-Ponty. It is produced through the work of the body.

> (Crossley, 1995, pp. 50–51)

In a sense, he transcends mind-body dualism by never acknowledging it in the first place (cf. Grosz, 1994, p. 11): taking life in the world as it is and on its own terms, Merleau-Ponty finds wholeness and continuity which only subsequently bifurcates—and bifurcation or folding back is an opening rather than a splitting; mind, he says, is "the other side of the body", "the perceiving mind is an incarnated body" (1962, pp. 3–4).

Nick Crossley (1995) argues that Merleau-Ponty's work can be used as the basis for a new approach to the sociology of the body—one for which Crossley coins the term "carnal sociology". Such an approach would be based on continuity rather than duality: in this case, continuity between the bodily and "the social with which we are in contact by the mere fact of existing, and which we carry about inseparably with us without any objectification" (Merleau-Ponty, 1962, p. 362). Like language—to which it is of course closely tied—the social for Merleau-Ponty is inherently embodied.

The feminist philosopher Iris Young sums up Merleau-Ponty's contribution to Western thought as:

> … locating consciousness and subjectivity in the body itself. This move to situate subjectivity in the lived body jeopardizes dualistic metaphysics altogether. There remains no basis for preserving the mutual exclusivity of the categories subject and object, inner and outer, I and world. (1990, p. 161)

There seems to me to be a striking convergence between this project and that of body psychotherapy—the one primarily in a theoretical register, the other in a practical register. Yet for body psychotherapists to stay exclusively in the realm of practice risks being over-influenced by the unconscious, habitual, deeply dualistic "folk theories" of our culture, which will always tend to drag us back into an unexamined splitting of mind and body.

We need to develop a theory sufficiently rich, nuanced, and broad-based to encompass the whole of our clinical experience, and in turn to help test, sharpen, and deepen it: a theory which recognises and corresponds to the "multiplicity of sites, knowledges and processes" (Budgeon, 2003, p. 52) in which embodiment is constructed. I have tried so far to indicate how social theory is a crucial resource in that project; next, I will take this process further, looking at how social theory can help account for our capacity to *produce* as well as to experience our embodiment.

CHAPTER SIX

Being, having, and becoming bodies

The title of this chapter derives from an editorial passage in Fraser and Greco's splendid compilation *The Body: A Reader* (2005), in which they argue that sociology has been taught by feminism and other human rights movements "to regard the body as highly relevant to any theorisation of socially situated subjectivity, and simultaneously to problematise any notion that 'the body' can be thought of as a single and coherent conceptual entity" (p. 3). I think that what has been said in the previous chapter confirms and illustrates their argument. They go on to suggest that much contemporary discussion of the body can be understood as falling into three categories: "the body as something we *have* (the body as object), as something we *are* (the body as subject), and as something we *become* (the body as process and performativity)" (p. 4).

The conventional wisdom in body psychotherapy is that the first of these three categories, the body as something we have, is an expression of Cartesian alienation—part of the problem for which our work tries to be a solution. Certainly this can be the case: to see our body as simply a possession, a tool via which our mind carries out its projects, is to deny that we *are* our body (though of course we are not only our body). This denial of embodiment and exclusive identification with mentality, so common in the mainstream of Western society, has been rightly highlighted by body psychotherapists and many others (for example, Abram, 1997; Berman, 1990). One of the most succinct and pointed formulations is Richard Grossinger's: "The majority treat their body like a date picked up at the singles bar. They hustle it, punish it and try to make it give them things they want" (1995, pp. 40–41).

Perhaps, though, we need to learn from the sociology of the body that the experience of *having* our bodies is in fact unavoidable— intrinsic to our human situation as tool users, who treat every aspect of our existence as tools for producing our selves; and that to simultaneously *both* be *and* have bodies is in many ways creative. By "having" my body, I mean experiencing it as an aspect of myself which, while not alien, is in some senses *alienable*: I and other people can *do things to it*, things that may permanently alter its being, and by doing things to it I and they can both express and create individual and social realities.

This is at least part of what Foucault means when he talks of "the use of the body" and "the production of the body" (1987a, 1987b, 1997). It is a way of understanding a wide range of situations, both familiar and more unusual ones—for example, hairstyles as markers of social rank; punishments which mutilate or remove parts of the body; tattoos in gangs, prisons, or military organisations, or indeed in other cultural groups and subgroups; breast enlargements, facelifts, and stomach tucks; dieting; delicate cutting; self-castration; exercise regimes; and, of course, the whole register of fashion, including subcultural fashions.

Social theory of the body has recently started to move on from a cataloguing of the many varieties of alienation from and disciplining of bodies, to tentative accounts of empowerment and self-creation through the production of embodiment. Shelley Budgeon's tremendous paper "Identity as an Embodied Event" (2003) makes the point very well, with specific reference to the experience of women:

> Being cannot be reduced to an effect of the consumption of images but instead is the result of various forms of self-inventions which occur within embodied practices .... The self/body configuration is one which is lived via its immersion in a multiplicity of sites, knowledges and processes, therefore, understanding the choices women make in "doing" embodied identity requires a move beyond reductionist accounts, away from questions about what women's bodies *mean* to questions about what women's bodies can *do*.

> (p. 52; my italics)

What Budgeon says about women's bodies applies also to the rest of us. "Embodiment", as I have stressed in Chapter One, is a term describing not a fixed state, but an ongoing *process of embodying*. Alternative terms like "corporeality" are much weaker, because they do indeed suggest a fixed state, something completed and passively experienced; while embodiment is always provisional and ongoing, something that we are both doing and having done to us. As Budgeon also writes:

> Bodies ... can be thought of not as *objects*, upon which culture writes meanings, but as *events* that are continually in the process of becoming—as multiplicities that are never just found but are made and remade.

> (p. 50)

This perception seems to be spreading rapidly through the sociological world, transmitted particularly by feminist writers. For example, Rebecca Lester discusses "embodiment not simply as a state of being, but as an ongoing *process* of transformation and meaning making" (2004, p. 416); and Abigail Bray and Clare Colebrook argue that:

> The body is not a prior fullness, anteriority, or plenitude that is subsequently identified and organised through restricting representations. Representations are not negations imposed on otherwise fluid bodies. Body images are not stereotypes that produce human beings as complicit subjects. On the contrary, images, representations, and significations (as well as bodies) are aspects of ongoing practices of negotiation, reformation, and encounter.

> (Bray & Colebrook, 1998, pp. 38–39)

This richly textured account of embodiment corresponds to the anthropologist Clifford Geertz's (1973) term "thick description", and we can oppose it to the "thin description" of traditional body psychotherapy, which tends to sheer away the social register entirely. But the "relational turn" in body psychotherapy can hardly be restricted to dyadic relationship; it means that the whole complex meshwork of direct and indirect social relating can and should be brought to bear on our understanding of each individual's situation.

In Chapter Three I have tried to describe and conceptualise the full force of what is traditionally called embodied transference and countertransference on the personal-historical level. I am now suggesting that we need also to stretch our awareness to the social and cultural levels of reciprocal embodied transference, and to track how embodiment as a social process of self-production resonates through the therapeutic relationship.

When we as therapists encounter the client's embodiment as it impacts upon our own, we directly experience in our *own* bodies its multiplicity, its compromises, its contradictions, the ways in which it is embedded in hegemonic social narratives, and also resists or evades such embedding, and indeed exploits it for its own purposes of self-production—all of this, for the length of the session, becomes part of our own lived embodiment, and resonates with our own multiplicity of compromises, contradictions, and self-productions. At times it becomes enacted in the therapeutic relationship. In the next section, I will try to indicate how this can be concretely experienced.

Two examples

Here is a composite and fictionalised case vignette. Naomi came to me with an eating disorder: she was anorexic, though not quite to the point of life threat, and also tending to exercise addiction. She was also very attractive (to me? to men in our culture? to the editors of glossy magazines?), with enormous eyes, high cheekbones, and long legs: a beauty which teetered right on the edge of emaciation, so that my perception of her veered, often within a single session, between desire, horror, and protective tenderness.

Naomi was Jewish; her grandmother had died in a concentration camp. It was impossible for either of us to experience her emaciation outside this context. Another context, of course, was the social pressure on women to shape their bodies in conformity with an exaggeratedly slim norm. Naomi was tall; in her early teens, she had, at least by her own account, tended to fat. Her stepmother was a much-admired beauty.

Most therapists could no doubt write the story from this point on their own. But what would they tend to leave out? What I myself struggled not to leave out of the picture was *my own investment* in Naomi's self-starvation: the extent to which I would have been repelled by a fat version of my client, the extent to which I was stimulated by the doe-like fragility of her embodied self-representation. In the countertransference,

I enacted the male gaze which demanded slimness—not only her father, whose appreciation she badly needed, but the collective male gaze of our culture. Also, more subtly, I colluded with a romantic image of the beautiful young Jewess in the concentration camp; demanded, perhaps, woundedness.

Our easiest alternative to this level of interaction was an intellectual one: Naomi was clever and sophisticated, and well able to understand all the issues I have outlined. But by escaping with her to the plane of thought, I was also collaborating with her anorexic rejection of the body (while still silently enjoying its visual presence). I experienced a bizarre double perception: rejecting and starving her body, Naomi was simultaneously creating a desirable artefact for my enjoyment, irrespective of her own libidinal emptiness. I came to dread our sessions.

The only way forward that we found—and I am not sure that it was an adequate solution—involved a sort of abjection on my part. I took on the enactment, sharing with her many of my responses and fantasies, including the fantasy that this interaction itself was an erotic intimacy. This process germinated in her a seed of rage which offered some new freedom within the structures of power that constrained her—an alternative freedom to self-starvation. We finished therapy at some emotional distance from each other; but Naomi was eating.

When I first offered this story (Totton, 2010), I felt uncertain and almost ashamed about my approach to working with Naomi. I ended up writing apologetically that:

> What we did not manage to address in our work together was precisely the body-in-itself, supposedly the core entity of body psychotherapy. Another way of saying this is that we didn't work (much) with the infantile, pre-oedipal levels of experience, with reconstructions of Naomi's early experience of her mother, who died when she was 7 years old. Our work privileged the oedipal, triangulated level, the little girl's hysterical response to what society, as mediated through her father, seemed to require of her. The extent to which my own post-oedipal requirement of her, which mostly drowned out my tender response to the infant (Ferenczi, 1999 [1933]), acted as an obstacle to therapy—and to what extent my countertransference accurately and usefully zeroed in on her primary issues—will remain unknown.

(p. 5)

Revisiting the story now, it feels entirely clear that, in perceiving my fantasies as something she was forced to ingest along with the nurturing she craved, Naomi re-experienced the emotional price of feeding which her mother had exacted from her—among much else, her forced internalisation of the grandmother's story. In other words my countertransference *did* "accurately and usefully zero in" on her pre-Oedipal issues, re-enacting the early attachment scenario as well as the later Oedipal one, which itself was thus—or at least was thus experienced as—a replay. Our inability to articulate these replays in the room together, and through our embodied enactment to explicitly connect Naomi's hysterical response to what her father seemed to require of her to the earlier and equivalent hysterical response to what her *mother* seemed to require of her, certainly acted to limit what the therapy could achieve.

However, I would no longer say that my erotic response to her acted as an *obstacle* to therapy. Rather, it *was* the therapy; and my ability to acknowledge the injustice of my implicit demands was a transformative element. I notice as I write now my use of "we" and "our" in previous paragraphs, and it feels very meaningful: the two of us did indeed establish a hard-won partnership, and the fact that elements of this were unspoken does not seem to have invalidated it. Perhaps the story supports a version of therapy which gives less privilege to the role of speech. My shame and uncertainty is an important part of what I was able to offer her: a small act of reparation between genders and between generations.

What I do want to underline is how hopeless it would have been to leave out the social dimension, and to treat our work together as purely a matter of individual relating. Our therapeutic "success" was partial and ambivalent; but I do not believe that even this could have been possible if I had been unable to place Naomi's difficulties, *and my own responses to her*, in the context of a set of cultural values around women's thinness and fragility. And it was only through this use of social context that I could also understand Naomi's production of her embodiment as a form of self-empowerment, the claiming of a victim/siren identity which was capable of exerting a powerful effect over others—including, certainly, over me.

Ken—another composite and fictionalised character—brought a rather different issue of embodiment to therapy: he was covered (as I initially perceived it) with piercings and tattoos, as well as wearing a spiky Mohican haircut and a sort of punk kilt over his trousers. (Ken was in his late forties.) Once I was able to get past the rather overwhelming first impression, there were about a dozen piercings, some visible and some hidden (including genital), a tattoo on his neck, tattoos on each arm, and, he told me, a large one on his back. Ken was at the same time a rather shy and quietly-spoken man, and his main presenting issue was his difficulty in handling the sort of public attention which his appearance created.

Naturally enough, I soon raised the question of the contrast between his professed dislike of standing out, and his chosen appearance. Ken tried to explain that I was missing the point. He was not "attention-seeking", but rather suffering from the fact that his expression of his core identity was unusual and often unacceptable to others. He was not asking me for help in changing his appearance, but for help in handling other people's reactions.

Never having worked with someone from Ken's subculture before, I was able to make some sense of what he was saying by thinking about the situation, which I had encountered with other clients, of gay people basically at ease with their sexual orientation but suffering from the effects of other people's prejudice. It made even more sense to think of a transvestite with parallel issues. It was not my job, it seemed to me, to *embody* society's difficulty in accepting Ken's self-presentation, but rather to support him in his rather problematic situation, and to see what new material emerged as trust developed between us. Had my own cultural placing been even slightly different, slightly more "conventional", I might have found this task—or even its articulation—impossible: a different engram might have been activated in me, one which was more about fulfilling Ken's expectation of rejection rather than exploring it.

The way that I found to support him was, as is so often the case, to be *interested* in his experience: to ask him about what his piercing and tattooing meant to him, the significance of the particular images he had had inscribed on his body, and also, of course, what it *felt* like— my own mildly prurient curiosity, part of a voyeuristic engram, was very useful here. ("Does it hurt? What happens when you pee?") This reaction of feeling very slightly but definitely turned-on by the conversation was not something I see as a *problem* in the work, but much more as a facilitating factor. I found out a great deal about not only Ken's individual take on body modification, but also—and I think this is crucial—the subculture of which he was part, what he called his "tribe".

Judging by my experience with this client, Sweetman (1999, pp. 52–53) is absolutely right to describe body modification as "a form of anti-fashion … an attempt to lend corporeal solidity to expressions of individuality." "Individuality" here is a complex concept, however: as is common in our culture, people frequently use "body mod", as it is known, to express their individuality by looking similar to each other. I am not mocking this behaviour: I think that for Ken, as for many other people, there was a very real fulfilment in coming together with those who shared his unusual taste in embodiment (something which the internet has of course made it enormously easier to do). The way in which other people's body mod and general appearance influenced him was primarily through his *recognition* in them of something which corresponded to his own desire. (This closely connects with groups of people drawn together by liking the same music.)

It would have been crass to make the "obvious" interpretation that Ken's body modification was a compensation for his shyness. To begin with, this shyness was only relative, and might not even have been defined in those terms except by contrast with the perceptual "loud-ness" of his tattoos, piercings, hairstyle and so on. But also, and more importantly, to think in terms of compensation would be to refuse valid-ity to his body mod *on its own terms*, and hence to frontally attack Ken's identity, his way of having a body. It would have been equivalent to "explaining" a client's gayness in terms of developmental deficit, while another client's heterosexuality passes without comment.

As it happens, Ken was in fact gay; and twenty years earlier he would no doubt have been subjected to reactions towards his sexual orienta-tion similar to those which he was now experiencing towards his body mod. And in another twenty years? We cannot know. But is the "early adopter" automatically to be perceived as deviant—or to put it another way, is the *socially* deviant person inherently *psychologically* deviant? Personally I often feel enormous admiration for the courage and uncon-scious skill of those who succeed in negotiating a space within culture for their deviant or "perverse" embodiment—for what we might call, in more than one sense, their queerness (Totton, 2006). Eventually, Ken and I did have some useful conversations about the deep significances for him of piercing, wounding, penetrating, and scarring—as one might explore the significances of any client's mode of sexual expression, het-erosexual or otherwise, "normal" or otherwise; but only after we had clearly established that I was not treating these significances as the "real", "fundamental" meaning of his embodiment style.

I want to be explicit that I am, and was at the time, conscious of the force of the countertransference engrams activated in me when with these two clients. (One referee of the original paper assumed that I had no idea what countertransference was or how to work with it.) The traditional way of processing this would have been internally to explore the personal-historical sources of my response, trying to do a quick fix on myself in order to regain some sort of therapeutic neutrality; and having done so, to address the various "narcissistic" and other clinical issues being presented by the clients. My overall argument here, of which these two examples form part, is that such a procedure would be neither therapeutic nor realistic. To in any sense "see through" socially conditioned versions of embodiment, we need to own, and indeed navigate by, our countertransference engrams, rather than strive for some imaginary neutrality. At this point social science approaches and relational body psychotherapy coincide.

The body as event

Body psychotherapy is not and cannot be a means of wiping the body clean of imposed meaning. The body is always already written upon— a palimpsest of superimposed and interpenetrating texts, alternative and sometimes contradictory layers of representation. These texts take the form of what Reich (1945a) called "armouring"—over- or under-investments of particular muscle groups, which through time affect the local connective tissue and hence associated organs and systems, and constellate into competing or cooperating elements of character structure (see Chapter Seven). The question is, who decides what is written next? It is through *having* bodies as tools for personal and political expression—tools always already compromised by the ways in which they have been used by others—that we are able to *become* bodies, to own our embodiment as process and achievement. But embodiment as expression is always an only relatively stable compromise, between domination and freedom, between "the physical, the symbolic and the sociological" (McNay, 1999, p. 98).

The body is always already written upon:

> The social body constrains the way the physical body is perceived.
> The physical experience of the body, always modified by the social

categories through which it is known, sustains a particular view of society. There is a continual exchange of meanings between the two kinds of bodily experience so that each reinforces the categories of the other.

(Douglas, 1973, p. 93)

In other words, there is also always already something upon which the messages have been written; and a sense in which, as Marshall McLuhan told us many years ago, the medium is the message— a sense in which the body itself writes its own representation: as Budgeon, again, puts it, "The body serves not simply as a natural foundation or passive surface upon which meanings are inscribed by systems of signification" (2003, p. 36). Rather, there is an active dialogue, a negotiation, between the body as biological given—but also, as constituted through the perspective of our assumptions—and the body as a cultural artefact—but also, as the biological ground of culture itself. Budgeon continues:

> In order to understand the ways in which young women [and equally, I would add, people in general] actively live their embodied identities, we need to develop an approach which can envision a body beyond the binary of materiality and representation—the body not as an *object* but as an *event*.

(p. 38)

I am not seeking to close off any of the various models of embodiment which are offered by body psychotherapy, neuroscience, or social theory, but rather to draw on all of them. If there is any "final" view of the body, it would be somewhat like a Cubist painting, overlaying many perspectives on embodiment simultaneously. For example, Charles Varela (2005) identifies two kinds of account of human beings which parallel the biology-culture dialogue I have just described, and which he calls the "human nature" paradigm and the "being human" paradigm. The "human nature" paradigm, he says, is individualistic in its assumptions: it construes humans as having a biological nature, which is lived psychologically and hence experienced socially. Both neuroscience and attachment theory, I suggest, are clear examples of this model. In contrast, Varela says the "being human" paradigm construes our nature as cultural (culture being ultimately a biological potential), lived socially, and therefore experienced psychologically. Hence it is holistic rather than individualistic.

Varela is inclined to choose between these two models, and in fact to prefer the second, which he specifically links to some contemporary thinking in dance and movement psychotherapy (Farnell, 1994, 1995; Sheets-Johnstone, 1990; Williams, 1998), and which seems to me also exemplified in several of the ideas with which this book is concerned. My own preference is to work with *both* models, and indeed with as many models as possible, at least while body psychotherapy is in its current state of creative flux, and until we have reached the point which Budgeon (2003, p. 38) identifies as envisaging the body "not as an *object* but as an *event*". After all, an event, one might suggest, does not have a "nature" in quite the sense Varela is arguing.

At times of paradigm shift, it is always tempting to combat anxiety by prematurely establishing a new orthodoxy; in some ways this is happening with current simplified versions of neuroscience-inflected trauma and attachment theory (for example, Gerhardt, 2004, which has become a sort of rulebook for many newly trained therapists). This perhaps represents a failure of nerve: it can be difficult to keep practising one's discipline while knowing that its theoretical basis is a work in progress. But let us keep our nerve, and keep our options open; and let us learn from all available accounts of embodiment, certainly including those offered by social theory.

Familial embodiment

We can all notice in daily life how family resemblance often goes beyond physiognomy to express itself in *patterns of embodiment*—the "way in which" (Reich, 1942, p. 300) family members inhabit their bodies: styles of posture and movement, habits of distance or closeness to other bodies, of tension or relaxation in particular bodily areas and systems, the extent to which a person is or isn't aware of and responsive to her body's sensations, position, and movement through space. The family, in the wide sense of the group in which a child is nurtured and grows up, is the immediate context for our learning of embodiment, our adoption of what Pierre Bourdieu calls "bodily *hexis*", which he defines as the socially conditioned way that individuals "carry themselves" (1984, p. 218). Hence bodily *hexis* is:

> Political mythology realized, *em-bodied*, turned into permanent dis-
> positions, a durable manner of standing, speaking, and thereby of
> feeling and *thinking* ... The principles em-bodied in this way are
> placed beyond the grasp of consciousness, and hence cannot be
> touched by voluntary, deliberate transformation, cannot even be
> made explicit.
>
> (Bourdieu, 1977, p. 94; original italics)

Bourdieu sums this up epigrammatically: "It is because subjects do not, strictly speaking, know what they are doing that what they do has more meaning than they know" (1977, p. 79).

The context which Bourdieu gives to bodily *hexis* is what he calls "habitus": "the way society becomes deposited in persons in the form of lasting dispositions, or trained capacities and structured propensi-ties to think, feel and act in determinant ways, which then guide them" (Wacquant, 2005, p. 316), unconsciously moulding each person's behav-iour along lines which seem to her simply "natural". In fact *habitus* is the Latin translation of the Ancient Greek *hexis*, a term much used by Aristotle in the sense of "acquired disposition". Charles Taylor offers a rough but useful English equivalent of both *hexis* and *habitus*, "bodily know-how" (Taylor, 1995, p. 170).

Bourdieu argues that it is our embodiment which carries "the deep-est dispositions of the habitus" (1984, p. 190). Echoing the concepts of extended mind discussed in Chapter Two, he discusses how a socie-ty's political relationships are displayed and enforced through ways of walking, sitting, or even standing still:

> If all societies ... set such store on the seemingly most insignificant
> details of *dress, bearing*, physical and verbal *manners*, the reason is
> that, treating the body as a memory, they entrust to it in abbrevi-
> ated and practical, i.e. mnemonic, form the fundamental princi-
> ples of the arbitrary content of culture. The principles embodied
> in this way are placed beyond the grasp of consciousness, and
> hence cannot be touched by voluntary, deliberate transformation,
> cannot even be made explicit; nothing seems more ineffable, more
> incommunicable, more intimable, and therefore more precious,

than the values given body, *made* body by the transsubstantiation
achieved by the hidden persuasion of an implicit pedagogy, capable of instilling a whole cosmology, an ethic, a metaphysic, a political philosophy, through injunctions as insignificant as "stand
up straight" or "don't hold your knife in your left hand". (1977,
pp. 94–95)

Plainly, it is through the habitus of family life that most of us develop
our bodily *hexis*. But what needs to be added to this, I think, is that children, at least in Western culture, frequently *reject* their parents' bodily
hexis, consciously and/or unconsciously; the resultant pattern of "*not-
being-like*" is of course just as dependent on their parents' patterns as
imitation would be. We can think of an individual's pattern of embodiment as a complex blend, sometimes smooth and sometimes conflict-
ual, of elements taken from or arising in opposition to those of both
parents, other important adults, siblings, role models like film and pop
stars, and so on, all adopted and adapted by an organismic individual
who already has some strong traits at and before birth, which flavour
the whole stew and make some patterns easier and others harder to
take on. A bodily narrative which can probably never become wholly
conscious, but parts of which will often be explored and perhaps will
change in the course of body psychotherapy. Gender identity and sexual orientation play an important role in all this, and to some extent
arise together with it; Judith Butler's concept of gender performativity
(2006) is helpful here—that our gender is constructed through embodied acts, the ways in which we speak and walk and hold ourselves.

Reich (1945a, 1945b) points out, however, that in giving shape to the
child's embodiment, the family is also acting as an agent of the wider
society and its hegemonic values: in most cases, the family, to at least
some extent, seeks to produce the child as the sort of individual which
society wants her to be. "The family—which is saturated with the ideolo-
gies of society and which, indeed, is the ideological nucleus of society—
is … the representative of society as a whole" (Reich, 1945a, p. 26); and
thus, in a capitalist society, shapes family members into subjects who
can be easily directed and manipulated into producing and consum-
ing as capitalism requires. It does this by, in effect, directly sculpting
its children's bodies, through the regulation of feeding, elimination,
movement, sleeping, touch, expression, sexuality, and so on, to create
particular character types. I will discuss this further in Chapter Seven.

What both Reich and Bourdieu perhaps underestimate is the extent to which families are the site of *struggle*, rather than simply the transmitters of social norms of embodiment. As Jacoby says critically of the 1970s radical therapy movement, which was strongly influenced by a particular reading of Reich, the family "is accepted as the *cause* of social oppression and not also its *victim*" (Jacoby, 1975, p. 133, my italics): a much richer and more nuanced picture of the shaping of our embodiment can be created through exploring the ambivalence of much family life, the resourcing and sanctuary which it offers as well as the discipline and deprivation, the ways in which a family may consciously or unconsciously seek to *shield* its members from social forces. Each family has its own habitus, which is often nonconformist in one way or another, and hence may produce a nonconformist bodily *hexis*; although what we of course also often see is the child of a nonconformist family rebelling by conforming to social norms (and surely her bodily *hexis* will be different from that of a child who reaches the same position through conforming with her family rather than rebelling against it).

However, Reich's placing of much of our social and familial experience under the rubric of patriarchy is as illuminating now as it was when he first wrote about it in the 1930s. He established—possibly for the first time—that the personal is indeed, as we used to say in the 1970s, political; and that the family, and the individual character structures it produces in the bodies of its members, occupy both these two registers. Muriel Dimen writes:

> Psychoanalysis takes up where social theory leaves off … Although social theory dissects the conditions of daily working and civic life, it does not unravel the personal and interpersonal tangles of domestic intimacy … Social theory leads right up to the bedroom door, to the hearth of family and psyche. Then it stops, defeated by the messy, tangled intangibles of domestic life, the same untidy interiority that constitutes the psychoanalytic meeting of minds.
>
> (2004, p. 40)

What Dimen says about psychoanalysis applies perhaps even more clearly, I suggest, to an embodied relational approach. In the next chapter we will explore in more detail the workings of the transformation of social power into individual character.

CHAPTER SEVEN

Character as embodied relating

Several of the authors whose work I have already explored discuss, each in their own way, how we develop structured ways of being bodies which simultaneously express and reproduce the condensed history of our family and cultural experience. This connects strongly with the discussion of motor imagery in Chapter Two. For example, Pierre Bourdieu, whose work has already featured prominently, writes:

> The child imitates not "models" but other people's actions. Body *hexis* speaks directly to the motor function, in the form of a pattern of postures that is both individual and systematic, because linked to a whole system of techniques involving the body and tools, and charged with a host of social meanings and values: in all societies, children are particularly attentive to the gestures and postures which, in their eyes, express everything that goes to make an accomplished adult—a way of walking, a tilt of the head, facial expressions, ways of sitting and of using implements, always associated with a tone of voice, a style of

speech, and (how could it be otherwise?) a certain subjective experience.

(1977, p. 87)

The final phrase here is very important: bodily *hexis* is not just about embodied *behaviour*, but about embodied *experience*. Merleau-Ponty writes that "[T]he body is our general means of having a world" (1962, p. 147): it is the body which apprehends the world, but in doing so forms it into *a* world, the specific version of reality which we are afforded through our early experience. Hence, "[M]y own body is the primordial habit, the one that conditions all others" (Merleau-Ponty, 1962, p. 93). In close parallel, Katharine Young says that "[C]hildren apprehend parents' bodies as solutions to the ontological problem of how to be in the world ... The body is one of our family traditions" (2002, pp. 25–26). There is another mutual causation loop operating here: the world we experience shapes our body into the instrument which perceives the world to be the way we believe it to be.

Merleau-Ponty's version of *hexis* is what he calls the "habit-body": "[O]ur body comprises as it were two distinct layers, that of the habit-body and that of the body at this moment" (1962, p. 82). As Young comments:

> The habit body, which sustains body image, is at once the locus of the condensation of memory and imagination in the present and the aperture through which the body adumbrates itself into its past and its future.
>
> (2002, p. 27)

It is only if we are able to dissolve and reconstitute our existing habit-body that we are able to absorb new experience and form a new view of the world: "The body, then, has understood ... when the body allows itself to be penetrated by a new signification, when it has assimilated a new meaningful core" (Merleau-Ponty, 1962, p. 148). Drew Leder states this reciprocity very clearly:

> Incorporation is the very means whereby new abilities are acquired, unlocking novel aspects of the world. However, it is

also by incorporation that abilities sediment into fixed habits. ... The world transforms my body, even as my body transforms the world. ... The demands and solicitations of the world gradually lead me to reshape the ability-structure of my body.

(1990, pp. 32–34)

Even without the hint of the chapter title, most body psychotherapists reading this will by now have found themselves thinking about *character structure*: the traditional way in which our modality understands the patterns that simultaneously shape our style of embodied relationship and our beliefs about the world. Character theory originates with Freud (1908b) and his circle (e.g., Abraham, 1921, 1924), and is still a part of mainstream psychoanalytic thinking (Lax, 1989; Totton & Jacobs, 2001, Chapter Two), though not much attention is paid to it these days. However, it was taken up and massively elaborated by Wilhelm Reich (1945a), and continues to have a central place in many forms of body psychotherapy (Totton & Jacobs, 2001, Chapter Three).

If we look at Reich's writings on character, we find passages that correspond with striking closeness, assuming that they did not know his work, to those quoted above from Bourdieu, Merleau-Ponty, Young, and Leder:

Character resistance is expressed not in terms of content but formally, in the way one typically behaves, in the manner in which one speaks, walks and gestures; and in one's characteristic habits (how one smiles or sneers, whether one speaks coherently or incoherently, *how* one is polite and *how* one is aggressive).

(1945a, pp. 51–52)

The entire world of past experiences was embodied in the present in the form of character attitudes. A person's character is the functional sum total of all past experiences.

(1942, p. 145)

The first and most important organ for the reproduction of the social order has been the patriarchal family, which lays in its children the characterological grounding for the later influencing by the authoritarian order.

(1945a, p. xxiv)

I believe that character theory can be of great use in thinking about embodied relating; however, it needs to be stripped of its traditional diagnostic, pathologising style, and reconceived as a way to think about the range of creative ways of being human. This work is already underway in Embodied-Relational Therapy (Totton & Priestman, 2012), as well as in some other styles of body psychotherapy like the Hakomi Method (Kurtz, 1985).

What makes character theory different from the many other ways of categorising people (Totton & Jacobs, 2001) is its grounding in embodiment, and specifically in each individual's *history* of embodiment. Character brings together several apparently very different aspects of a person, and shows them to be profoundly linked: developmental history, body structure, emotional attitudes, underlying belief system, relationship style, all emerge as different facets of a fundamental style of being-in-the-world.

Character tracks the energetic focus of a child's development as it moves through the body over the first few years of life, down from the head and eyes to the pelvis and legs; and identifies particular points in that journey where a particular child's vitality may be checked, her needs unmet, and where energy therefore continues to be focused as the child grows up through what Gestalt therapy would call an "uncompleted gestalt". For each of these body areas, there is a developmental window during which, if something significant happens which captures the child's creative/defensive attention, a whole bodymind posture will crystallise and a character position will come into being.

What I mean by "creative/defensive attention" is that human beings come into the world with two equally urgent priorities: to *express* ourselves, and to *protect* ourselves. If we cannot maintain our physical and psychological integrity, then there will be no self to express; but equally, without self-expression there is nothing much to protect. The ongoing tension and reciprocity between these two poles, as they are conditioned by the different circumstances, restrictions, and possibilities afforded to each individual, create the space within which an embodied human personality is shaped (This is a function of the fact that a human being is a non-linear dynamic system: see Chapter Ten).

Where character differs significantly as a concept from Bourdieu's bodily *hexis* and Merleau-Ponty's habit-body is that, as well as expressing and reproducing the condensed history of how our family and culture have impinged on our experience, character also *contends against* the negative aspects of this impact, the ways in which society, acting through the family, represses our spontaneous vitality. Character defends and expresses our desire at the same time as, and in the same ways in which, it expresses the repression of desire.

In this respect character operates like a symptom, bringing together desire and its repression in a single complex bodymind phenomenon. In Freud's view, the symptom of his client Dora's chronic cough expressed both her desire for oral sex and her denial of that desire (1905e). In just the same way, an individual's characteristic combination of traits of orderliness, parsimony, and obstinacy represents both a childhood desire for anal pleasure and the denial of it (Freud, 1908b). This makes character into a much more dynamic force than *hexis* or habit-body—a point of entry for the political into our embodiment, the site of both power and freedom (Foucault, 1997, p. 292). It meets some of the common objections (e.g., Calhoun, 1993) raised to Bourdieu's habitus and *hexis* as politically inert and conservative concepts which offer no purchase point for challenge. Character is inherently a potential challenge to the very forces which have brought it into existence.

Character and developmental affordances

It is noticeable that character theory in some ways dovetails with James and Eleanor Gibson's ecological psychology. A human being can only develop in relation to the developmental affordances that her environment provides. The family environment, the character structure of parents and other carers, and the events and circumstances of childhood limit the possibilities of the child's fundamental concerns and interests; from the palette provided by the universal developmental thresholds as she encounters them in the specific form allowed by her environment, she creates a unique picture of her world and her place in it which constitutes her character structure.

When our developmental environment enables us to meet the needs that become figural at each threshold, this achievement becomes a permanent part of our embodied resources: we've been there, done that, got the T-shirt to prove it. But when our need is not met by a reciprocal capacity of our environment to satisfy it, we are left with a specific deficit, a hole that wants to be filled. This leaves two options. Either we interpret every situation we encounter as evoking that same unmet need, and wander the world looking for some way it can be satisfied; or else we build a structure of denial that represses the very existence of the need. Neither of these options achieves closure: if we permanently yearn, then we also script every situation to repeat the original failure; and if we permanently deny, then we also script every situation to threaten to reveal our need.

The reality is obviously a lot more complex than this. Both later and previous events will either support or weaken, "justify" or challenge the character position that has formed, and will give it a particular flavour and emphasis. Not very many people occupy just one character position; much more often, they will have two or three positions in play, sometimes taking turns to emerge in different situations, sometimes chiming together, sometimes clashing with each other. And, of course, there are many different ways to perceive the "set" of character positions; different body psychotherapy sub-modalities each have their own lists, with their own names, emphases, and omissions. However, there is a good deal of common ground—enough so that it will suffice to stay with the set that we use in Embodied-Relational Therapy (ERT), with new names that are intended to avoid the pathologising tone of the traditional set—"schizoid", "psychopathic", "masochistic", and so on—inherited from psychoanalysis (See Kamalamani, 2012; Totton & Edmondson, 2009; Totton & Jacobs, 2001, Chapter Three).

In ERT we identify three forms of each position: the *creative* version, where the position simply affords a theme, a focus through which the person's life energy expresses itself; the *yearning* version, where people continually search for something crucial which they feel is missing from their world; and the *denying* version, where they compensate for and deny the underlying yearning. The creative position is effectively inherent and syntonic to the individual—in order to be in the world we all have to be *someone*, to have a particular style, a particular set of concerns—a particular character, in fact, which will arise partly from our life circumstances and partly no doubt from our biochemistry. The other two positions, though, are layers which in unfavourable circumstances (these being almost universally present to some extent) can accrete onto and obscure the creative position.

With each position, the direction of increasing limitation is creative > yearning > denying.

In therapy, therefore, growth will typically take place in the reverse direction, denying > yearning > creative, as the individual becomes increasingly able to acknowledge her need and to find positive ways of expressing and satisfying it. The crucial move from denying to yearning, from "*I don't want*" to "*I want*", the conscious owning of repressed desire, is what enables the political challenge inherent in character to begin to actualise; but only insofar as this desire is able to ground itself and take creative forms does its challenge to "business as usual" become concrete.

However, elements of all three positions will usually coexist at the same time, and often wax and wane depending on how much stress the person is under. For example, there is a strong oral component to my own character; when things are going well for me, this is expressed (or so I believe) in an enthusiasm and gusto for life, a savouring of experience, and a desire to articulate it in words—but under stress I tend first of all to become needily dependent on other people's understanding and positive feedback, then increasingly hard to soothe, and eventually I close down and refuse to communicate about my pain: the limitation sequence from creative > yearning > denying. If I am able to process this pattern, as I increasingly am, then it is possible for me first of all to acknowledge the neediness I am trying to repress, then to face the difficulty of trying to get my needs met by others and the inevitably partial extent to which that will be possible, and then, strengthened by successful relational nurturing, to regain an autonomous capacity for satisfaction: the opportunity sequence from denying > yearning > creative.

Here is a chart summarising—in very simplified terms, inevitably—some of the typical qualities and relational issues of each of the six basic character positions. As may be evident even from this brief outline, character theory in effect brings together into one schema many themes of attachment theory, object relations, and classic Oedipal theory, showing how each can be applicable to different parts of an individual's history as it condenses into a style of embodied relating.

But why bother with such a complicated framework? There is of course a risk of letting a characterological grid dominate and obscure our direct experience of the other; and this certainly tends to happen temporarily when someone is learning to make use of the system. As with all learning, though, once the knowledge of character becomes

Table 1.

Character position	Key relational issue	Developmental stage	Typical body	Typical concerns	Relational style (creative)	Relational style (yearning and denying)	Effect on others
Boundary	Presence	Birth and first weeks of life	Awkward, under-occupied, strange	Theories, systems, spirituality, science, internet. "Nerd", "geek"	Inspiring others through intellectual, spiritual or artistic vision	Distant/lonely/telepathic/awkward—too much or too little	Either deeply uncomfortable, or deeply "in tune"
Oral	Support	Breast/bottle feeding, weaning, teething	Long and thin, either wiry or floppy	Appetite, sensual pleasure, justice & fairness, using language to get needs met	Gusto and appetite for life; passionate about justice and fairness	Needy or self-sufficient	Eliciting either caring (ending in frustration) or contempt/rejection
Control	Trust	"Terrible Twos"	Pronounced chest, dominating stance	Being in charge, being taken seriously	Leadership, protecting others, generosity	Self-centred, manipulative or bullying—or desperate for acknowledgement	Charismatic and/or frightening

Holding	Autonomy	Potty training	Squashed, square, sturdy	Getting it right, avoiding shame	Quietly getting on with what needs doing, taking care of the world	Binding self and others to "the rules"; petty, shortsighted; over organised or chaotic	Frustrating, reliable
Thrusting	Achievement	Start of independence	Athletic, physical, dashing	Competition, testing self against others and the world	Courageous, adventurous, stepping up	Cruel, dominating, obsessive	Draws out everyone's competitive or submissive streak
Crisis	Surrender	Gender identity, relational erotic charge. "First puberty"	Lithe, rounded, sexually charged	Being liked, finding entertainment, flirting with danger	Challenging the rigid and rule bound to play and experiment. "Let's have fun"	Chaotic, unreliable, manufacturing emergencies. "Let's talk about me"	Seductive, entertaining, infuriating

implicit and procedural, rather than explicit and theoretical—a visceral rather than visual understanding (see Chapter Two) grounded in our own embodied experience and not just in observation and deduction—it enables deeper and richer embodied connection with the other. After all, one crucial aspect of character is that it conditions each person's unconscious theory and practice of embodied relating. In the following section, I apply character theory to this crucial aspect of life. My use of "she" and "her" for the generic individual should not be taken as implying that any character positions are inherently gendered.

Relating with character

I am going to look briefly at each of the six basic character positions—the six basic varieties, we might say, of being embodied in the world; with each in turn, I will try to sketch the implications of that position for someone's style of embodied relating. We of course need to bear in mind that no one is a "pure" example of only one character position; we are all more or less complex mixtures, with different positions, different engrams, coming to the fore in different situations (for example, everyone's boundary aspect will tend to appear in new and strange environments)—but always flavoured by the other character positions which form an important part of that person's make-up.

How, after all, could it be otherwise, given that the different characters reflect developmental thresholds which we have all had to traverse? No one can grow up without being born into a pre-existing world, without learning to feed and to ask for support, learning to use other people to validate ourselves, learning to regulate our sphincters and our spontaneity, learning to assert ourselves in the world, and learning to play, to surrender, and to meta-communicate. And in passing through these territories with varying degrees of ease or difficulty, we form our own way of seeing and being in the world, seeing and being in relationship.

Character can be entirely *creative* in nature: we can be very beautifully and impressively the particular kind of person that we are, following the particular path through life that we follow. However, we can also get stuck in a groove, fixated on one particular aspect of life to the exclusion of all others, trying to open every door we encounter with the same key—or perhaps, if our early experience has been unlucky, with a bit of broken metal that we *think* is a key. Character can function as a channel for energy, or as a block on it. Usually, it has some of each quality.

Boundary character

The boundary position—most widely, and off-puttingly, referred to as "schizoid", but also as "ocular" or "sensitive/analytic"—is associated with the very earliest phases of life, pre-birth, birth, and the first days or weeks thereafter. Hence the experience of the boundary aspect of ourselves is of extreme sensitivity and vulnerability. If the individual feels welcomed, made safe and cherished, her sensitivity becomes an asset, something which she can use on behalf of herself and her community as a visionary, an artist, a creative thinker.

If she feels less than fully welcomed, however, some degree of alienation will develop in her make-up: she will protect herself through distance or through armouring. I supervised someone who became aware that her client felt uncomfortably close to her as they sat in the therapy room. They started to experiment with finding a tolerable distance— and ended up standing on opposite sides of a large field, with the client saying over his mobile phone, "This feels about right"!

Symbolically at least, this is how it often feels to work with someone who has a strong boundary component to her character. She will not come into contact until she feels safe enough; and yet being out of contact *also* makes her unsafe. So she will often use quite indirect ways of connecting with us, talking about theory or about "safe" topics (like the trumpeter client I will mention in Chapter Nine), or communicating non-verbally or apparently telepathically. Unless we are able to allow her enough psychic distance, and to pick up her clues, it will be very difficult to establish a working relationship.

However, we could look at it differently, and accept that this *is* the working relationship for someone in the boundary position. Quite a lot of therapists know this place in themselves quite well, which is fortunate—though it does not immunise them against an engram-based enactment, which can feel like being on the ocean at night, trying to make out the shape of another ship in the distance through the murk and the rolling waves, and to find some way of signalling to it; or, even worse, impatiently ignoring the other's vulnerability and rolling over her frontiers like a tank regiment.

Boundary material often expresses itself in the eyes, an important avenue of connection or disconnection for the newborn baby: the adult boundary character's eyes can be blank and cut-off, or deep and dreamy; she may be unwilling to make eye contact or equally unwilling to break it. The person's overall embodiment can also seem childlike, with an overlarge head, or generally "odd", muddled together in a way that expresses inner chaos, as if she has picked her body parts out at a jumble sale.

As I have said, there are three versions of each position, which we can call the yearning, the denying, and the creative. Here are the three versions of the boundary character, emphasising relational issues.

Yearning version: *I am desperate for contact with others, but also feel it will disintegrate me. I am not real in the way that other people seem to be: I need them to make me real, but also fear they will damage my reality still further.*

Denying version: *Only I am real; other people are all robots, aliens, phantoms, hypnotised, figments of my own imagination. I have infinite resources in my own mind; I am complete in myself. I choose to stay outside the world.*

Creative version: *I am connected to the infinite web of existence and information. Through reason and/or intuition I can reveal and create pattern, make sense of the whole. I can make subtle contact with others and share visions with them.*

Oral character

As its name suggests, the oral position originates in developmental issues relating to the mouth: feeding, weaning, teething, and talking, all thresholds which can be extremely difficult for the infant and carer to negotiate, and which can structure lifelong relational patterns. The oral position also expresses itself in the legs and arms—issues around supporting oneself, being "grown up", or reaching out to be picked up and held.

The oral aspect of us is focused on how or whether we can get our needs met. It leads us to relate to others as sources of nurturing and support, or as rivals for it. The individual struggles with feelings of intense need and inability to cope, and also with a reaction of "well, I don't need anyone anyway"; it is hard for her to find a middle ground where she can recognise and tolerate in herself and others a human need for mutual help and support. There is often an oscillation, echoing infant feeding experiences, between phases of feeling full and content and phases of desperate emptiness. But once an oral character finds that middle ground, and accepts that all organisms need to support themselves and fairness doesn't come into it, she can develop a great gusto for life, a capacity to feed herself and others and to fight for justice in a wide range of situations.

Therapy which involves a client's oral position tends to be very stormy, with the therapist feeling under pressure to meet the client's needs, yet never able actually to do so in a stable way—more unmet needs will always keep appearing, inviting an enactment of failure and rejection. The therapist is likely to feel a reciprocal sense of rejection, and to feel too small and "not enough" for the client. The meeting of both people's engrams produces a difficult dance where feelings of contempt, dissatisfaction, and shame are passed from one to the other. This will continue indefinitely until the therapist is able to remember that she is not there to meet the client's needs—or to reject them—but to help what is happening emerge into shared awareness.

Yearning version: *I lack the internal resources to look after myself, and need constant top-ups from outside. I resent other people because they don't see how hard it is for me, and never give me quite what I want or need. I feel both envy and contempt for them, I am potentially so much better than they are—if only I was given a fair chance.*

Denying version: *I am strong because I am self-sufficient. I go through this empty world alone; like a desert plant, I have formed a tough skin and learned to wait. I will stand up for justice, and sometimes may look after others, but really I despise their weakness—if I can do it on my own, why can't they?*

Creative version: *I have a good appetite for life, and enjoy taking nourishment in all its forms. I am ready to knuckle down and work to get my needs met, and also for pure pleasure—and to strive for justice and equality in the world.*

Control character

Also known as "psychopathic" and "tough/generous", the control position originates in a struggle to be recognised and validated. We can think about the period in childhood when the child is able to move about and play independently, but still very much in need of the adult gaze: "Look at me, Mummy!" "Daddy, did you see what I did!" Along with this goes the need to *use* the adult as part of the child's fantasy—in Andrew Samuels's wonderful example, "You be the daddy, Daddy" (1993, p. 171).

A difficult experience at this developmental stage leaves the individual permanently struggling to be attended to and to feel she has an influence on others. Because she has not been treated as real herself—although by this stage of development, unlike boundary characters, she knows that she *is* real—she has great difficulty in believing in anyone else's right to claim full reality. In a rageful reaction, she may treat others as pawns to be manipulated, either by force or by charm. Since other people are unreal, the control character need feel no responsibility for their fate. The great example here is Orson Welles in *The Third Man*—"Would you honestly care if one of those dots stopped moving?"

Denying control characters can often appear puffed up, like Mr. Toad, sticking out their chests and throwing their heads back in an attempt to dominate. They will try to take control of the therapy and to subtly or openly diminish the therapist, unless we can convince them of our genuineness; and this is not easy, since they will suspect trickery at every point. If they manage to process their woundedness, however, they often become "big" people in a positive sense, able to offer leadership and help to others and to society as a whole.

There are two obvious relational engrams which the therapist of a denying control character is likely to experience. One is counter-control, an urge to puff ourselves up even bigger than the client; the other is to yield, be small, and admire the client's apparent superiority—perhaps ending up accepting an offer of networking opportunities, for example. With a yearning control character, we may find ourselves entering an enactment where we miss what she is showing us and ignore her communications. In reality, of course, yearning and denying are generally mingled, so that to buy into the denying position is itself to miss the yearning position.

Yearning version: *I need to be noticed, seen and responded to—to make my mark on others. I know I am real, but other people don't seem to see me—this must be because they are only shadows themselves. How can I find someone real who will see me for who I am?*

Denying version: *"Relationships" are weak and stupid. Like everyone else, ultimately I am out for myself—the trick is to win the battle: to the victor the spoils. Other people are transparent fools, and I enjoy deceiving and manipulating them.*

Creative version: *I am a big, powerful person, who needs to get involved with people and be useful in the world. I am big enough to give generously, and in turn receive a lot in approval and recognition.*

Holding character

The holding character was the first to be identified, as the "anal" character (Freud, 1908b), and much of what Freud said about it still holds true today. Other names that have been used are "masochistic" and "burdened/enduring". The core issue here is about self-regulation, and has its clear origins in toilet training and all the forms of anxious interference that can go along with it.

Rather than being supported in recognising and following their own body rhythms and needs, denying/yearning holding characters have been subjected to externally based regimes corresponding to other people's needs: timetabling, cleanliness, emotional control, "being good". All this has given them the message that their insides are unacceptable, bad and shitty, and must be kept hidden. This naturally produces a great deal of rage and resentment, which appears to the person as confirmation of how bad and unacceptable her insides are.

The holding character's shameful rage is expressed in one of two ways in adulthood: either the individual uses self-repression to repress others, sitting down heavily on all freedom and spontaneity; or she acts chaotically in ways that impact subtly on other people—being late, forgetting commitments, leaving things behind, praising people in a fawning, "greasy" way that leaves a bad taste, spilling secrets—in effect, smearing invisible excrement over those around her.

The typical style of embodiment for holding characters is an apparently "squashed" appearance—short and wide, with not much neck or waist, and sunken, suffering eyes. The more creativity they can access, the more their appearance reads as "sturdy and grounded" rather than "stuck and burdened". Because of their groundedness they are often surprisingly good dancers, and on very good terms with the material world.

Holding characters who manage to deny their rage often live small and impoverished lives, afraid to take any risks or have any adventures, to show their heads above the parapet. On the other hand, they can be in touch with the creative aspects of the character, and have a genuine humility, kindness, and straightforwardness; they look after what needs doing and keep the world going round. In therapy they will often be quietly terrified of letting go and spilling their guts; and a therapist who, with the best intentions, pressurises them to relax and be spontaneous will only re-enact the original trauma and cause them to seize up further—the holding character is structured so as to absorb any pressure, physical or emotional, and make it part of her resistance. In therapy they need to be given space to feel how they are restricting themselves, and very slowly to release the restriction. This process can be intensely painful for therapist as well as client.

Yearning version: *I need to let go and push—to splurge, make a mess, spread myself all over things and people. I want to knead and shape and play with physical matter, to bring my insides outside and admire them; but I also need to keep this secret and unseen. I'll "blamelessly" spoil and crush whoever I can; or sabotage them with "mistakes".*

Denying version: *I won't—can't—mustn't—let go; I must stick to the rules at all costs, or I'll mess up and be shamed, expose my insides to ridicule, others will be disgusted and reject me. I can only express my anger by forcing others to follow the rules, and by boring and frustrating them.*

Creative version: *I have the strength to stand for myself, as a natural being in the natural world; the patience to attend to detail, do things the right way, follow through. I am not afraid to be simple and nothing special, to serve, to get my hands dirty. I follow my own rhythm, and honour the rhythm of all beings.*

Thrusting character

The last two character positions are in some ways the most complex, and also the most politically charged, because they have been taken up culturally as reflections of gender norms; hence individual and social forces meet in them. Historically in the West, the thrusting position has been understood as typically masculine—as is apparent in its well known name of the "phallic" character. Its embodied expression approaches a masculine ideal, lean, powerful, and athletic, with narrow waist and wide shoulders; paralleled by stereotypically "masculine" character traits like initiative, ruthlessness, competitiveness, and courage.

These traits are a reactively exaggerated version of the assertiveness which is part of normal growing up for both genders (and both genders can of course enter the thrusting position). When this assertiveness is crushed and punished by parents who cannot tolerate it—perhaps because they themselves are thrusting characters—the frustration and rage of this experience turns assertion into competition, and competition into a need to defeat and destroy everyone experienced as a rival.

This can come out on a macro-level, for example as ambition and workaholism; and on a micro-level, as a tendency for thrusting characters to find more or less subtle ways to humiliate and denigrate anyone around them. People stuck in the denying or yearning thrusting position tend to see sex as conquest—pleasure is dangerously close to surrender, which in turn feels like collapse. Therapy can also easily feel like an invitation to surrender, so that the therapist becomes someone who must be defeated at all costs; in fact few thrusting characters come for therapy, unless they have a stubborn "psychosomatic" symptom, or are themselves training to be therapists.

The relational engram here can be very powerful, and as therapists we need to work hard at not losing our perspective as we are drawn into fighting back, and subtly refocusing our invitation to spontaneity as a push for compliance. Instead, we can try to model soft strength for them, a tenderness which is not weakness; but the competitive engram may be so strong that we can only go with it, and seek ways to bring it usefully into awareness.

Yearning version: *In order to feel successful and proud, I will take any risks and defeat any opponent. Life is about working and fighting, stimulus and challenge. There will always be another mountain to climb; it's never time to relax and let go, always time to try a little bit harder.*

Denying version: *Life is dog eat dog—I look out for number one. Feelings are weakening, and I have none. Other people are to be despised and humiliated, especially the opposite sex. I won't enjoy myself, and nor will you—if I catch you doing so, I'll smash you.*

Creative version: *I seek to stretch my abilities, to aspire, do the impossible, test myself against the world. Nothing feels so good as trying my hardest, especially in a worthwhile cause—then basking in my achievement. Life is to be lived, and I seek out chances to do so.*

Crisis character

This is well known as the "hysteric" or "histrionic" character, and also called "expressive-clinging". It is the most complicated position to describe and account for—appropriately enough, since people in the crisis position tend to feel complicated both to themselves and to others. But what really makes the position complicated is that it is in many ways a response to the complexity of the social sphere. (As the well known crisis character Jessica Rabbit says in *Who Killed Roger Rabbit*, "I'm not bad, I'm just drawn that way": https://www.youtube.com/watch?v=yy5THitqPBw.) Compared with the other positions, the crisis position is less fully mediated through the private life of the family: it develops at a stage when the developing child is exposed willy-nilly to society and its rules, and in particular to rules about sexuality and gender.

In a sense, therefore, the problems faced by the crisis character parallel those of the boundary character: they are about entering into a new and unknown world, and finding out how to make contact with others. However, the crisis character has already traversed the developmental sequence from crown to pelvis, on a journey of embodiment; the contact she now needs to negotiate is embodied, gendered, erotically charged. The crisis position is crystallised in the "first puberty" at around four or five years old, when developmental energy arrives explosively in the genitals, disturbing everyone's careful arrangements and throwing the whole family into—and hence, partly, the name—crisis.

The whole process will replay itself far more obviously in the "second puberty" of adolescence; but what happens then has been at least partly already set up in this first iteration of the themes. There are many ways in which the child can try to handle her situation, and some of these will employ the engrams of earlier character positions already developed in previous phases. The crisis position, however, uses skills and capacities which were not available earlier: in particular, the ability to metacommunicate and to achieve relational metapositions. Put more simply, the child, and later the adult, discerns in her situation the hidden rules which govern it, and uses this perception to play with her own and other people's positions. Examples of this serious play are flirting, exaggeration, and paradox. "Serious play" is itself half paradoxical, and a good example of how the position works. A lot of what I talk about in Chapter Eight is connected to the crisis position.

The key theme of crisis embodiment is *fascination*. The crisis body has a way of always drawing the attention, by its frequently ripe and full build, and/or by its graceful, lithe, expressive style of movement, which can be very disturbing to others and sometimes to the self. Or the denying crisis embodiment can be completely frozen, awkward and sexless—yet still somehow drawing sexual attention. There is often an element of androgyny; and an underlying communication we might sum up as "Go away … closer". These complex, contradictory embodied messages keep drawing the attention back as we try to pin down what is being expressed and decide how to respond to it.

The relational engram, then, is explicitly embodied: as with boundary characters, the issue here is mingled desire and anxiety around contact, but the desire is much more bodily, sexually charged, and, often, active. The crisis character generally keeps approaching, attracting, fascinating, but at the crunch will do anything rather than simply be present with the other. Both the attraction and the underlying panic are contagious.

Yearning version: *It's all too much!—exciting and terrifying things happen all the time! I need your attention, but can't bear to keep still and be really seen. I have to find out the rules in any situation—by breaking them if possible. Everything is sexual, exciting, and dangerous.*

Denying version: *I feel no excitement of any kind; I am passive, the victim of other people's actions. All the excitement and danger is outside me, in other people or in the surrounding situation. Nothing is sexual (but other people keep trying to have sex with me); nothing is exciting (but other people keep being excited by me).*

Creative version: *I can have fun with the rules, while knowing that it's just a (serious) game. I can choose in each moment how close to get to you, and take responsibility for my choices, and their effect on others. I love to play, to pretend, to be wild and exaggerated and exciting. There is a sexual side to everything, but it doesn't have to be acted out.*

Thinking further about character and habit

Character is our unique response to the circumstances of our development. But its uniqueness is only relative: it also falls into a limited number of recognisable, stereotyped patterns—the more so, the more it tends towards the yearning and denying versions of each position. Growing up with a character position increases our chances of inheriting it: we imitate what is presented to us as *the* way of becoming an adult. Through what we say and do, but even more through *how* we say it and do it, we express the state and history of our embodiment, the history of our family relationships and of our class and culture. Young points out that our style of embodiment develops through imitation or rejection of family models of adulthood, masculinity and femininity, our judgement of how we should be:

> Out of a family repertoire of such judgements, children shape a corporeal self. Whether by imitation or resistance, their bodies memorialize the family's way of being in the world.

> (2002, p. 26)

Hence:

> This haunting of our own bodies by the bodies of others is constant, a persistent familiar in our ordinary lives. … The body is the flesh of memory.

> (p. 45)

Body psychotherapy's ways of thinking about character need to be broadened to include what Young and Bourdieu focus on: character as inheritance, the familially and culturally sanctioned ways in which we seek purchase on the world. In a formulation very similar to Reich's thinking in *The Mass Psychology of Fascism* (1945b), Bourdieu describes bodily hexis as "political mythology realised, embodied, turned into a permanent disposition, a durable manner of standing, speaking and thereby of feeling and thinking" (1977, p. 93).

Steph Lawler (2004) points out how for Bourdieu, "… the subject is not the instantaneous *ego* of a sort of singular *cogito*, but the individual trace of an entire collective history" (Bourdieu, 1990, p. 91); and habitus is "embodied history, internalized as a second nature and so forgotten as history" (Bourdieu, 1990, p. 56). The body:

> … does not represent what it performs, it does not memorize the past, it *enacts* the past, bringing it back to life. What is "learned by

the body" is not something one has, like knowledge that can be brandished, but something that one is.

(Bourdieu, 1990, p. 73)

Katharine Young takes the same position, except that for her the enactment of the past does not so much bring it back to life as *raise its ghost*, "the ancestral ghost in the flesh of the present" (2002, p. 45).

Young's strong implication is that freedom lies in the rejection of this ancestral ghost; Bourdieu, as many have commented, seems to imply that we are powerless even to recognise how we embody history, let alone put it to rest. The tenor of character theory, certainly in its more recent forms, is that we can transmute both inherited and acquired character through *owning* it, mourning the loss, and celebrating the potential creativity.

THE STORY SO FAR, 2

Here is a summary of the most important points in Chapters Five, Six, and Seven.

1. As well as the effects of our personal history, embodiment also shapes and is shaped by the ensemble of present and past familial and social relations, on every level from the personal to the global, which provides a guiding context for individual relationships.
2. This context is a mixture in varying proportions of the benign and the repressive, and often includes contradictory elements, which tend to be held out of consciousness.
3. We each use our environment as a set of "exograms", an extension of our thought processes into the world. In particular, we use other people in this way, as they equally use us. Hence "our" minds are not wholly "ours", but part of larger collective projects.
4. Embodiment and embodied relating are constrained by socially constructed understandings of what they are and can be, which encode complex organisations of power in relation to class, gender, race, and other categories.

5. Hence it can be said that bodies are *produced by discourse*. However, it is also true that language itself is produced by and through the body; a further example of circular causality.

6. As a framework for these complex relationships, it is helpful to consider embodiment in three aspects: the body as something we *have* (object), as something we *are* (subject), and as something we *become* (process).

7. In the embodied therapeutic relationship, we as therapists directly and concretely experience how the client's embodiment is embedded in social narratives, and also how it resists or evades this embedding, and even exploits it for its own purposes.

8. Social structurings of power mediated through the family, together with our resistance to them, place us in character positions which embody the history of our embodied relationships with significant others and with the social structures that their bodies transmit to us. Character structure is the matrix formed by and forming ensembles of engrams. As with every other consequence of power, character also contains within it the possibility of freedom.

9. From the earliest part of life a person's character structure filters and gives a particular spin to new relational experiences, at the same time as it—reluctantly—adjusts its own assumptions in the light of those new experiences, and feeds that adjustment back onto its picture of previous experiences.

In the remainder of the book, I will build on this foundation to explore other aspects of embodied relating, ending with the clinical and with the ecopsychological aspects.

CHAPTER EIGHT

Therapy as play

In the early 1950s, two very intelligent and far-sighted people, one in England and the other in California, were both thinking about play. It seems a great pity that they apparently knew nothing about each other, because their work dovetails in complex ways which they themselves could probably have explored more effectively than I can. But I will do my best, because between them they were saying something about psychotherapy which seems to me enormously important—and more so if both are taken into account than if either one's ideas are pursued on their own. The two people were Donald Winnicott (1953, later included and extended in 1971) and Gregory Bateson (1955). Not only were they both talking about play, they were both connecting it with therapy: while Bateson argues that "[T]he resemblance between the process of therapy and the phenomenon of play is ... profound" (1955, p. 191), Winnicott if anything goes further: "*Psychotherapy has to do with two people playing together*" (1971, p. 38; original italics).

I am certainly not the first person to have noticed the parallels in their work (see, for example, Hamilton, 1982; Iacono, 2002; Pateman, 2006). But I haven't come across anyone who has done what I intend to do now, which is to place both authors in the context of embodied relating: a move which is made possible by the increasingly well known work of Stephen Porges (2011) on the social engagement system (SES). Porges, in turn, gives no sign of knowing the work of either Winnicott or Bateson.

Porges focuses on a group of several cranial nerves which all originate in the same area of the brain: an area which, in our early aquatic ancestors, was concerned with the function of the gills. If we put together the operation of all these cranial nerves, we get a very interesting picture. Some of them are still concerned with breath, and also with sucking, swallowing, salivation, and vocalisation—in other words, with all the mechanisms which allow first of all, breastfeeding without suffocation, and then eventually, articulate speech. Others let us tense the muscles of the middle ear, strengthening the ability to pick out and discriminate the frequencies of speech from the hum of background noise. Others control the expressive muscles of the face, and the muscles of the eyelids, influencing eye contact. And one branch of the vagal nerve allows us to smoothly ramp up and ramp down the activity of the heart.

These nerves together map the social engagement system, described by Porges as a complex interactive network of cranial nerves and functional systems which in earlier species was devoted to absorbing oxygen from water; gradually developed in mammals into a system for absorbing food and comfort from the mother's breast; and then in humans merged with systems of visual, facial, and vocal interaction with our carer, becoming in adults a way for absorbing *relational* nourishment from our social context. What was once literal absorption gradually became an embedded, embodied metaphor. All in all, this is an elaborate and subtle system for interrelating with other people, first as infants and then as adults: a system developed over evolutionary time by co-opting and synthesising pre-existing anatomy and physiology for new purposes. This sort of process, where a mechanism evolved for one purpose is co-opted for a different one, is called "exaptation".

In terms of the up-hierarchy discussed in Chapter One, Porges's work is largely concerned with the crucial transition from physiology to feeling. I will discuss it further in Chapter Twelve. For the purposes of this chapter, though, I am going to pick out one aspect, which is in a sense far from the centre of Porges's work, concerned with the role of *play*. Porges (2011, p. 278) identifies five physiological states of activation, which we could think of as species-wide—in fact, mammalian-wide— engrams, ancient but living skeletons on which our personal engrams are fleshed out. Four of these states are: *social engagement* (the polyvagal system); *mobilisation* (fight-flight); *immobilisation* (freeze-faint); and *immobilisation without fear* (making possible various forms of physical intimacy). The fifth state is *play*, which Porges suggests is a combination of mobilisation with social engagement (Play is also identified as a "hard-wired" human behaviour by Jaak Panksepp, 2004).

All of these states are of enormous interest in relation to therapy, especially immobilisation without fear; but I am focusing here on play, which Porges describes like this:

> Access to the social engagement system is critical in defining mobilization as play and not aggression. ... A "polyvagal" definition of play requires reciprocal interactions and a constant awareness of the actions of others. Play is different than fight-flight behaviors. Although fight-flight behaviors often require an awareness of others, they do not require reciprocal interactions and an ability to restrain mobilization. Play recruits another circuit [social engagement] that enables aggressive and defensive behaviors to be contained.
>
> (2011, p. 276)

It seems to me that this is very relevant to the "as-if" nature of psychotherapy, where—if we are working relationally—both client and therapist need to experience deep feelings towards each other, both positive and negative, while they however simultaneously inhibit the sorts of action which their feelings would normally imply, and hold a meta-perspective which says "I am not *really* loving or hating this person in front of me—although I *am* feeling *real* love or hate". Both Winnicott and Bateson make this same connection between play and therapy.

In his paper on play and fantasy (Bateson, 1955), which was a key document in the development of systemic family therapy, Gregory Bateson argues (pp. 178–180) that play in humans and other mammals is structured through meta-signals conveying the message "this is not what it seems" (for example, I am not really about to rip your throat out). He relates this to a number of other human activities, including threat, deceit, dramatisation, ritual, and psychotherapy. In a characteristic procedure, Bateson uses this list as a highly condensed argument in its own right: if we can see what these very varied activities have in common, then we have already grasped his point. And what they have in common, essentially, is that various acts are *represented* but not literally *performed*. Winnicott actually offers a parallel and overlapping though distinct list of activities which begin with play and include artistic creativity and its appreciation, religious feeling, dreaming, fetishism, lying, and stealing, "the origin and loss of affectionate feeling", drug addiction, obsessional rituals, etc. (1953, p. 233); this list can only be understood through Winnicott's concept of transitional space, which is discussed below.

Play in the therapy room

If Bateson and Winnicott are right that play is the fundamental form out of which all these activities develop, then it is clearly very important to human life, for adults as well as children. And as should already be clear, both of them believe that it is also very important, indeed foundational, to the practice of psychotherapy. In fact, Winnicott goes so far as to say that "psychoanalysis has been developed as a highly specialized form of playing in the service of communication with oneself and others" (1971, p. 41). Actually, *both* participants need to play: "*Psychotherapy needs to take place in the overlap of two areas of playing, that of the patient and that of the therapist*" (p. 38; original italics).

Winnicott sees the capacity for play as *essential* to the process of therapy, so that "[W]hen a patient cannot play the therapist must attend to this major symptom before interpreting fragments of behaviour" (p. 47). Winnicott doesn't say so, but it is generally trauma that damages a person's capacity to play; I will discuss this below, and also in Chapter Ten. "If the therapist cannot play", however, Winnicott states flatly that "he [sic] is not suitable for the work" (p. 54). Bateson would certainly agree. In the terms I have been developing, the capacity for play is an *engram*, a habitual pattern of activation. If the client cannot play because the engram has not been formed in childhood, it may be possible for her to learn from the therapist; but if the therapist cannot play, will she be able—willing—to learn from the client?

However we do it—and neither Bateson nor Winnicott express any interest in the nuts and bolts, probably because there was no way at the time to investigate further—it is undoubtedly true that neurotypical humans, like other mammals, can read—or rather, sense—the signs which bring into being what Bateson calls a "frame", and Winnicott a "transitional space" or "third area". This is in some ways the equivalent of the pitch or field of play in the special form of play called sport, which is invisibly signposted, "While we are in this space, different rules are in operation". The overarching rule in question is: "These actions in which we now engage do not denote what those actions *for which they stand* would denote" (Bateson, 1955, p. 180; original italics). A key element in what defines therapy as play seems to be the frame within which it takes place. Bateson's term "frame" is of course commonly used to denote the set of rules which are special to the activity of therapy. We will return to this.

Winnicott's concept of the third, or potential, or transitional space is complex, and we need to explore it in order to grasp its full relevance to therapy. Winnicott developed this shifting set of terms to describe a series of what we might call "inbetweennesses". There is the space between mother and child, which both connects and separates them; the space connecting and separating internal and external reality; the space which is neither self nor non-self. The transitional space of therapy partakes of all these; and they all share a special quality—which is in fact a recurring theme in this book—of being simultaneously "both" yet "neither": both yet neither internal and external, both yet neither reality and illusion, both yet neither me and you. This is all paradoxical, of course; and as Winnicott says:

> My contribution is to ask for a paradox to be accepted and tolerated and respected, and for it not to be resolved. By flight or by split-off intellectual functioning it is possible to resolve the paradox, but the price of this is the loss of the value of the paradox itself.

> (1971, p. xii)

How far is this related to Bateson's concept of the frame? The two men bring very different styles of mind to bear on the theme of play: Bateson is thinking much more rigorously about paradox, in the context of Russell's theory of logical types: "It is our hypothesis that the message 'this is play' establishes a paradoxical frame" (1955, p. 184). Bateson's explanation of this is rather untypically confused and unconvincing, but the simplest example would be the statement: "This statement is untrue": if it is true then it is untrue, but if it is untrue then it is true, and so on *ad infinitum*. The statement is both true and untrue, yet neither true nor untrue. So Bateson, although he comes at it from another angle, emphatically shares Winnicott's appreciation of the paradoxes involved in "as-if":

> Paradox is doubly present in the signals which are exchanged within the context of play, fantasy, threat, etc. Not only does the playful nip not denote what would be denoted by the bite for which it stands, but, in addition, the bite itself is fictional.

> (1955, p. 182)

The paradox establishes a space where some very important phenomena can exist: for example play, culture, art, and therapy. And what is especially important for my argument in this book, embodied relating also takes place in the transitional, in-between space, where what we experience is *both* mine and the client's, yet *neither* mine nor the client's, but belonging to the field that is brought into existence between us. The fruitless question that practitioners so often raise in relation to all kinds of countertransference experience—"Is this mine or theirs?"—tries to collapse the paradox which is essential to bringing the experience into being: that it is both, yet neither.

Recognising play

The paradox is itself an *embodied* one. We don't tend to think of embodiment as able to carry a logical message, but Bateson points out that in fact it can and does communicate not just logic, but logical paradox:

> Not only do the playing animals not quite mean what they are saying, but, also, they are usually communicating about something which does not exist.

> (1955, p. 182)

As with Porges's description of the embodied signalling of intention to play, the "saying" and "communicating" to which Bateson refers is clearly not happening in language. Until fairly recently, ethologists assumed that it must be happening in language-like "signals"; but this has been thrown into question, as we are about to see.

In his original paper, Bateson writes about a research expedition in 1952 to a San Francisco zoo.

What I encountered at the zoo was a phenomenon well known to everybody: I saw two young monkeys playing, i.e., engaged in an interactive sequence of which the unit actions or signals were similar to but not the same as those of combat. It was evident, even to the human observer, that the sequence as a whole was not combat, and evident to the human observer that to the participant monkeys this was "not combat."

(1955, p. 179)

As I have already mentioned, Bateson makes no attempt to consider just *how* this was "evident", both to the monkeys themselves and, across species, to the human observer. And still today it appears that there is remarkably little consensus about how play is signalled, either in humans or in other mammals (Burghardt, 2005; Mitchell, 1991; Pellis & Pellis, 1997).

I am in no way an expert on ethology, but there seems to be at least a respectable position that:

… not only are most so-called play signals not universal amongst species that engage in play fighting, but also … many such signals are not unique to play.

(Pellis & Pellis, 1996, p. 250)

In a slightly later paper the same authors argue:

Play signals have not been identified in all species which play fight, and when present, appear to be used only in a minority of play fights. … In most cases, the interactants appear to differentiate playful from serious fighting by contextual and stylistic cues.

(1997, p. 123)

In other words, if the interaction looks like play and feels like play, it is play. But what does it mean for something to *feel like play*?

We may safely assume that, for humans, language plays an important role in identifying play; but given the similarities between human and other-than-human play, plus the huge importance of preverbal play for babies, language is clearly not a required factor for identification. The specific question which interests me here is: how do we "signal" intent to play in the therapy room? How do we indicate that what is going on will be treated as pretend, as "as-if"—even though much of it is clearly quite serious?

To begin with, seriousness is in any case not foreign to ordinary play—in other words, play is not necessarily *playful*. Tina Bruce writes, describing a piece of video:

> The baby who is playing with the red and blue ball ... is very serious as he plays. This links with the view of play held by Froebel, that play is the highest and most serious form of learning, because it helps children to make sense of their lives, the ideas, feelings and relationships they are coming to know about and understand, and the way their learning is embodied in their physical selves.
>
> (2004, p. 133)

This really sounds quite like play in the therapy room. But what, again, is the quintessential quality of play which can be so readily recognised?

Actually, I think Bateson's description of play as *self-evident* is right on the button. He, like the monkeys themselves, could recognise play *through the response of his own body*. As Merleau-Ponty writes, "It is through my body that I understand other people" (1962, pp. 184–185)—or other animals. When we combine Bateson's rather dry and abstract formulations with Porges's description of the *embodied communication* of play, we get something very different. Whether we think of the communication of play as happening through mirror neurons or through the Flesh, it is neither a deduction nor a signal, but a direct and immediate embodied experience.

Porges himself, however, has recourse to the platitudes of old school ethology to describe the meta-signals of play; his account is a little simplistic and positivist, focused mainly on expressions of concern if something goes wrong:

> The social engagement system cues others that the "intentionality" of the behavior is benign. For example, a fight is likely to occur if the individual who accidentally hits another in the face while playing basketball walks away without diffusing the tension through a face-to-face expression of concern. Similarly, play will

not continue if dogs playing do not make face-to-face engagements after an accidental, but hurtful bite.

(2011, p. 276)

This is all no doubt true, but doesn't really tell us anything about the subtle meta-signals that Bateson focuses on, the ones that tell us right from the start, "This is a game".

It seems reasonable to think that these meta-signals are also conveyed at least in part through the SES, through micro-expressions—the "play face" (Burrows, 2008; Pellis & Pellis, 1997)—and vocal intonations as well as postural and gestural elements; and sites in the brain have been identified where the process of distinguishing very precisely between safety and danger via the facial expressions of others seems to be carried out (Adolphs, Baron-Cohen, & Tramel, 2002; Fosha, Siegel, & Solomon, 2009, pp. 46ff; Porges, 2011, p. 12; Winston, Strange, O'Doherty, & Dolan, 2002). However, it is hard to conceptualise just how these fine discriminations can take place: is it really possible for a specific brain location to identify complex, socially and culturally constructed expressions like flirtatiousness (Adolphs, 2002)—or, relevantly to this chapter, playfulness? It's pretty difficult, after all, *consciously* to identify what tells me that someone else is being playful rather than serious. There is something more global going on, a direct embodied experience which gives relevance and meaning to the detail—that cues us to look for it in the first place.

One way of thinking about this is in terms of *style*: a subtle shift of vitality affect (Massumi, 2014; Stern, 1985, 2010), a combination of exaggeration and distancing which establishes the frame indicating that "these actions ... do not denote what would be denoted by the actions which these actions denote" (Bateson, 1955, p. 180). Brian Massumi (2014, p. 9) rather brilliantly identifies this vitality affect as "-esque"— for example, not *combat*, but *combatesque*; he says of this quality that it represents "a surplus: an excess of energy or spirit"—*brio* might be another useful word. And like all vitality affects, the -esqueness of play is not primarily something that we *see*, but something that we *feel*.

-Esqueness, in fact, is what Reich is pointing at when he says that what matters is not only *what* someone says or does, but "the *way in which*" (1945a, p. 49) she does it: character, in fact, "is expressed not in terms of content but formally, in the way one typically behaves, in the manner in which one speaks, walks and gestures" (pp. 51–52). In particular, although there is an essential element of exaggeration in every character position—"this is the *only* thing that matters"—it is the crisis position which is most fully -esque, which specialises in the complexities of play, of pose, of surplus, and of paradox—in fact, all the elements which Bateson and Winnicott discuss.

Like embodied relating in general, playfulness isn't really some sort of coded message flashing between the protagonists, but a contagious state of physiological activation, transmitted through the Flesh (Merleau-Ponty, 1968; cf. Reich, 1945a, pp. 382–383). We can think of this activation as a particular kind of *relaxation*, a loosening of anxiety, which translates further up the up-hierarchy as the "realization that signals are signals" rather than reality (Bateson, 1955, p. 178). This state of relaxation connects with the state of "immobilization without fear" also described by Porges (2011, pp. 178–179), and also essential to therapy: what else, after all, apart from repressive socialisation, could keep us emotionally charged yet sat in our chairs for an hour?

The realisation involved, though, can go deeper still, to an awareness of the distinction between social rules and reality—an awareness which potentially frees us from impossible internalised demands (cf. Wilden, 1987a). As I have already emphasised, while our embodiment is the ground of social relations it is also constructed *through* social relations. This is paradoxical from the viewpoint of formal Western logic, but such chains of mutual or circular causation are common from the perspective of ecological and other cybernetic systems, and are the foundation of Buddhist ontology (Macy, 1991a, 1991b). And it would seem as though the relaxed physiological state of play, which allows us to sort out the sign from the reality, the map from the territory, is a part of what can be reached through meditation and other similar practices, especially in the Zen tradition (Watts, 1969).

The value of therapy as play

At this point it feels necessary to disentangle some different senses of the word "play" which have already appeared in this chapter. They are not wholly separate in the first place; and once we have distinguished them, we will find ourselves needing to re-braid them into a fresh pattern. The three senses I have in mind are play as *consensual pretending*;

play as *fun*; and play as in *the play of feelings and images* which we experience for example in daydreaming, free association, and fantasy.

Most of our attention so far in this chapter has been on play as consensual pretending, and on the circumstances which allow this to happen. Bateson begins from the observation of playing animals, and Winnicott from the play of mother and baby, but both end up in the therapy room, discussing the "as-if" nature of the psychotherapeutic relationship. As I have already pointed out, play in this sense can be very serious, and not fun at all; however, playfulness and fun perhaps always contain an element of "as-if"—for example the rough-and-tumble of young animals, including humans, which as Bateson realises depends on an ability to recognise that this is not literally the fighting which it closely resembles, but only an "as-if". In fact, the relaxation that follows from this realisation—"No one is trying to kill me"—may be a direct element of what makes something fun. In a quite different context, the linguist Chris Knight, whose work we will be considering shortly, writes:

> What makes an animal's play gestures so different from the displays staged when under serious competitive pressure? Clearly, freedom from anxiety is decisive in making the difference.
>
> (2000, p. 106)

Terry Marks-Tarlow (2012a, 2012b, 2014) argues strongly for the value of playfulness in therapy:

> Sometimes we therapists succumb to the instinct to play in order to lighten up the atmosphere. At other times, the intuitive urge to play marks an open, nondefensive attitude towards ourselves and others. Whether initiated by therapist or patient, the instinct to play encourages the experience of fun during experimentation with new possibilities.
>
> (2012b, p. 353)

"Succumb" perhaps indicates a residual shamefacedness about bowing to the "instinctive", "intuitive" urge to have fun. But Marks-Tarlow goes a lot further than presenting play as a way to sugar the pill of novelty. She draws on research that shows the role of play in fostering "a host of affective, cognitive, social and motor capacities", including:

> ... brain growth, self-regulation of behavior and emotions, the development of imagination and symbolic representation, the making of meaning, the development of language and narrative, metacommunication ... creativity and divergent thinking, self-transformation, social confidence, gender identity, community awareness, and cultural awareness and creation.
>
> (p. 354)

"Therapists draw from the creativity that inheres in play," she suggests, "to animate the intersubjective space between patient and therapist" (p. 354).

Play and playfulness, we might summarise, are juicy! And this juice is something generated in and coursing through the bodies of client and therapist, as they entrain into Porges's fifth state of physiological activation. Marks-Tarlow is zeroing in on fun as a powerful form of enticement to participate in the therapeutic game—and also as a solvent, enabling the client to let go of old and unsatisfactory patterns and form new and more creative ones. But running through her paper are a number of conscious allusions to "the play of language", "the play of expressions" (both 2012b, p. 353), "the play of intuition" (p. 356), "the play of imagination" (p. 361); all of which signal the third aspect of play which I identified at the start of this section, the same aspect highlighted by Winnicott in *Playing and Reality* when he identifies the need for therapy "to afford opportunity for formless experience, and for creative impulses, motor and sensory, which are the stuff of playing" (1971, p. 64).

Winnicott is referring back to what he has already described earlier in the paper as "the essentials that make relaxation possible"—relaxation being in his view a *sine qua non* for therapy:

> The patient on the couch or the child patient among the toys on the floor must be allowed to communicate a succession of ideas, thoughts, impulses, sensations that are not linked except in some way that is neurological or physiological and perhaps beyond detection.
>
> (1971, p. 55)

This is a hugely significant idea, and one which brings out some little-noticed aspects of Freud's original conception of free association. Winnicott goes on:

> It is where there is purpose or where there is anxiety or where there is lack of trust based on the need for defence that the analyst will be able to recognise and to point out the connection (or several connections) between the various components of free association material.
>
> (p. 55)

In other words, truly free association—the unconstricted play and playfulness of "ideas, thoughts, impulses, sensations" without defensive control—is something which comes about only when trust and relaxation have been established, when anxiety is loosened. As Ferenczi pointed out, free association "represents an ideal which ... can only be fulfilled after the analysis has ended" (1927, p. 147): it is the goal, not the starting point, of therapy. Adam Phillips suggests, "the patient is not cured by free-associating, he is cured *when he can free-associate*" (1995, p. 102; original italics).

This, I think, takes us to the heart of why play is crucial to therapy. It is an agent in the alchemical process of *solve et coagula*, the coming apart which enables us to come together again in a new settlement of our personality. Terry Marks-Tarlow writes:

> Play, imagination, and change all go hand in hand. As a psychotherapist, when I work with people, I'm not satisfied with surface changes. Instead, I want to address the very embodied core of things, which includes nonconscious levels of automatic, spontaneous response.
>
> (2014, p. 307)

Play reaches right to "the very embodied core of things", connecting us to "how young animals learn and grow" (ibid.); it has the power to render what has become hard and rigid in our personality plastic and flexible, as it was when we were young.

There are a number of parallels to this solvent action of play in various bodywork approaches. Rolfing seeks to stimulate the connective tissue in a client's body—more specifically, the colloidal "ground substance" which is one component of connective tissue—into shifting its phase state from *gel* to *sol*—from cold and immobile to warm and fluid (Juhan, 2003, Chapter Three; Schultz & Feitis, 1996, p. 31). Craniosacral therapy invites the pulse of craniosacral fluid to pause and enter a "stillpoint", a "free space" which is the "fulcrum for … transmutation" (Ridley, 2006, pp. 53–54). In a parallel way, embodied-relational play creates a "potential space" (Winnicott, 1971, p. 41) in which it is possible for us to begin again.

This needs to happen on both mental and physical levels; otherwise the aspect of our being which has been left unchanged, whether that is body or mind, will instantly start to *recreate* the familiar pattern in the other aspect, whether mind or body, acting as a template to "re-grow" character structure as RNA is a template for re-growing DNA. Richard Grossinger describes how, through six hours of cranial work, he felt a chronic motion sickness disappear from his system:

> When I stood up from the table at the end of the day, I knew at once that the motion sickness was gone; I felt its core pretty much dissolved. Yet, contradictorily, the removal of the hard mechanism had little effect on my sense of the imminence of dizziness or its inevitability. I felt myself floating through a vast internal chasm, about to get dizzy right then and there. The physical component of motion sickness was missing, but its presence was, if anything, more daunting. As I began to try to fill the void, what I ushered in automatically was a ghost of dizziness, a dizziness that wasn't sup-ported by structures in the bones of the face and cranium except as I clung to them in warding it off.
>
> The … therapist remarked on this common consequence. "We remove the problem," she said, "then the person quickly finds a way to begin reestablishing it."

(1998, p. 95)

However, Grossinger has previously described his similar frustra-tion with years of verbal therapy that failed to make inroads into his core material as it was anchored in his bodily structure. The title of his chapter is even-handed: "Why Somatic Therapies Deserve As Much Attention As Psychoanalysis in The New York Review of Books, and Why Bodyworkers Treating Neuroses Should Study Psychoanalysis". *"And"* being the operative word: neither psyche nor soma, addressed separately, can readily lead to deep change.

In the same chapter, Grossinger describes a moment of epiphany:

> Suddenly I understood how psychosomatic patterns come into
> being and are fixed in tissue. A rip occurs in the social and psycho-
> logical fabric, and the body creates kinesthetic material to occupy
> it—no doubt something innocent and idle at first—which then
> takes on its own life and creates its own inflated topology, which
> then steals space from mobility and natural function, which then
> ossifies and institutionalizes itself. All of these generate iconogra-
> phy and ego structure over a lifetime.

(p. 95)

The "rip" that Grossinger identifies is individual and social trauma.
I will be discussing this in depth in Chapter Ten; for now I just want to
point out that play, inside and outside therapy, is medicine for trauma.
Repetitive play calms and soothes, steadily, rhythmically closing up the
wound with small, regular stitches; while "deep play" summons the
transitional space in which "ossified, institutionalized" hard psychic
tissue can soften and reshape itself. Running through the braided pattern, playful fun and lightness smooth and gentle the process of healing.

Fleshing out the third space

I have already mentioned the strong similarity between Winnicott's
third or transitional space, and Merleau-Ponty's Flesh. I have quoted
David Abram on the latter, bringing out the connection with transitional space very clearly:

> The Flesh is the mysterious tissue or matrix that underlies and
> gives rise to both the perceiver and the perceived as interdependent
> aspects of its own spontaneous activity. It is the reciprocal presence
> of the sentient in the sensible and of the sensible in the sentient,
> a mystery of which we have always, at least tacitly, been aware
> since we have never been able to affirm one of the phenomena, the
> perceivable world or the perceiving self, without implicitly affirm-
> ing the existence of the other.

(1997, p. 66)

In a nutshell, what the two share is the deep sense of *reciprocity* between
perceiver and perceived, mother and child, therapist and client; and

the experience of a matrix holding and held by that reciprocity, a little like the ether which scientists once thought pervaded space. It brings to mind powerfully some passages from the surrealist Andre Breton which I have used in writing about the paranormal. Breton describes how in his vision of society, "surreality" will:

> ... reside in reality itself and will be neither superior nor exterior to it. And conversely, because the container will also be the contained. One might almost say that it will be a *communicating vessel* placed between the container and the contained.
>
> (1932, p. 126; my italics)

This image of the *"vase communicante"* was supremely important to Breton. In his work of that title, he speaks of:

> ... *a capillary tissue* in ignorance of which one works in vain to understand mental circulation. The role of this tissue is visibly to assure the constant interchange which must take place in thought between exterior and inner worlds ...
>
> (1932, p. 71; original italics)

There is a striking synchrony between Abram's description of the Flesh and Breton's "capillary tissue". Both of these, like Winnicott's third space, are descriptions of a paradoxical matrix which overcomes apparent contradiction and creates circulation between opposites. The paranormal, as I have been calling it (see Chapter Four), is a similar "capillary tissue", putting back into circulation whatever the ego attempts to bind to itself, while simultaneously exerting a magnetic counter-force to the "repulsion" that Freud describes between "each single ego and the others". What the ego says is mine, the paranormal shows to be other; and what the ego says is other, the paranormal shows to be profoundly mine.

Play and language

Metacommunicative language is generally assumed to be subsequent to and dependent on denotative language: a reasonable enough idea, since to talk *about* statements the statements need to be there in the first place. Bateson makes the radical suggestion that things are really the other way around:

> Denotative communication as it occurs at the human level is only possible *after* the development of a complex set of metalinguistic (but not verbalized) rules which govern how words and sentences should be related to objects and events.

(1955, p. 180)

Bateson sees the embodied metacommunication of play as providing the template for these metalinguistic rules. Chris Knight (2000) is operating in similar territory with his unusual theory of the origins of speech (a topic which attracts many plausible but unproven theories). He suggests that speech itself may emerge from play: from the relaxed murmuring vocalisations of resting groups of primates. In parallel to Bateson, Knight takes the ability to discriminate and reproduce complex "digital" patterns of vocalisation, as a mode of social bonding, to *precede*, and make possible, the coding of phonemes on which speech as communication is based. Only in relaxed play can primates experiment with complicating and elaborating the calls which in "real life" need urgently to be simple and unambiguous; and Knight's paper gives many examples of different species engaging in such playful elaboration.

For Knight, language originates in transitional space. And certainly, the language which emerges from the transitional play-space of the therapy room has a unique, fresh-minted, and mutative quality which seems to match his hypothesis. In the next chapter we will look at how therapy can help transform the embodied quality of speech.

CHAPTER NINE

Full and empty speech

The body as unthought known

There is a widespread idea in psychoanalytic circles—perhaps closer to an assumption than an idea—that bodily experience, or at least some of it (perhaps the pre-Oedipal part) cannot be put into language. Hence for example Claudia Zanardi writes of "a body with a language that cannot be verbalized and which is perhaps only traceable in the emotional experience of a primary relation or in the loss of a primary relation" (1995, p. 427). In a paper that I generally very much like, Muriel Dimen summarises this approach (which she also throws into question):

> The body is not only excessive, it is also deep. The fathoms of the unconscious are "written on the body." ... The body is, in this sense, almost paradigmatic for psychoanalysis. Body matters are so weighty, so deeply important, they often cannot be spoken. Untellable, they can only be shown ...
>
> (1998, p. 66)

This view is, as I say, enormously common, often expressed in passing (see, for example, Bucci, 2005, p. 171; Pally, 2001; Wrye, 1996, p. 290), and quite frequently goes along with the characterisation of embodied experience as "archaic" or "primitive"; its extreme form, of course, is Lacan's assignment of direct bodily experience to the wholly unsymbolised register of the Real (Fink, 1995, p. 24).

Most analysts don't go as far as Lacan, but express or imply regret that bodily experience, while on the one hand a powerful source of information, on the other hand cannot be brought to bear through verbal description—which is generally seen as identical with thinking. In his influential book *The Shadow of the Object: Psychoanalysis of the Unthought Known* (1987), Christopher Bollas writes:

> Some analysands enable us to feel somatically rested and receptive, while others precipitate complex body tensions ... This is not a peculiarity of psychoanalysis, as in all our relations with people, we somatically register our sense of a person; we "carry" their effect on our psyche-soma, and this constitutes a form of somatic knowledge, which again is not thought.
>
> (p. 282)

The sting is in that final phrase: we may know it, but we can't think (speak) it. Bollas in effect briefly contemplates body psychotherapy, but turns aside.

Body psychotherapy has itself historically tended to take a similar position on the incompatibility of speech/thought and embodied experience—though taking, one might simplistically say, the other side of the argument, and privileging embodiment over language. This originates with Wilhelm Reich himself, who wrote *"The living organism has its own mode of expressing movement which simply cannot be comprehended with words"* (1945a, p. 359; original italics). He goes on to draw an analogy from music:

> Every musically inclined person is familiar with the emotional state evoked by great music. However, if one attempts to translate these emotional experiences into words, one's musical perception rebels. *Music is wordless and wants to remain that way.* Yet music gives expression to the inner movement of the living organism.
>
> (p. 359; my italics)

Hence, Reich situates his developed technique of body psychotherapy "essentially outside the sphere of human language" (p. 361). The body is wordless and wants to remain so.

The trouble is that the whole notion of embodied experience being outside language is simply false. Bodily experience is no harder—though certainly no easier—to language than mental experience. A writer like Proust, for example, performs equal near-miracles in either register, and also shows clearly how inseparable bodily and mental experience are from each other; also, of course, through his partial success he makes us acutely aware that *complete* transcription is impossible. The map is never the territory, and the description is never the experience; this is universally the case, but no more deeply so of embodiment than of any other aspect of existence.

Reich actually touches on the way out of his own dualism when he points out, just after the passages quoted above, that we understand "body language" through an intuitive response in our own bodies—an anticipation both of mirror neurons and of Merleau-Ponty:

> The patient's expressive movements involuntarily bring about an imitation in our own organism. By imitating these movements we "sense" and understand the expression in ourselves and, consequently, in the patient. ... The language of facial and bodily expressions becomes an essential means of communicating with the patient.
>
> (p. 362)

Here Reich acknowledges an intermediate zone between symbolic communication through language, and internal bodily experience: his own undeveloped version of the Flesh. Since he has already said that "[L]anguage is clearly derived from ... inner movements and organ sensations, and the words that describe emotional conditions directly reflect the corresponding expressive movement of the living organism" (p. 259), the concept of semiotic language (see the discussion below of Julia Kristeva's work) is only a step away; a step which Reich unfortunately never takes.

Embodied language in practice

To set up a radical disjunction between language/thought and embodiment problematises the role of feelings, which by general agreement bridge these gaps: a feeling occurs simultaneously in the body and the mind. In her very useful paper "Understanding Feelings", Liz Bondi takes a more moderate and nuanced position towards the relationship between feelings, embodiment, and language, in line with Bollas but reframing the issue as a problem that can be *solved* rather than endured:

> Psychoanalytic ideas about unconscious processes suggest that feelings are communicated easily enough and may be registered ("known") by those to whom they are communicated. Indeed, the psychoanalytic concepts on which I have drawn presume that feelings arise and take shape relationally. The challenge for researchers lies in the capacity to think about what we register and work from within our emotional entanglement with others. Moreover, because much communication happens outside of our conscious awareness, and because our affective boundaries are so permeable, there is ample scope for confusion about the relationship between our own bodily sensations and the feelings of others.
>
> (2014, p. 53)

As I have argued throughout this book, the "confusion" of bodily sensations and feelings between self and other is much more than that; but as I hope I have demonstrated, it is entirely possible to learn to think about it. For apparently "unthought" reasons, however, embodiment has been isolated as a uniquely unspeakable, unthinkable aspect of experience. This certainly meshes with the place traditionally given to the body in the patriarchal pyramid which I described in Chapter One. And both of these positionings correspond with the reality that in practice embodiment is relatively absent from most people's speech and thought.

As James Kepner says, speaking of life in general, but in terms applicable to much therapeutic work, embodiment has been largely erased from cultural awareness:

> Most often, our conversation and common contact includes little of our embodied experience in its content, little reference to embodiment in gesture, and little conscious experience of

ourselves or the other as embodied beings. Even when we report emotions they are rarely acknowledged as bodily events, located in our bodily self, even though one cannot experience emotion without bodily location. We keep it all very abstract with little bodily referent. It is as if our emotions had no bodily origin or location, but are something we "thought up".

(2003, p. 7)

In contrast, Kepner suggests, "[A] body therapist must have access to their own deep embodiment and relate to the client in a deeply embodied way" (p. 9): "To be deeply embodied is to have access to one's body experience as *self-experience*" (p. 12; original italics).

We frequently experience a split between this "self-experience" and experience mediated through language. In Daniel Stern's view:

Language ... causes a split in the experience of the self. It ... moves relatedness onto the impersonal, abstract level intrinsic to language and away from the personal immediate level intrinsic to ... other domains of relatedness.

(1985, pp. 162–163)

Stern is not of course arguing that language is a negative development; just that its enormous benefits come at a price of alienation from the immediacy of experience. We can sometimes perceive the languaged and the embodied aspects of experience as *opposed*, or sometimes as *complementary*; what makes the difference?

Speaking the body/the body speaking

Full speech is speech which aims at, which forms, the truth such as it becomes established in the recognition of one person by another. Full speech is speech which performs [*qui fait acte*].

(Lacan, 1988, p. 107)

The psychoanalyst Jacques Lacan argued in his earlier work that therapy seeks, or should seek, to enable the production of "full" rather than "empty" speech (1977, p. 253; 1988, p. 107). He means several complex things by this, but we can usefully borrow his terminology without borrowing his whole theory, especially since Reich makes a fairly closely related point (for an extended discussion of Reich's and Lacan's positions, see Totton, 1998, pp. 122–128):

> In many cases the function of speech has deteriorated to such a degree that the words express nothing whatever and merely represent a continuous, hollow activity on the part of the musculature of the neck and the organs of speech. ... In many psychoanalyses which have gone on for years the treatment has become stuck in this pathological use of language.
>
> (1945a, pp. 360–361)

As Lacan says of empty speech, "The subject seems to be talking in vain about someone who ... can never become one with the assumption of his desire" (1977, p. 45).

Empty speech, then, can be understood as *disembodied* speech. Fully embodied speech, in contrast, is a complex modulation of the spontaneous and pleasurable breath. It has resonance, timbre, and rhythm; it emerges from chest (heart) and belly, not just from throat and mouth; in fact at its fullest it comes all the way from the feet, out of the ground. Crucially, it is also filled out by resonances of metaphor and imagery, which derive entirely from the physical world and largely from bodily experience. The psychoanalyst Ella Sharpe wrote that "A subterranean passage between mind and body underlies all analogy" (1940, p. 202), and in several books written together and separately, starting with *Metaphors We Live By* (1981) and culminating in *Philosophy in the Flesh* (1999), George Lakoff and Mark Johnson have demonstrated the truth of Sharpe's statement. Lakoff and Johnson propose (a) that all metaphor is based on embodied experience, and (b) that all conceptual language is metaphorical:

> Our conceptual system is grounded in, neurally makes use of, and is crucially shaped by our perceptual and motor systems. ... We can only form concepts through the body. Therefore, every understanding that we can have of the world, ourselves, and others can only be framed in terms of concepts shaped by our bodies.
>
> (1999, p. 555)

Maxine Sheets-Johnstone's *The Roots of Thinking* (1990) uses a very different body of evidence, mostly from evolutionary anthropology, to make the case that "thinking is modelled on the body" (p. 5), and further, that language arises in the body rather than in the mind ("body" and "mind" standing, of course, for two aspects of a unified whole):

> The origin of language lies in the discovery of certain sensory-kinetic powers, the discovery of certain bodily *I can's* in the form of lingual [i.e., tongue] articulations and discriminations. The original elements of language were a consequence of that discovery. ... Not only are sound and meaning physiognomically congruent ...; the tactile-kinetic gesture—the bodily making of the sound—is also physiognomically congruent with the meaning.
>
> (1990, p. 162)

Sheets-Johnstone quotes the linguistics expert Philip Lieberman:

> The listener responds as though he is interpreting the acoustic signal in terms of the articulatory gestures that a speaker would employ to generate the word ... The perception of human speech is generally structured in terms of the articulatory gestures that underlie the acoustic signal.
>
> (Lieberman, 1975, p. 535)

This immediately brings to mind the sign language of the deaf, where "articulatory gestures" play a major role. Nicaraguan sign language, developed only in the last thirty-odd years, shows very clearly how over a few generations of learners these gestures transform from their role of speech accompaniment into language elements in their own right (Senghas, Kita, & Ozyrek, 2004), organised by the left hemisphere language area of the brain (Hickock, Bellugi, & Klima, 1996).

Signing is fascinating, because it constitutes a limit case, a fully developed language which is gestural and three-dimensional rather than vocal and linear. In his book *Seeing Voices* (2011), Oliver Sacks shows how Sign enables an extraordinary complexity through its

> ... unique linguistic use of space ... a use that is amazingly complex, for much of what occurs linearly, sequentially, temporally in

speech, becomes simultaneous, concurrent, multileveled in Sign. The "surface" of Sign may appear simple to the eye, like that of gesture or mime, but one soon finds that this is an illusion, and what looks so simple is extraordinarily complex and consists of innumerable spatial patterns nested, three-dimensionally in each other.

(pp. 69–70)

Hence he characterises Sign as employing "a new and extraordinarily sophisticated way of representing space; a new sort of space, a formal space, which has no analogue in those of us who do not sign" (p. 76). It appears that signing involves a cooperative effort between the spatial skills of the brain's right hemisphere, and the language skills of the left hemisphere:

The left hemisphere in signers "takes over" a realm of visual-spatial perception, modifies it, sharpens it, in an unprecedented way, giving it a new, highly analytical and abstract character, making a visual language and visual conception possible.

(p. 76)

The example of Sign helps us to remember that language, like the brain, is inherently multi-modal, and able to manifest in any available embodied channel:

Circuitry across brain regions links modalities, infusing each with properties of others. The sensory-motor system of the brain is thus "multimodal" rather than modular. Accordingly, language is inherently multimodal in this sense, that is, it uses many modalities linked together—sight, hearing, touch, motor actions, and so on. Language exploits the pre-existing multimodal character of the sensory-motor system.

(Gallese & Lakoff, 2005, p. 473; see also Legrand, 2006)

All of this is very close to a passage from Merleau-Ponty:

If we were to make completely explicit the architectonics of the human body, its ontological framework, and how it sees itself and hears itself, we would see the possibilities of language already given in it.

(1968, p. 155)

Far from wanting to remain wordless, the body seems to desire language. Speech is always already embodied in the first of the two senses outlined in Chapter Two: it grows out of the *state* of being a self-aware organism, something which all living human beings share. To become full speech, I am suggesting, it needs to be embodied in the second sense—to flow from a self-aware *owning* and expression of embodiment. As Christopher Kinman writes:

> If I am to give any credence to my speaking, I must speak from my walking and from my touching and tasting and smelling. From those places of lived experience come words that are received into the circles and flows of ongoing conversation.

(2001, p. 37)

I acknowledge that what I am discussing is not what Lacan himself means by "full speech": it hardly could be, since he does not recognise the possibility of embodiment as I have described it, assigning the body to the realm of the unspeakable Real and speech to the realm of the Symbolic and Imaginary. From my perspective, though, it seems entirely plausible that what he *does* mean by full speech is something that actually depends upon and flowers out of embodied self-awareness. "Full speech, in effect, is defined by its identity with that which it speaks about" (Lacan, 1966, p. 381); and the only sense in which speech can be identical with what it speaks about—the map identical with the territory—is, surely, through bodily mimesis.

The semiotic

As well as the symbolic register of denotative meaning, embodied speech occupies what Julia Kristeva calls the *semiotic* register:

> I therefore distinguish between the semiotic, which consists of drive-related and affective meaning organized according to primary processes whose sensory aspects are often non-verbal (sound

and melody, rhythm, colors, odors and so forth), on the one hand, and linguistic signification, that is manifested in linguistic signs and their logico-syntactic organization, on the other.

(1995, p. 104)

The semiotic uses language as a direct expression of the body and its energies, partaking of the musicality and playfulness of vocal expression which we find in the interaction of infant and carer. This is a pre-symbolic form of language, arising in "the fragmented body—pre-Oedipal, but always already invested with semiosis" (Kristeva, 1984, p. 22). Kristeva sets the task of restoring "gestural and vocal play ... on the level of the socialized body" (p. 26). Her concept of the semiotic parallels Chris Knight's theory of the playful origins of language (2000), which I summarised at the end of Chapter Eight.

But embodied or semiotic speech as it exists now is not the yardstick of some idealised state of health: as well as the joy of self-expression, it bears the marks of pain, trauma, and repression. It expresses the tensions imposed on the body to facilitate both the physical act of speech—the precise, synchronised micro-movements of lips, tongue, jaw, palate, vocal chords, and lungs, which have no close correspondence to any other bodily activity outside specialised forms of work—and other socially required behaviours which inscribe themselves upon our bodies in the form of chronic muscular tensions, particularly tensions regulating our sphincters.

Kristeva describes the semiotic as:

> ... a psychosomatic modality of the signifying process ... articulating ... a continuum: the connections between the (glottal and anal) sphincters in (rhythmic and intonational) vocal modulations, and those between the sphincters and family protagonists, for example.

(pp. 28–29)

But also of great importance, and directly relevant to speech production, is the diaphragm, which powers our breathing—not strictly a sphincter, since it has permanent openings, but contracting and relaxing in a similar way, and deeply implicated in tensions around the throat and anus—contractions in all three areas tend to mirror each other or to be passed from sphincter to sphincter.

Ella Sharpe's extraordinary 1940 article "Psycho-physical problems revealed in language: An examination of metaphor", from which I have already briefly quoted, both anticipates and clarifies Kristeva's argument:

> My theory is that metaphor can only evolve in language or in the arts when the bodily orifices become controlled. Then only can the angers, pleasures, desires of the infantile life find metaphorical expression and the immaterial express itself in terms of the material. A subterranean passage between mind and body underlies all analogy.
>
> (p. 202)

Sharpe offers an example of what she sees as "the pattern on which all metaphor evolves":

> I was told by a young husband that his wife had been confiding to him how angry she felt about their young son's frequent "accidents" [i.e., incontinence]. He had replied to her: "Of course you feel angry, that's natural, but don't let John see your anger. Think to yourself you must keep your anger in and hold it in till you get to another room and then you can let it out." This is metaphor.
>
> (p. 202)

Sharpe makes clear, without actually spelling it out, that the father is consciously or unconsciously offering his wife a further metaphor, drawing a parallel between the self-control being asked of her, and that being asked of their son:

> In time the young son will go through this same process of thinking with regard to his actual urine and fæces: "I must hold it, and hold it in until I get to another room." When the ego stabilizes this achievement of body control and it becomes automatic, the emotions of anger and pleasure which heretofore accompanied bodily discharges must be dealt with in other ways.
>
> (p. 202)

Sharpe then generalises from this to describe the semiotic aspect of language and its origins in sphincter control, which redirects energetic discharge from the rest of the body into speech:

> At the same time as sphincter control over anus and urethra is being established, the child is acquiring the power of speech, and so an avenue of "outer-ance" present from birth becomes of immense importance. First of all the discharge of feeling tension, when this is no longer relieved by physical discharge, can take place through speech. The activity of speaking is substituted for the physical activity now restricted at other openings of the body, while words themselves become the very substitutes for the bodily substances. Speech secondly becomes a way of expressing, discharging ideas. So that *we may say speech in itself is a metaphor, that metaphor is as ultimate as speech.*

> (p. 203; my italics)

Both Kristeva's and Sharpe's work leads us to see that the semiotic is the expression of character structure in speech and language; while character structure itself is the expression both of desire and of its social-familial repression (Chapter Seven, this volume; Kristeva, 1984, pp. 28–29; Totton, 1998, Chapter Eight). Through what we say, but even more through *how* we say it (Reich, 1945a, pp. 49ff), we express the history of our embodiment, the history of our family relationships and the family relationships which preceded us—what Katharine Young describes as "the ancestral ghost in the flesh of the present" (2002, p. 45).

Kristeva describes the semiotic as "a signifying process which, although produced in language, is only intelligible *through* it" (1984, p. 15): in other words, one has to "see through" the ordinary symbolising functions of language in order to see/hear the semiotic at play. The semiotic enters communicative speech as a rebellious surplus:

> The way in which the semiotic enters the symbolic constitutes a return, a repetition of language in its origins, in its past, and thus a regression. At the same time, it is a transformation, revolution, then, in the sense of repetition of children's language, of the repetition of oneiric regression, of the unconscious, of the most archaic elements: fear, passion, abjection ... It is also the elaboration of the archaic material in an outlook of revolt, insubmission, and defiance.

> (Kristeva, 1996, p. 213)

Both symbolic and semiotic aspects of speech are functioning at all times, though to different degrees (cf. Sharpe, 1940, pp. 203ff):

> These two modalities are inseparable within the signifying process that constitutes language, and the dialectic between them determines the type of discourse (narrative, metalanguage, theory, poetry, etc.) involved ... Because the subject is always both semiotic and symbolic, no signifying system he produces can be either "exclusively" semiotic or "exclusively" symbolic, and is instead necessarily marked by an indebtedness to both.
>
> (Kristeva, 1984, p. 24)

Perhaps the most important thing about Kristeva's work for the purposes of this book is her rejection of the break between bodily and languaged experience which is proposed (or assumed) in so much psychoanalytic theory.

> Instead of lamenting what is lost, absent, or impossible in language, Kristeva marvels at this other realm that makes its way into language. ... Signification is like a transfusion of the living body into language. This is why psychoanalysis can be effective: the analyst can diagnose the active drive force as it is manifest in the analysand's language. Language is not cut off from the body.
>
> (Oliver, 1993, p. xx)

Also importantly, though, Kristeva emphasises the *playful*, excessive origins and function of semiotic language, underwriting the role of full speech in the play of psychotherapy:

> Magic, shamanism, esoterism, the carnival and "incomprehensible" poetry all underscore the limits of socially useful discourse and attest to what it represses: the process that exceeds the subject and his communicative structures.
>
> (1984, p. 15)

Full speech in practice

I can best make clear what I mean by fully embodied speech through some therapy vignettes. James was a man in his forties who worked in the finance department of a large company. His immediate reason for seeking therapy was a persistent cough for which no medical cause could be identified; but he very soon also told me that he found his life meaningless and unsatisfying. One striking thing about James was that his voice was very quiet, strangulated and somehow *muffled*, as though he was speaking through a mask or scarf, or on the other end of a poor phone connection. Listening to him one day I found myself fantasising that he was a kidnap victim phoning his family, and trying to communicate information about where he was being held without alerting his listening captors. But if he was speaking through a scarf which disguised his voice, surely that meant he himself was the kidnapper—both criminal and victim?

James was not really available for this sort of imaginative play; he preferred to stay with the concrete and rational. Luckily, however, he *was* interested in using body psychotherapy to address his cough—perhaps he saw this as more concrete and rational than speculating about its psychological causes. I fed back to him how I experienced his voice (though not my fantasy about it), and he saw the possible relevance—he was aware of how quietly his speech emerged, and said that he felt as if he was forcing it out against an obstacle of some sort, but he had no idea why this was.

We began with James focusing on his jaw (which was visibly tense), mouth, and throat, and telling me what he experienced as he followed the movement of breath through his throat. At first it was hard for him to talk and stay focused on his body; it became clear that for me to "observe" him made the process more difficult, so I turned my chair slightly to the side and looked across the room as he talked about his experience. Over a few sessions he became fully conscious of the tension in his jaw and throat; and this consciousness extended to how uncomfortable, even painful, it was to tighten his muscles in this way. However, this awareness didn't make it possible for him to relax the muscles involved—he experienced them as outside his control, which he found surprising and frustrating.

James was therefore willing to let me use touch to explore and intervene in what was happening in his jaw and throat. I made it clear to him that he could ask me to pause or stop altogether at any point, and that this was an experiment to see whether we could find out more about his process. James lay down on a mat and focused on his breathing, while I touched and pressed on his jaw and the sides of his throat—without obstructing his breathing in any way—at points which I knew from experience were likely to be useful. I invited him, if the pressure was painful, as I expected it to be, to try making a sound in response before asking me to stop.

It took a while before James felt safe enough to really explore the experience, and we continued to work verbally in-between these bodywork experiments. The fourth time we tried it, I pressed in the angle of James's jaw and invited him to make a sound. This time, he did: a terrible, grinding, groaning noise, which seemed to rise from the depths of his being and to rip his jaws apart. As his mouth opened, the sound became fuller, developing into a yell of profound grief. James began to sob deeply; I gradually realised that the sobs contained words—he was saying over and over again "I'm sorry, I'm sorry, I'm sorry."

James was obviously stirred and shocked by this eruption; but, impressively, he did not run away from what had happened. This was partly because he felt an immediate gain from it: his throat and jaw were relaxed in a way he could not remember ever experiencing before, and his voice was clear and resonant. Although shaky, he felt good; and wanted to tell me straight away about what he had remembered: a point in his early childhood when he had soiled himself and been punished by his father.

This may seem too neat to be true, and certainly things don't always unfold so clearly. And of course this one session and the accompanying memory turned out to be far from the whole story; what gradually emerged as central was James's anger, which he had had to suppress in the face of a bullying father (I find that coughing can often signal suppressed anger). As in Sharpe's example, the need to control his anger became equated with the need to control his bowels, with the threat of punishment and shaming hanging over both. Tension in the anus and pelvis often happens in parallel with tension in the jaw and throat—we can all experience this when constipated.

As James gradually re-owned his capacity to stand up for himself and fight back, many things changed in his life: he became *present* rather than *absent*, released from the self-captivity which he had felt forced to impose on himself. Not only was the quality of his voice fuller and more resonant, but also the content of his speech: he became able to play with language, to use metaphor and imagery, in a way that had not been possible before.

One interesting aspect of this work is that in many ways it was not very relational: James could not acknowledge any relational charge between us, but throughout tried to keep me safely in the role of expert technician. But it would be more accurate to say that the relationship was *wholly and only embodied*. Our bodies responded to each other, and this made the whole work possible: my body adopting a caring relationship to the kidnapped boy on the phone, while his body entrusted itself to me so as to open up his grief and anger, even though the process was painful and frightening. Eventually I had the thought that his quiet, muffled voice was also communicating "Come closer, I'll tell you a secret."

The route to full speech was very different for Roz, a university lecturer who came to see me because of an interest in therapy (she used psychoanalytic theory in her work) and, like James, a general dissatisfaction with life. She was extremely articulate, but in a rather abstractly intellectual way: language clearly excited her, and she would wave her arms furiously and contort her body to squeeze out the exact phrase she was looking for, but what she talked *about* related only indirectly to her immediate experience, and was always mediated through one intellectual language or another, usually feminist theory and/or psychoanalysis. She almost always referred to herself as "one": "One finds ...", "One tends to believe ..."

It was on balance useful that I could follow her into the intellectual uplands where she was most comfortable—otherwise I don't think the work could have developed successfully; however, I had to maintain an alertness to the seductions of theory, and remind myself constantly to translate Roz's abstract formulations (sometimes out loud, sometimes internally) into more concrete experience: "When you say that 'one finds ...' I'm hearing that also as about what is actually happening to you," and so on. She was a little condescending about this, treating me as a plodding literalist.

After several months we were having a fairly typical semi-intellectual discussion around Jane Gallop's book, *Thinking Through the Body* (1988). For once I became exasperated with her abstract verbalising—in relation to a book whose title pointed so directly to embodiment. I grabbed the book off my shelves, thrust it at her, and said rather forcibly. "Why don't you just *look* at it?"

What I consciously had in mind was the title, and the general nature of the image, a photograph of a woman giving medicalised birth (which Roz had done herself). But what Roz zeroed in on—what Gallop herself emphasises in the introduction to her book (p. 8), where she also plays (pp. 1–2) with the idea of decapitation, losing one's head—is that right near the bottom of the photograph we can see a tiny, furious, agonised head just emerging from the birth canal. For the first time since we had met, Roz became actually lost for words: she entered a state of dissociation, swaying and holding her head, occasionally struggling to produce a few disjointed words: "I ... I never ... what ... that is ..." Not "one", I thought afterwards, but "I".

After a few minutes her thinking started to re-emerge, like the baby's head peeking out of its mother's body. She gradually spoke about the "enormous pressure" that she felt under to produce words and concepts, to "squeeze them out" as "a matter of life and death". She felt a clear, embodied connection between this demand on herself, and the threat to survival experienced in the birth process. Our work together continued for some years; "mind" and "body" remained connected in a way that had never previously been the case.

Jane Gallop's book in fact directly addresses my theme of embodied speech/thought, and the difficulty of creating a space for it within the dominant culture:

> At this point in history, thinking that passes through the body only occurs in brief intervals, soon to be reabsorbed by the powerful narrative of mind over matter.
>
> (1988, p. 8)

These two clinical examples illustrate, I think, both the difficulty and the possibility of achieving moments when thinking does pass through the body.

I don't want to give the impression that full speech is always the result of embodied psychotherapy, or indeed that it should be. I worked for some time with Al, a professional trumpeter, whose partner had strongly encouraged him to enter therapy because she experienced him as detached and uncommitted. He talked a lot about trumpets: which kinds and which makes were best, whether an electric trumpet might be useful for some purposes, where to find the best mouthpiece, a little shop in Chicago which he phoned up regularly for technical advice ... I learnt a great deal about trumpets and how to play them, which was more interesting than I expected. And without my confronting Al with explicit interpretations of his musings—which would have been tactless at best—we managed implicitly to explore many of his difficulties around choice, decision, and commitment. He and his partner eventually married; which of course might have happened anyway.

The role of language in embodied psychotherapy

Some of what I have said in the client vignettes above helps to illustrate an attitude towards the role of language in the "talking therapies"—of which body psychotherapy is a member—which is more flexible, in a sense more sceptical, than the traditional view. Language starts out as play, but soon becomes work: from being an expression of attunement between mother and baby, it becomes a means of trying to get our needs met, a means of bringing ourselves into conformity with the demands of family and society: a means, on several different levels, of *getting hold of the world*. If as I argued in the previous chapter play is a crucial aspect of therapy, then it may be counterproductive to place too much emphasis on language as work, even if the work involved is one of liberation.

As Richard Grossinger writes:

> When psychotherapy works, it is rarely because of the quality of verbalized insights. As long as the patient hears these coming to him in the hierarchicalized voice of the therapist, they will remain on-again, off-again New Year's resolutions, difficult to apply in the heat of life's battle.
>
> Only the initiation and empowerment of the patient's own inner voice leads to lasting change, for that voice is with the patient all the time, consciously and subconsciously, awake and asleep. It is much more efficient to have a stream of continuous insight and perspective than to rely on remembered instructions from one hour a week. Thus, the therapist must inculcate not his own voice but the patient's voice—the voice of his intrinsic sanity—which may not even affirm the therapist's beliefs.
>
> (1998, pp. 97–98)

There are probably very few therapists who would not sign up to this statement. But theory and practice can be two different things; and it is very easy, especially with certain clients, to get drawn into perceiving the sound of one's own voice as containing magical power. (Ursula Le Guin offers a brilliant portrait of such a therapist in *The Lathe of Heaven* (1972)). Attention to the semiotic aspect of language, to the signs in the client's speech of "revolt, insubmission, and defiance" (Kristeva, 1996, p. 213), may help to puncture the bubble and bring playfulness back into the therapy.

But Grossinger goes on to make an even deeper point:

> The reason certain problems seem vast and insoluble is that they begin before we have language and they arrange themselves out-side of language. Any attempt to heal them must also go outside of language. Unquestionably, somatic therapies do this—that is a big part of their value. But their dilemma is that the way in which they go outside language … is not necessarily the way in which a neu-rosis or other emotional pathology was structured primally … The actual horror or trauma, primal and outside of language, no longer looks like itself anymore. Too painful to be viewed in its raw skel-etal manifestation, it could not be recognized in any adult language or by any symbolic system of visualization. This is why bodywork that succeeds at a visceral level does not necessarily translate to an emotional level.
>
> (1998, pp. 98–99)

Have we simply circled back here to the idea which I started the chapter by criticising—that there is a realm of bodily experience which stands outside language? I think Grossinger is saying something more subtle and limited. He is saying that it is *trauma* which in a sense stands out-side language, creates (as I quoted in the previous chapter) "a rip … in the social and psychological fabric" (1998, p. 95) which psychosomatic material then fills. Really, he is pointing to the way that trauma stands outside, creates a rip in, *consciousness*, and the conscious use of lan-guage. To understand this, we next need to look at embodied trauma.

CHAPTER TEN

Embodied trauma and complexity

Some history

Trauma has been an important concept in psychotherapy right from the beginning. This is perhaps particularly so for body psychotherapy, because the concept has always been body-centred, starting out from the analogy implied by its name—"trauma" literally means "wound", the sort of wound which bleeds and needs to be closed up. Psychological trauma is conceived, therefore—sometimes explicitly, sometimes implicitly—as like a raw wound in the skin of the psyche; often, as caused by the invasion of some splinter-like foreign object which persists as an alien, encysted aspect of the self (Totton, 2002), and may result in "a tearing of the network of signification which supports symbolic relationships" (Kirshner, 1994, p. 238).

This vision goes back to the origins of psychoanalysis:

> The psychical trauma—or more precisely the memory of the trauma—acts like a foreign body which long after its entry must continue to be regarded as an agent that is still at work.
>
> (Freud & Breuer, 1895d, p. 56)

However, therapeutic discussions of trauma have tended to downplay its bodily nature and, as the quotation from Kirshner illustrates, to focus on a psychologically inflected version of its impact, even though this is frequently organised around a bodily metaphor. In order to understand the role of trauma in embodied relating we need to look at the historical development of the concept and see how its connection with the body has moved in and out of focus.

Freud's first psychotherapeutic discovery was also an embodied one, and closely linked with trauma: he called it the "hysterical attack" (Freud & Breuer, 1895d, pp. 64–68; Freud, 1909a): a dramatic crisis of liberation, which through bodily convulsions and contortions accompanied by screams and sobs enabled memories to emerge of the traumatic events which had created chronic hysterical symptoms (Freud & Breuer, 1895d, p. 66). These symptoms themselves, in Freud's view, often symbolically represented memories of actual sexual attack.

Freud worked in very physical ways with his hysterical clients, lying on the floor with them, rubbing their legs, pressing on their heads or their chests, so as to encourage catharsis (Totton, 2002, p. 9). He wrote in 1895:

> Yesterday Mrs. K again sent for me because of cramplike pains in her chest; generally it has been because of headaches. In her case I have invented a strange therapy of my own: I search for sensitive areas, press on them, and thus provoke fits of shaking that free her.
>
> (Freud to Fliess, March 13, 1895, quoted in Masson, 1985, p. 120)

The important function of shaking in trauma recovery has been rediscovered by contemporary therapists (Levine, 1997). Freud initially believed that the hysterical crisis removed the hysterical symptom "immediately and permanently", allowing the renewed flow of unlocked memories along with emotional discharge (Freud & Breuer, 1895d, p. 57).

Belief in the clinical efficacy of the hysterical crisis led to the first of many therapeutic disappointments suffered by practitioners over the last century or so. Like several other innovations, the "cathartic technique" turned out to be far less reliable and effective than it first seemed; it became clear that it depended on an intensive positive transference towards the practitioner, which could not always be produced. In a brilliant turnaround, Freud suggested (1912b) that *negative* transference was itself a fresh symbolisation of past traumatic experience (the therapist being identified with the source of the trauma), and thus offered a different and more easily accessed therapeutic route. Working with the transference, rather than with the body itself and its memories—that is, in line with my argument throughout this book, *rebranding embodied relationship as transference*—became the core of the analytic process.

What draws one's attention, however, is the way in which, ever since it was first rejected, Freud's original cathartic theory and technique has repeatedly re-emerged. The first to readopt it was Freud's close disciple and ally Sándor Ferenczi, who had played a large role in developing transference analysis (Ferenczi & Rank, 1925), but eventually found himself, in response to his clients, reinventing Freud's early use of bodily discharge as a core method of treatment and encouraging therapeutic hysterical attacks, "*trances*, in which fragments of the past were relived … one was forced to compare them with the Breuer-Freud *catharsis*" (Ferenczi, 1929b, p. 298; original italics).

Ferenczi doubted his own work—"I must confess that at first this was a disagreeable surprise, almost a shock, to me" (p. 298)—but eventually concluded that psychoanalysis, in concentrating on transference interpretation, had been going up a blind alley. He identified as the other essential component of treatment, along with "neo-catharsis", a humane, respectful, and open attitude from the therapist towards the client (For all this, see Harris & Kuchuk, 2015; Rudnytsky, Bokay, & Gampieri-Deutsch, 2000; Stanton, 1991).

Ferenczi's return to the cathartic approach, and the accompanying critique of transference interpretation as potentially persecutory, led to his estrangement from Freud and isolation within the analytic community, and possibly hastened his early death. The cathartic approach to trauma was taken up and developed in the work of Wilhelm Reich (1942, 1945a), and became embedded in body psychotherapy. It later resurfaced independently in the psychotherapy mainstream in the 1990s, this time supported by neuroscience (Levine, 1997; Perry, 1997; Perry, Pollard, Blakley, Baker, & Vigilante, 1995; Van der Kolk, 1994, 2014). "Trauma", together with the accompanying idea of "dissociation", became an omnipresent concept both in psychotherapy and in the culture at large.

The concept of dissociation, though only rarely the term itself, was central to both Freud's and Ferenczi's thinking, and is bound up with the "foreign body" image discussed above. Trauma is seen as causing a split in the psyche, whereby unbearable feelings and memories are encapsulated out of everyday consciousness, like a cyst or abscess—unavailable to awareness, but still exerting an effect, both psychologically and physiologically (Siegel, 1995; van der Kolk, 1994, 2014). Just as for Freud, Ferenczi, and Reich, the 1990s (and subsequent) approach to treatment involved cathartic abreaction which is intended to lead to reintegration of dissociated memories and feelings:

> A "therapeutic" abreaction emphasizes processing, both cognitively and emotionally, of dissociated elements of previously inaccessible or partially inaccessible memory.
>
> (Siegel, 1995, p. 117)

Each time the trauma/dissociation/abreaction model has reappeared, it has been subject to the same cogent criticisms: in essence, that its efficacy is doubtful; that it emphasises one cause of distress at the expense of an overall view of the client's psychological organisation, including the ways in which traumatic experience may be taken up in the service of defence (Piers, 1998); that it is deeply vulnerable to creating factitious catharsis and constructed "memories"; that it can become a vehicle for unexamined, histrionic transference/countertransference collusion (Lacanians might say that it takes place in the Imaginary); and that it abandons the role of the therapist as fair witness. As Ferenczi asked himself in self-doubt:

> Was it really worthwhile to make that enormous detour of analysis of associations and resistances, to unravel the maze of the elements of ego-psychology, and even to traverse the whole metapsychology in order to arrive at the good old "friendly attitude" to the patient and the method of catharsis, long believed to be discarded?
>
> (1929b, p. 298)

These criticisms nevertheless fail to address the question of why, despite its many problems, the trauma/abreaction model has repeatedly resurfaced. What is it that this model addresses which is left out of the more sober approach of orthodoxy? And is there a possibility of going beyond the ping-pong alternation of models to some sort of synthesis?

Hysteria and embodiment

I suggest that what is repressed by mainstream therapy, and what returns repeatedly in the form of trauma/abreaction theory, is embodiment. Trauma theory in psychotherapy represents not only a specific response to distressed clients in the therapy room: over and above that, it represents *the body itself*. More than a century ago, Freud's and Breuer's hysterical patients, with irresistible force and much against the better judgement of the practitioners involved, brought the body into the consulting room. Psychoanalytic theory originated as simultaneously an attempt to respond to this invasion of the body, and an attempt to fend it off. Ferenczi revisits this ambiguity and sides decisively with the body:

> In *all* cases where I penetrated deeply enough, I found uncovered the traumatic-hysterical basis of the illness ... Where the patient and I succeeded in this, the therapeutic effect was far more significant. ... Psychoanalysis deals far too one-sidedly with ... ego-psychology—while neglecting the organic-hysterical basis of the analysis. This results from overestimating the role of fantasy, and underestimating that of traumatic reality. (Ferenczi, letter to Freud, quoted in Ferenczi, 1988, p. xii)

Hysteria itself, on one level, was the forcible return of the body into a culture which denies it; but it returned not as *embodiment*, since there was no cultural space for a conscious identification with the body, but as the *foreign* body, the body as an intrusion of the real. Hence Ferenczi's jamming together, in the above quotation, of these three elements: trauma, hysteria, and the organism. On the one hand, hysteria represents the trauma suffered by the child's embodiment as she is forced into culture. At the same time, it represents the trauma which embodiment then re-presents to the dissociated mind of the adult: to be embodied is to remember and re-own one's traumatic experience.

Childhood sexual abuse in particular turns the child's body into a foreign body. But any overwhelming trauma does something similar: the intensity of the bodily activation caused by trauma attacks and threatens to overwhelm its victim, who takes the only escape route available to her and dissociates from her own embodiment. Trauma is often seen as a damaged capacity to think; but the connections which it breaks are connections with and through the body. Through the effect which this has on our thinking, trauma demonstrates that *we need our body to think with* (see Chapter Two). Embodiment represents the threat, the site of unbearable experience; but later, it also represents recovery. It is by learning to own her embodied experience in titrated, gradually increasing quantities that an acutely traumatised person becomes able to function fully again (Heitzler, 2013; Levine, 1997; Ogden, Minton, & Paine, 2006).

Body psychotherapy, not surprisingly, has tended to preserve and develop the most embodied aspects of the trauma model which originated with Freud. Like Ferenczi, Reich maintains the particular importance which Freud originally gave to hysteria, where "body" and "mind" meet and interact most chaotically (in the technical sense given to "chaos" by complexity theory: see later in this chapter). Reich agrees with the position Ferenczi had reached: that hysteria is a fundamental traumatised "layer" which must be reached in any analysis.

In a summary of the "typical phases" of successful character-analytic work, Reich moves through ego interpretation to "breakthrough of the deepest layers of strongly affect-charged material: *reactivation of the infant hysteria*" (1945a, p. 292; my italics). In Reich's developed work, the approach to this fundamental "infant hysteria"—Ferenczi's "organic-hysterical basis of the analysis" (1988, p. xii)—is through releasing the tension of the voluntary musculature, and thus releasing the feelings and memories "contained" in the muscles (Reich, 1942, Chapter Eight).

We can consider trauma as an embodied-relational engram (Chapter Three). PTSD "flashbacks'" are a clear example of how an extreme state of overwhelmed activation can become habitual, and triggered by apparently very minor stimuli in the environment. But equally, the characteristic hyperarousal and hypervigilance of the trauma engram appear in the therapy room and shape the relational field between client and therapist, creating macro- and micro-enactments often organised around themes of embodiment.

A new client told me in the initial meeting that he wanted to "do bodywork", without explaining (and without me asking) what he meant by this; when he arrived for the first actual session, however, he threw himself down full length on the sofa and proceeded to talk continuously about the dramas of his daily life, allowing me very little room to comment. Two or three sessions passed like this, and I found myself very conscious of his initial request for "bodywork", and trying to work out how I could bring this in. (This would certainly not always happen—often I would simply yield to where the work was going and let go of agendas, whether mine or the client's.) Eventually, he gave me an opening by referring obliquely to his psoriasis. I seized the opportunity to suggest that I move my chair a bit closer to the sofa so that I could see what he was talking about. My hope was to use this as a gentle way in to "bodywork".

My client immediately panicked and started hyperventilating. This led to my promising *never* to come physically close unless specifically invited; and to a long conversation about his psoriasis, what it meant to him, and its connection with traumatic childhood situations, both acute and chronic (see the next section). We never did have any further physical interaction: this conversation turned out to be what "bodywork" meant. The need was to bring the trauma of bodily invasion concretely into the therapy; and between us (most of the credit being due to my client) we managed to do this as a symbolic rather than a literal enactment.

Acute and chronic trauma

If we take a step back from the dramatic examples of child sexual and physical abuse, we see that trauma is omnipresent. Placing this sort of event at one end of a spectrum as *acute* trauma, then we find at the other end of the spectrum *chronic* trauma, the effectively universal (at least in our culture) childhood experience of forced adaptation, inadequate holding, and misrecognition. Between these two poles is where most of us live, somewhere in the "normal" middle part, having suffered a few major wounds which in memory often stand for and represent a continuous low level suffering, while our processing of these larger wounds is also organised by our adaptation to chronic trauma.

Philip Bromberg (2011, pp. 57–58) writes of these two poles as "massive" trauma and "developmental" or "relational" trauma; he points out that the way in which people deal with acute trauma, especially in adulthood, is very much shaped and influenced by their experience of chronic developmental trauma, and that the latter makes them more vulnerable to the former. He writes of developmental trauma in these terms:

> A person's core self ... is defined by who the parental objects both perceive him to be and deny him to be. That is, ... the parents

"disconfirm" the relational existence of those aspects of the child's self that they perceptually dissociate. ... "Disconfirmation", because it is relationally nonnegotiable, is traumatic by definition.

(p. 57)

This description picks up on one of Ferenczi's key points, that "Trauma doesn't primarily concern what has happened, but what has not happened" (Borgogno, 2007, p. 145): in other words, it is very often about a deficit—about not experiencing being loved enough, recognised enough, validated enough—about being what Ferenczi calls "*unwelcome guests of the family*" (1929a, p. 270). Either the whole child or, as Bromberg says, certain aspects of her, are systematically ignored. But what seems to me strikingly absent from Bromberg's account is of course embodiment: recognition of how "disconfirmation" is experienced and communicated through bodily avoidance, coldness, and hardness, and of how it fosters bodily engrams (see Chapter Three) which, unless revised, will carry the traumatic experience forward indefinitely through life.

Chronic trauma is a rather wider concept than developmental/relational trauma, including the latter but also including many intolerably painful experiences which are usually regarded as normal aspects of life in our society. These include, for example, rigid gender stereotypes, so that children have to fit themselves into often ill-fitting expectations; the cruel and dissociated treatment of both human and other-than-human beings, which often horrifies children; and a general expectation of toughness and self-sufficiency. In an earlier paper on education, Ferenczi describes the effect of chronic trauma as "*introspective blindness*" (Ferenczi, 1908, p. 27; original italics)—dissociation, in other words, from all the aspects of subjective experience which are incompatible with what the individual believes is required of her. Boarding school is a great breeding house for introspective blindness (Duffell, 2000), but it can be found everywhere.

Emphatically, the distinction between chronic and acute trauma is *not* about whether the experience can or can't be put into language. Chronic trauma is often as far from conscious, language-using awareness as acute trauma, sometimes even further from it. Depending on the specific experience and make-up of the individual, there are endless variations in how readily memory can be languaged—for example, a person may be thoroughly aware of an acute traumatic experience but unable to talk about it—in other words, there is a specific block to communication, often because an abuser threatened terrible consequences if the child told anyone (sometimes the client is able to write it down instead). Alternatively she may be unconscious of her own experience, but it emerges in speech through slips of the tongue and choice of imagery. As for chronic trauma, we will see in the next section that it is usually processed through character formation; and the very nature of character is that it feels "natural" to us, and not in need of explanation. In its denying mode, it is specifically a way of staying unaware of our experience—though, again, it will emerge indirectly in "the way in which" we speak and act.

So the issue of language is distinct from the issue of "psychic representation" which is so often regarded as the key to trauma treatment (Bichi, 2008; Laub & Auerhahn, 1993; Laub & Lee, 2003). It is a dogma for many verbal therapists that the work is about "transforming" bodily experience into mental experience. While it is clearly true that being able to think about things is often helpful, the elevation of this simple fact into a central pillar of therapy is baffling to body psychotherapists who have frequently experienced change taking place independently of conceptualisation, which may or may not follow afterwards.

Character as trauma

As well as the triad of fight, flight, and freezing, there is another embodied strategy available to us for withstanding the impact of trauma: we can absorb it, "bind" it as Reich says, into a character structure. Character performs exactly the sort of "introspective blindness" to which Ferenczi refers:

> The dynamics of character include patients' reflexive, active, and contemporaneous reactions against aspects of their own subjective tendencies, because these aspects run counter to their preferred style, and thereby stimulate intense discomfort and anxiety. ... Patients develop through life experiences ways of binding and forestalling anxiety that feel tolerable or, at least, necessary. These characterologically based yet consciously unrecognized or

unarticulated reactions have the effect of narrowing the patients' awareness of themselves.

(Piers, 1998, p. 18)

Piers sets up an opposition between character theory and trauma theory which is, I think, exaggerated, because he doesn't realise that Reich originally describes character precisely as *a response to trauma*. The difference between chronic and acute trauma is exactly that the former can be dealt with, at great cost, by repression and character formation, which "binds" the traumatic charge into muscular and attitudinal rigidity or "armouring"; while the latter can only be dealt with by splitting and dissociation. So the opposition—which is still overstated—is between chronic, bindable trauma, and acute, unbindable trauma: between toxic experiences which are absorbed into the tissues, and toxic experiences which are encysted like abscesses.

This opposition is still exaggerated because repression and character formation themselves involve dissociation and splitting, while dissociation and splitting themselves involve repression and character formation. The distinction remains one of degree, of the balance between different strategies. The more that a traumatic experience is sudden, unexpected, and shocking, the more likely it is that emergency strategies of dissociation have to come into play (Levine, 1997). And, of course, the individual's capacity to manage sudden trauma very much depends on what sort of characterological accommodation she has already come to. A denying boundary character, for example (see Chapter Seven), has already chosen a strategy of dissociation between "mind" and "body" as their fundamental approach to life; while at the other extreme, a denying holding character has already chosen to bind suffering into bodily rigidity; and at a third angle, a crisis character has chosen to make a huge fuss about it.

One implication of this which is worth emphasising is that dissociation as a strategy, though difficult and sometimes disabling, has one advantage over binding. In dissociation, both the original trauma *and the personality which suffered it* are still present, frozen in the moment of catastrophe (Ferenczi, 1988, p. 82), still potentially available in a much more immediate way than is generally the case with character structure, where both the original free energy and its trauma have been passed through a long series of adaptations and compromises. The recovery of the original personality cannot always be achieved, but almost miraculous events do happen. Some survivors of extreme trauma manifest a striking goodness and wisdom.

Trauma and embodied relating

Ferenczi's reconceptualising of trauma and its effects was the place where, in retrospect, relational psychotherapy can be seen to have started (cf. Aron, 1990, p. 477). In his view, what analysis called "transference" was in fact primarily an *enactment*: the alignment between the therapist as the "foreign body"—the invasive, abusive, and/or seductive external force—and the subsequent threat from one's *own* bodily impulses. By inviting, encouraging, or, in the client's fantasy, and perhaps to some extent in reality, *compelling* her to yield to the spontaneity of the body, the therapist recapitulates and is identified with the early "traumatic-hysterical" crisis and with the adults who took part in it, in whatever role. Ferenczi believes that this is not a useful experience, certainly not a curative one: "The similarity of the analytical to the infantile situation impels patients to repetition, the contrast between the two encourages recollection" (Ferenczi, 1929b, p. 124). Only by giving up her authority and invulnerability can the therapist establish a new situation "different from the actually traumatic one" (Ferenczi, 1988, p. 108). Hence his experiments with "mutual analysis" and with comforting touch.

Both chronic and acute traumatic experience leads us to experience *our own body* as "foreign", in its spontaneous impulses to surrender and flow: if it feels vital to suppress feeling and emotional expression, then this can only be achieved by alienating ourselves from our own bodies, in particular from our sexuality, which has attracted punishment and exploitation.

> As heroically as they [clients] once wrestled with the "devil" in themselves, i.e., sexual pleasure, they now senselessly defend themselves against the cherished capacity for pleasure.
>
> An abreaction of quantities of the trauma is not enough: *the situation must be different from the actually traumatic* one in order to make possible a different, favourable outcome. The most essential aspect of the altered repetition is the relinquishing of one's own rigid authority and the hostility hidden in it. (Ferenczi, 1988, p. 108; my italics)

This conclusion leaves us with a dilemma. The notion of "cure" and "putting right" can be seen as a regressive one—a mutual transference fantasy, which identifies the therapist as a magical rescuer and smoothes away the trauma in the act of exposing it. This is just one of a group of fantasies to which body psychotherapy is perhaps uniquely prone. Intimate physical contact, in our culture, generally implies one or more of the following: a sexual relationship, an adult-child relationship, a child-child relationship, and a "making better" relationship (doctor, nurse, dentist, etc.). If the therapist cannot bring awareness to these implications, a mutual trance may develop where both people fantasise about their relationship in one or more of the ways outlined, *without owning* those fantasies. The fantasies can potentially be very useful as a way of exploring core beliefs and patterns of relationship—but only if we can name and study them openly.

But in criticising the transference fantasies in this way, don't we render ourselves liable to Ferenczi's criticism—that the fundamental reason why regression and catharsis fail is the persecutory attitude of the therapist? Ferenczi resurrects what he calls "the good old 'friendly attitude' to the patient ... long believed to be discarded" (1929b, p. 298); and shows how problematic the apparently straightforward issue of *trust* becomes when we are working with primal, traumatic material, and how difficult it is to create:

> ... *this confidence that establishes the contrast between the present and the unbearable traumatogenic past*, the contrast which is absolutely necessary for the patient in order to enable him to re-experience the past no longer as hallucinatory reproduction but as an objective memory.

(1933, p. 296; original italics)

But the problem is two-sided. Many bodyworkers, including some body psychotherapists, believe that a simplistic "friendly attitude" and an assumption of goodwill on both parts is sufficient to facilitate therapy—ignoring our inevitable involvement, through the embodied-relational structure of the therapeutic encounter, in the client's trauma-tised experience.

Body psychotherapy has a particular struggle around the fantasy of "making better", because of its close association with techniques of skilled physical manipulation. No rigid boundary can be drawn between, for example, body psychotherapy and corrective massage; Reich's own work overlaps between the two, and his successor in orgonomy, Elsworth Baker, offers specific physical techniques as part of his textbook on body psychotherapy (1980). This creates real and persistent relational difficulties: the therapist may enjoy the sense of power and effectiveness offered by this identification as an expert who will cure the client, or may employ a psychological "white coat" to cover up more frightening feelings in herself and her clients. It must be said, however, that many practitioners of purely verbal therapy have a similar countertransference problem, often without seeing it as a problem; simply inviting the client to lie down, as in psychoanalysis, sets up some of the same fantasies, and interpretation itself often attracts fantasies of surgical intervention.

Because of these problems I was convinced for some years that body psychotherapy, and therapy in general, needed to sternly resist the wish to heal our clients, to treat it only and always as a regressive fantasy. This no longer feels adequate. It is our caring, our wish to help, which provides the engine for therapeutic work; if we try not to feel love and compassion for our clients, we are crippling ourselves as practitioners, and opening the door to persecution. At the same time, though, we need to hold firmly to the knowledge that we can only help by not "being helpful", by studying the client's life with her rather than trying to fix it.

These difficulties and dilemmas, and how to find an appropriate therapeutic response to trauma, as well as several other aspects of embodied relationship, can be illuminated through complexity theory.

Embodied complexity

At the risk of overcomplication, I want to introduce another model which offers a different way of conceptualising much of what this book has already discussed, and which in fact has been at the back, or sometimes near the front, of my mind at many points during writing it. This model is widely known as *complexity theory*, or the theory of nonlinear dynamic systems (NDS): originating in mathematics, it has emerged as a powerful and revelatory way of modelling many phenomena which were previously opaque to us. A number of writers have already applied complexity theory to psychotherapy (among others, Boston Change Process Study Group, 1998; Galatzer-Levy, 1978, 2004;

Palombo, 1999, 2007; Spruiell, 1993), especially for the purpose of better understanding therapeutic change; and I think it will also be useful to apply it specifically to embodied relating.

Complexity theory shows that in nonlinear systems, which include both living organisms and relationships *between* living organisms, change happens not only gradually and incrementally but also through sudden shifts into "self-organisation". NDS are never static, but in constant flux to one degree or another; and when the system moves sufficiently far from equilibrium and towards "the edge of chaos" (Kauffman, 1995), a very small change of conditions can flip it from one stable state into a different one, like a liquid suddenly freezing when it becomes only very slightly colder, or turning to gas when it becomes slightly warmer.

> When the control parameters reach critical levels the current steady state becomes unstable and self-organization ensues. ... In these far-from-equilibrium conditions the internal potentialities of the system are released moving the system to a qualitatively different steady state.
>
> (Piers, 2000, p. 14)

Craig Piers, from whom I have just quoted, applies this idea very effectively to thinking about character structure (see Chapter Seven), its stubborn stability, and its unpredictable shifts:

> [NDS theory] accounts for both healthy and pathological conditions of character within a single systemic model. ... Chaotic systems in particular account for the local variability, context sensitivity, and adaptation in response to changing internal and external conditions, as well as the underlying continuity and integrity we see in people of relative psychological health. ... With the notion of self-organization NDS accounts for the qualitative, nonproportional, and unpredictable transitions people make through the course of development and treatment.
>
> (2000, p. 30)

However, he unfortunately defines character in entirely mental terms, as representing "an underlying consistency and coherence to the way individuals speak, think, experience affect, interact, and remember" (2000, p. 7)—ignoring Reich's equal or greater emphasis on the way in which people move, hold themselves, gesture, grimace, vocalise, and so on: the whole realm of vitality affect (Stern, 1985, 2010), what Reich also calls a person's "bearing" (1945, p. 292). It is not the mind alone which constitutes the nonlinear dynamic system, but the mind-body-environment.

Returning to the idea of movement from equilibrium to the edge of chaos, this can helpfully be understood in terms of "attractors". An attractor is basically a mathematical concept: if one tracks the changes in a nonlinear system in "phase space"—basically a multidimensional graph—then one sees repeated patterns of activity, which show as a return to the same area of the graph; this area is the "attractor". Although it is ultimately a misconception to imagine an attractor exerting a literal pull on the system, this is certainly what it looks like, and, for human beings, also often what it *feels* like; and indeed, some attractors do literally function in this way—for example, a whirlpool is an attractor in a nonlinear dynamic system, which persists and stays almost the same while water constantly flows through it (Kauffman, 1995, p. 187). The area of phase space around an attractor is termed an "attractor basin", and could be imagined as similar to a planet's gravity well: once a system enters into the attractor basin, it is bound eventually to end up back at the attractor.

We can visualise—and here I am moving even further away from an exact account of complexity theory—the terrain of human life as a plane pocked by a series of dimpled craters of various sizes, each of which is an attractor basin. It is perfectly possible to stay within one attractor basin, circling back and forth around one stable attractor, for many years. As with a gravity well, achieving escape velocity requires a large energy investment. But if something impels us sufficiently far up the side of the basin, we reach a far-from-equilibrium point where we are out under the stars, teetering between two or more slopes, on what is known as "the edge of chaos"; a very small event can precipitate us down into another basin, towards a new attractor.

So what is it in the therapeutic process that might donate us the energy to shift up the side of the attractor basin away from our habitual "fixed-point attractor" towards "the edge of chaos"—a place where new possibilities are born? One source of such energy is indeed hysteria, the chaotic bodily protest which Freud's early patients brought into the work, and which still appears today in new forms; this is perhaps why both Ferenczi and Reich talked of the need to get back to the hysteria underlying other manifestations of distress. But more often, and perhaps more usefully, the shift to the edge of chaos emerges from the *coupling* of client and therapist: their organisms come into entrained synchrony, so that a new and unpredictable system is created.

Terry Marks-Tarlow writes:

> The essence of the nonlinear element within psychotherapy stems from the coupled dynamics between people, where mind/body/brain rhythms get synchronized ... This holds not just for the flow of emotions but also for autonomic physiological processes. ... These kinds of coupled dynamics are central to psychotherapy, especially as they occur beneath the level of consciousness, where arousal levels, facial expression, emotional perceptions and response, body rhythms, even pupil size, all significant indicators of empathy, get synchronized ... The patient alone may be either stuck in an underlying stable attractor or lurching toward chaos in a problematic way. By contrast, the newly coupled system created by the therapy allows the self-organized evolution of the "analytic third" away from these pathological extremes towards the edge of chaos.
>
> (2011, pp. 119–120)

We are looking here at the same processes which we have been considering throughout this book, but using a new language to do so, a language which helps us understand how the embodied relationship sets up the potential for such dramatic change.

Complexity theory doesn't really offer us any direct suggestions for therapeutic technique—which may be frustrating, given the effort it takes to understand it. However, what it does offer is something which seems to me even more valuable: a reason for keeping our nerve, for staying committed when therapy becomes frightening and confusing for both participants—because we know that *this is precisely when there is real potential for change*: "Life exists at the edge of chaos" (Kauffman, 1995, p. 26).

No success like failure

The coupling of client and therapist within the relational field is a powerful force, and, given its situation at the edge of chaos, frequently also a wild ride. As Stanley Palombo writes: "Near the edge of chaos, analyst and patient are in tune. Their contributions, usually complementary, now overlap and reinforce each other" (2007, p. 11). The overlapping and reinforcement is not necessarily wholly benign, however, and what is shared may be an old and repetitive "tune", in which a client/therapist system maintains stuckness around a repetitive attractor, constituting:

> A psychotherapeutic impasse … when the therapist responds to the patient's pathological periodicity in a periodic manner, in a form of transference–countertransference entrainment. … This appears to overlap with the concept of "enactment" which describes the way the therapist and patient collude unconsciously to enact meaningful repetitions from the patient's life. That is, instead of developing a unique form of relatedness, the pair fall back into periodic, but meaningful, patterns of relating.
>
> (Piers, 2000, p. 31)

However, an acute enactment is very often organised instead around a "strange attractor", with a fractal structure which reproduces itself on every scale, so that once arrived at it is enormously difficult to leave: like a cunning labyrinth, every movement away from it brings the therapeutic pair back to the same place via a different route. This is one way of understanding chaotic enactments, where the only way out is further in, a deeper yielding to chaos which eventually permits the shift to a new attractor basin (Piers, 2000, p. 31). As I have been saying throughout the book, the therapist's holding back and refusal to engage cannot succeed in keeping her uncoupled from the client, it only ensures that the coupling will be malignant and enact a repetition of abandonment.

Stanley Palombo writes:

> The mother–infant relationship is often evoked to illustrate the attunement of the analytic process near the edge of chaos. This analogy is misleading, however. It attributes an unrealistic asymmetry to the analytic pair. More apt would be the image of a vocalist and her coach working together at the piano.
>
> (2007, p. 11)

When client and therapist do fall into a mother–infant embodied relational engram, they can be in deep trouble if this engram is traumatic in nature. They are caught in a fractal strange attractor, where every attempt to work reparatively and "reparent" the client finds itself retraumatising them instead, because for them parenting *means* trauma. This is the dilemma which I wrote about at the end of the previous section: trauma, especially acute trauma, tends to draw out of the therapist a powerful urge to hold and heal the damaged baby which she perceives in the client. But unless she is willing to yield to the edge of chaos, and to allow much less kindly feelings to appear—in fact, to risk failure—she is unlikely to help the client move to a new attractor.

The description of someone teetering on the edge between attractors may have reminded some readers, as it does me, of the image of The Fool in the Tarot deck: a young person balanced on the edge of a chasm, staring up at the sky, and with a small dog jumping up at his or her back. The Fool tells us of a fresh start, new possibilities, a step into the unknown. The dog can be seen as a warning voice trying to hold The Fool back, or equally as an energy propelling him or her forward into risk and novelty; perhaps the fundamental message is that there is always a second element, always an Other, constellated in the move to a new attractor (what Arnold Mindell (1985b, pp. 42–43) calls a "dream figure", supportive or critical, who pops up as we approach an edge). And this is the role which the therapist is drawn to take on in the situation, perhaps encouraging or discouraging or both, perhaps helping or hindering or both, but always committed to the coupled relationship of therapist and client which impels the system to the edge of chaos.

THE STORY SO FAR, 3

Now a brief summary of the major points made in Chapters Eight to Ten.

1. Play is a basic human activation pattern, shared in its essentials with all other mammals. It enables us to operate in an "as-if" frame, where actions do not mean what they would normally mean.
2. Rather than "signals" informing us that the other is playing, we have direct embodied experience through the resonance between our embodiment and hers.
3. This activation pattern is of vital importance to psychotherapy, which takes place largely within an "as-if" frame, allowing us to experience intense relational feelings without acting on them in the ways we otherwise would.
4. Play also gives us access to the "transitional space" described by Winnicott, the space within which creativity and relaxation can occur. It makes deep change possible.
5. The widespread belief among therapists that language and embodiment occupy separate spheres, between which little traffic can pass, is untrue. Embodied experience is not fundamentally

any more difficult (or any easier) to language than other complex phenomena.

6. Speech can be either embodied or disembodied—"full" or "empty". Full speech is embodied both in the physical sense of emerging from a vibrant body awareness, and in the sense that it reflects our embodied experience and understanding. These two aspects are entwined together.

7. To be fully effective, psychotherapy requires both embodied experience and embodied languaging.

8. Trauma is an attack on all aspects of our being, but most fundamentally on our body, as is indicated by the metaphors we use about it.

9. It tends to create a dissociation between "mind" and "body", such that a person's embodied experience is no longer fully available to her. This has a crippling effect on the psyche.

10. There is a doubling effect in psychotherapy between the disembodiment created in our traumatised clients, and the disembodiment of psychotherapy itself, which makes it very hard for us to stay centred around trauma.

11. We can usefully identify two sorts of trauma, although there is no gap between them but rather an overlapping continuity. These are "acute" or "massive" trauma, managed by dissociation, and "chronic" or "developmental" trauma, managed by repression and the formation of character.

12. Therapy with severely traumatised people—which in some ways means all of us—demands that we approach our clients in a humane, authentic, and gentle way, including being open when necessary about our own traumatised state. Trauma demands enactment, the playing out of its origins in the therapeutic relationship; any quality of "ungenuineness" or persecution will render the enactment unresolvable.

CHAPTER ELEVEN

Therapy grounded in embodied relating

I have been arguing throughout this book that embodied relating is already present in important ways in every therapeutic modality. Because we *are* bodies, and because our embodiment shapes our feelings, thoughts, and relationships, even the most mind-centred forms of therapy are still continuously drawing on bodily experience, though they may only address it once it has been translated into mental and verbal representations.

So I will be doing two things in this chapter: firstly, discussing how practitioners who are interested in what I am saying (and I imagine that must include any who are still reading at this point) can apply it to their work without going too far outside their comfort zone, or getting into difficulties with their peers or their training organisation; and secondly, describing the therapeutic modality in which I myself operate, Embodied-Relational Therapy, and how it works with relationship and with embodiment.

Embodied relating for mainstream therapists

A necessary and sufficient condition for working with embodied relationship, I suggest, is simply this: that *the therapist continuously tracks and brings into the work her own embodied experience while with the client.*

I have found that, offered this idea, a lot of therapists will say that it is what they already do, or part of it; and for some of them this is genuinely so. Body psychotherapists have no monopoly on embodiment! However, in many cases, when I ask one of these practitioners in supervision "So, what did you feel in your body when they said that?" the reply is "Nothing in particular." In reality our bodies are *always* feeling things, always processing and responding to what is happening: not usually in big and dramatic ways, but always in ways which on examination are meaningful, and which in a therapy session actually constitute our embodied relationship with the other. The psychoanalyst Sue Shapiro writes:

> All treatments, whether or not there is touch, involve body-to-body communication and the better we as therapists can tune in to these experiences in ourselves and are aware of changes in our patients' bodies, the more we have to work with.

> (2009, p. 100)

So my first, second, and third recommendation to someone who wants to explore embodied relationship is: practise attending to your embodiment. You don't need to get hung up on *understanding* it: meaning will come later. For now—possibly for quite a long time—just get used to the fact that things are always going on in your body: twitches, itches, trembles, gurgles, grumbles, sighs, swallows, pulses, jerks, yawns: hot and cold bits, hard and soft bits, tense and relaxed bits, wakeful and sleepy bits. Apart from body psychotherapists, it is mostly only hypochondriacs who notice all this activity: hypochondriacs are on to something, but unfortunately it scares them.

I have been consciously practising tracking my bodily experience for over forty years, and I really recommend it: it is good for one in all sorts of ways. But what we are focusing on right now is how it can bring us into relationship with the other. Most of what has been written about this process as it applies to therapy has taken a quite distancing attitude, which brings out what I referred to earlier in the book as *the difference between the visual and the visceral.* Visual consciousness thinks in terms of perceiving the other's behaviour and deducing experience from it; while visceral consciousness is about sharing and resonating with the experience of the other.

So a lot of the writing about "embodied countertransference"—that is, about how my embodied experience relates to that of my client—discusses how to identify something happening in me, and then how to try to work out what it might mean about what is happening in the client. This can produce very interesting and creative ideas, and I have written about it like this in the past; but over the years my focus has shifted to thinking of my embodied process as *direct information* about the field between myself and the other person, in the way that I discussed in the early part of this book. And by the way, I also think of factors like what I notice of how a person looks and how he sounds—where my visual and auditory attention is drawn—as aspects of my embodied process: the Flesh drawing me to "look here; listen to this".

My embodied response is happening in the overlapping transitional space between us, rather than exclusively inside either me or the client (see Chapter Eight). In order for me both to recognise it, and to distinguish it from my usual internal life, I need to be deeply familiar with what goes on in my body from moment to moment. And this of course also gives me much deeper and richer access to my emotional life, and even to my intellectual life: feelings primarily happen in and to bodies, and even thoughts cannot be corralled off in some sort of "psychosphere". I am a thinking, feeling, sensing body, encountering another thinking, feeling, sensing body, being changed by her presence and changing her by my presence in a way which creates a third, transitional space between us.

Bringing our embodied response into the work can happen in a very wide range of ways: including, but not restricted to, simply sharing our experience with the client, in a spirit of collaboration, and seeing what if anything we both make of it. I often feel that this is the most straightforward and effective thing to do: "Listening to you, I'm finding my belly getting tenser and tenser, and I'm starting to wonder what this is about." "When you told me about what happened, I felt a sudden electric jolt go through me, so I'm imagining that it was really important." "I've been fighting back tears for the last few minutes." "My tummy's thinking about my dinner."

Some of these responses depend on a good deal of trust between us, others are less risky. I tend to rely on my internal resonance to tell me whether or not my experience can be shared in a useful way. If I decide not to share it right now, then I ask *myself* the same sorts of questions that I might have invited my client to think about—how does this relate to everything else that is going on inside and outside the room? What I try to keep firmly in mind is the perspective of both-yet-neither inbe-tweenness (see Chapter Eight): my bodily experience has to do with both myself and the client, and is also about neither of us as separate individuals but about the field between us. So—what are we co-creating that emerges in my body's reaction? Where else is it emerging in our work—in what is being said, in dreams, in the relational weather between us? Arnold Mindell (e.g., 1985a, 1985b) has a great deal to say about these parallels.

So that is my recipe for working with, or in, embodied relationship, while still using whatever style and techniques you are already familiar and comfortable with. Doing so will change your work, but probably not very visibly so, unless you choose to let that happen. I think per-haps one of the most striking effects of tracking and using one's embod-iment is that it gently encourages us to let go of the need to *understand* in each moment the meaning of what is going on: encourages us to hold the overall project of understanding more lightly, trusting that mean-ing will fall into place on its own without too much effort on our part (though an engram of "efforting" may be drawn out of us by the recip-rocal embodied field). This means that we can be more spontaneous, more playful, more genuinely present, because we don't have a part of us holding back all the time to observe and make sense.

Now I want to move on to giving a picture of the therapeutic style which I, with help from clients, from trainees, and from co-trainers (Totton & Priestman, 2011), have developed specifically as a way of foregrounding the embodied relationship. Of course I don't believe that this is the only good, or necessarily the best, way of practising; only that it is the best way for me.

Embodied-Relational Therapy

Perhaps the biggest way that Embodied-Relational Therapy (ERT) goes beyond what I have described above is that it places at the centre of its work the project of *offering and modelling embodiment* to and for our clients. The more fully and consciously embodied a person is, the more able she is to live in the world and relate effectively to other humans and other-than-humans—so many of the problems our clients bring are bound up with issues of embodiment. And as I have emphasised in this book, embodiment is not an either/or deal, something to be achieved as a finality, but an ongoing process of becoming, an exploration of and dialogue with the organismic aspect of our being, without which we cannot exist, but which at the same time we always have difficulty fully accepting.

Relational therapy (Mitchell, 2000) is a shared attempt to work through mutual feelings of distress and pain, as well as love and enjoyment. And all of its psychological complexity develops on a platform of embodied experience. It is enormously helpful in negotiating these difficult feelings to have an awareness of and openness to the bodily experience which underlies them—and at the same time, the fundamental firm and soothing quality of embodiment, the simple sway of the breath, the gurgle of the belly, the feet on the ground. Body psychotherapists have, hopefully, worked through their own relationship with embodiment to the extent that they can regularly find comfort in it, and communicate this comfort to their clients.

The body-oriented Gestalt psychotherapist James Kepner stresses the importance of:

> The capacity of the therapist to hold [the embodied] aspect of experience as figural (bounded, central and relevant) even if, or especially if, it is not figural for the client. ... To work with embodiment ... the therapist must be able to hold a constant awareness and appreciation that the body is intrinsic to *all* human process.
>
> (2003, p. 9; original italics)

He says, perhaps idealistically, that "The therapist must, each hour, foster an embodied field powerful enough to support the client in holding their bodily life and experience as *intrinsic* to their ongoing experience" (p. 10; original italics). I certainly agree that this is what we should endeavour to do—although failures to do so may be equally useful to explore; and in this context, the significance of the "embodied field" is that it supports the client *and the therapist* in contacting the embodied ground on which their complex and difficult feelings and fantasies about each other have been erected.

An important route into deeper embodiment is to be in touch with our moment-by-moment experience. The ability to do this is a natural human resource, but it gets suppressed and switched off in various ways. It involves continuous attention to internal sensations, movement impulses, muscle states, feelings, fantasies, thoughts—an unbroken continuum from "bodily" to "mental" processes. For many people, bodily processes are less integrated than mental ones: either they tend to be partly or wholly out of awareness, or else awareness of them is invasive and alarming, as in hypochondria. Many of us would benefit from being more embodied—just as many of us whose mental processes are less integrated would also benefit from being more "enminded", more able to think about experience; and these need not be opposite directions or specialisations, as they tend to become in Western culture: we can be good at both!

Embodiment is a rich source of information, vital for our interaction with others. Complex, subtle, contradictory information and unconscious material gets processed much more effectively through our bodies than in our rational conscious minds alone. But ERT is acutely aware that processing may occur in *any* channel of information—visceral, proprioceptive and kinesthetic sensation, movement, emotion, vision, hearing, speech, thought, relationship, and more, even including aspects of our environment which seem to solicit our attention—the bird at the window, the ambulance siren, the article in the newspaper, last night's dream. To privilege embodied relationship would be as limiting as privileging language: we endeavour to let our attention float freely (Freud, 1912e, pp. 111–112), available to be drawn to any phenomenon, in any channel, that appears to carry energy. This may in conventional terms be something happening "in" the client, "in" the practitioner, or "outside" or "between" both of them—it makes little difference.

Whatever draws our own or the client's attention, we approach it in an open, curious, and playful way, turning it this way and that to see how the light catches it, considering how it might parallel or conflict with other pieces of the situation. We think in terms of finding ways to "amplify"—to fill out and enrich—something which might at first appear very small and insignificant, but which has managed to bend gravity around itself in such a way as to attract our embodied attention. Attention is itself the first and most fundamental way to amplify; other methods include talking about it, associating to it, taking it into other channels, using movement, role play, drawing, taking it outside the room—anything that occurs to either of us and feels good to both of us. Often channel-switching will happen spontaneously; and we have noticed empirically that there is a particular tendency for the process to switch in either direction between embodiment and relationship.

Channel-switching is something to which we need to be very alert: if we miss it, then we may waste a lot of time trying to explore something which is no longer happening where we think it is: the client's process may have moved from relationship to feeling, from seeing to sensation, from hearing to thinking. This missed connection can itself create a switch to the relational channel, if the client gets frustrated with us because we have lost the plot! We need to stay flexible and unattached, able to drop our fixed notions at any point.

This includes ideas about "who is who": ERT gives a lot of attention to "figures"—for example the dictator, the child, the animal, the complainer, the disturber, the carer—which can manifest at one minute in the therapist, the next minute in the client, and the minute after in a reported dream figure or someone from the client's life. In our experience it is safe and indeed useful to let things get muddled up and unclear: "muddle" is where the energy for change comes from, and by trusting the "edge of chaos" we are allowing a phase shift to take place. Of course we also need to pay attention to what the client needs to have available in order to feel safe enough to go to the edge of chaos; and a playful context, together with a willingness to dip in and out, is often important.

Having said all this, ERT, as the name suggests, does *specialise* in embodied relating: partly because it is downplayed in many other therapeutic approaches, but mainly because it seems to us a very central, powerful, and fruitful aspect of therapy—also a very safe one, because it brings into awareness aspects which are better not left unconscious. As I have been saying throughout this book, when we are impacted by the client's embodiment, we directly experience in our embodied response its compromises, its contradictions, how it is incorporated (literally!) into social narratives and also resists or evades such incorporation—all of this, for the length of the session, becomes part of our own lived embodiment, and resonates with our own multiplicity of compromises and contradictions. In the "third space" created by a melding of two embodiments, there is a creative opportunity for something new to arrive, something which can be transformative not only for the client but also perhaps for the therapist.

It is crucial to acknowledge our own defences against embodied relationship. To engage in this way makes us very vulnerable as it loosens our character defences (see Chapter Seven) and moves us into a state of "liminal awareness" (Bernstein, 2005; Totton, 2011) where we can feel at the mercy of the other's feelings. Really these are now *our* feelings, or we could not be having them; but this in itself is confusing, and sometimes alarming, if we don't like being a person who is having these feelings.

Sometimes, as therapists, we will just not be up for all this; sometimes the client will be more embodied than us, more relational than us—and sometimes we will experience this as an intolerable demand, to which we react with coldness, distance, or even disguised aggression (Winnicott, 1947b). None of this is catastrophic so long as we can allow it into awareness without denial—even when the client has noticed it first!—and explore, with the client, what is happening for us and why, and what needs to be done about it.

It is often very hard to hold on to the knowledge that the embodied response we experience is not a response *from* us *to* the client, but co-created in transitional space. A lot of the time we can only know this theoretically: our actual *experience* is of feeling pushed, seduced, lured, lulled, charmed, hustled, ambushed, and challenged into certain shapes by our clients. Often the shape feels familiar, since there has to be a "receptor site" in us which responds to the client's cue. Sometimes it is a shape that we like—the helpful, compassionate, accepting therapist or the intelligent, knowledgeable, experienced practitioner; sometimes one we don't like so much—the judge, the parent, the impatient, tired, imperfect human being.

Other shapes we find ourselves in are more unusual for us, more stretching, perhaps illuminating adventures. We need at times to be able to support our clients in moving us into shapes that we don't like or don't know, and to allow them to take up shapes that they don't like or don't know. Each of us has a different set of behaviours and emotions which we find difficult to support in ourselves and others; and we need to find out what these are. Feeling ourselves experiencing or receiving anger, hatred, mistrust, seduction, uncertainty, can be very hard.

Somewhere in ourselves, though, we are trying to hold on to the knowledge that this is not the best description of what is going on: that we are not, ultimately, being moved around by our clients, but that we are equal partners in the dance that is happening. To work well in the relational channel, we need to hold a double perspective: one from inside the relationship, where we feel as though our client and ourselves are two separate people doing things to and having feelings about each other; and one where we recognise that we are two *places* in an embodied-relational field, and witness what is happening in the field as a whole without attaching to just one aspect of it.

Neither of these perspectives is enough on its own: we need to hold both and to move our focus between them. Relational work—perhaps like life—depends on a combination of *commitment* and *detachment*: both taking our own side, and recognising that this position is part of a larger meaningful whole. Fully owning and identifying our emotional response to how our clients relate to us, and also witnessing it (which may be the main way we become aware of what they are doing); staying with this tension around our reaction to our clients and how much we can and can't inhibit our response; all this is central to working relationally. It is also in some sense impossible—another of the paradoxes which are associated with transitional spaces: we cannot simultaneously be both fully committed and fully detached, yet that is what we need to be.

When we feel pushed out of shape by the embodied relationship, we are challenged to hold on to our sense of being good enough as a therapist. Sometimes it can be hard not to collapse into what it seems our clients are showing us: that we're failing them, misunderstanding them. When we begin to get lost in such thoughts, it's good to remind ourselves that this is part of the territory, and therapeutically valuable *whether or not it is accurate*. Whatever the regulators say, therapy is an intrinsically risky undertaking, which cannot be made wholly safe if it is to be effective; and this is one of the areas where riskiness becomes foregrounded. Very often, the trauma from which our client has been suffering can only be fully brought into the therapy by being *re-enacted* there.

The debate over embodiment in psychotherapy

The form of mainstream, verbally-oriented psychotherapy which has so far expressed the deepest interest in embodiment is, I think, relational psychoanalysis. Even there, however, there has been considerable unwillingness to be drawn into active work with and through the body. This is illuminated in a fascinating debate between Bill Cornell, a relational body psychotherapist with a background in transactional analysis, and Sue Shapiro, a relational psychoanalyst with a deep interest in embodiment (Cornell, 2009a, 2009b; Shapiro, 2009; see also Shapiro, 1996). As is so often the case with discussions of body psychotherapy, the question of touch seems to act as a powerful attractor in this debate.

In his initial paper, Cornell presents "a detailed case discussion to illustrate the use of body-centered interventions within a psychoanalytically informed psychotherapy" (2009a, p. 75). He discusses his work with a client he calls Elizabeth, and deliberately cuts straight to the chase:

> Elizabeth and I lay on our backs, side by side on the carpet of my office. We were in close proximity to each other, but our bodies did not quite touch. I asked Elizabeth to notice any impulses within her body in relation to mine and, if she wished, to explore any of those impulses through movement between her body and mine. This therapeutic invitation proved to be a complex, disturbing, and nearly impossible process of exploration.
>
> (p. 75)

As Cornell immediately goes on to say:

> Elizabeth's therapy did not start on my office floor. We began our work together seated in chairs talking to each other about the ways in which Elizabeth felt immobilized in her life. Successful in her career, with a wide circle of friends and warm relationships with her family, Elizabeth lived alone, never having been able to sustain an intimate relationship, never having had a sexual relationship.
>
> (p. 75)

Elizabeth found that her previous verbal therapy did not get to the heart of her problems, and her therapist referred her to Cornell specifically for body psychotherapy. Her refrain of "I don't know what to do with my body" was what led them to active exploration of their embodied relationship (p. 76).

This is a long and detailed case account, which Cornell presented in a relational psychoanalytic journal for the deliberate purpose of trying to influence analysts towards working with the body in ways that go beyond talking about it:

> I think it is essential that the field of activity in psychoanalytic treatment open up to the field of actual movement between analyst and patient. ... The central function of direct work with body experience and activity in psychotherapy and psychoanalysis is that of providing space, a space within which to move and acquire new emotional and sensorimotor skills. ... That space is a place to try again, in the presence of a skilled and attentive therapist, to challenge one's psychosomatic vulnerabilities and rigidities, to revive and complete one's patterns of interrupted gestures, to discover new possibilities for delight and desire.
>
> (p. 89)

This is a fairly traditionalist description of body psychotherapy, though I would agree with everything Cornell says—he strongly emphasises what I have been calling the visceral over the visual; but the paper itself is clearly about embodied relational work, which in the case of Elizabeth was evidently transformative.

Sue Shapiro's response is in many ways welcoming: she agrees that:

> ... all treatments, whether or not there is touch, involve body-to-body communication and the better we as therapists can tune in to these experiences in ourselves and are aware of changes in our patients' bodies, the more we have to work with.
>
> (2009, p. 100)

"Our bodies speak incessantly," she continues, "We are unconsciously processing this corporeal speech all the time" (p. 100).

This framing of intercorporeality as a form of *speech*, which so dramatically misses the point, provides the context for her critique of Cornell's approach:

> However ... body therapies that involve physical contact and psychoanalytic therapy are two modalities that do better separately

than together. I have, over the years, become increasingly comfortable giving patients a hug or finding some way of being in physical contact ... When someone is exceedingly dissociated, I might place a hand on his or her knee or a back when I am as certain as I can be that my touch is welcome and will not cause further dissociation. But this supportive or grounding touch differs from bodily action aimed at opening up new experiences and behaviors, such as the touch in the body-based therapies I have mentioned.

(pp. 100–101)

The boundary which Shapiro draws is an often-repeated one. What makes her version of it unusual and interesting is that she grounds it in *her own embodied response* to reading the paper:

Upon every reading, I have a strong visceral response. The case opens shockingly: "Elizabeth and I lay next to each other on the floor." I feel anxious, tight, as I read this. My body is scared? My breath held. Where do I feel it? Back, chest, arms, legs—in fact, everywhere. I feel as if I'm slipping into being Elizabeth, my Elizabeth; this happens automatically for me, the way I sometimes scream in movies even if I've seen them before. *I don't want to do this, why are you making me, I trust you but this feels weird and scary and I don't think I will feel any impulse, but what if I do? What do you want from me? What are you feeling in your body?*

(p. 94)

Shapiro concludes:

Psychoanalysts and their patients feel relatively safe with each other because ... there is an absence of large actions within the consulting room. A patient or analyst can feel intense love, hatred, sexual feelings, but the expectation is that these will be expressed through language, although of course they are expressed nonverbally as well and are enacted, but generally these enactments are microactions. There is a great deal a patient can learn about being more embodied without direct engagement with the analyst's body. And if there is an agreed-upon need for more work with the body, the patient can be referred to someone else for this work.

(p. 101)

Cornell responds—and I strongly agree—that:

> ... any treatment modality represents an act upon the patient's body (and mind). I would argue that the entire technical paradigm of psychoanalysis is an action upon patients' bodies, which has not been sufficiently examined.
>
> (2009b, p. 110)

He points out the oddness of Shapiro's throwaway suggestion that "a patient in the midst of a deep psychoanalytic involvement" can be referred on for more work with the body to:

> ... a bodywork practitioner, who likely has had little or no training in transference and countertransference dynamics, unconscious processes, or other aspects of an analytic experience.
>
> (p. 110)

I would also add that the safety Shapiro appeals to is not ultimately created by the "absence of large actions", but by the "as-if" transitional space which I discussed in Chapter Eight.

Cornell eloquently restates his central argument:

> There are enduring, organizing systems of movement, sensation, and sensorimotor processes that are forms of knowing and showing carried in a different realm from that of speech ... and as such may need to be met first within that realm of experience. ... In psychotherapy and psychoanalysis the movement into a languaged narrative is usually sought, though language is not necessary for all learning. In the more classical psychoanalytic literature, when the body is written about at all, it is likely to be presented as a primitive, regressed, infantile body. ... Still to my reading most analysts present accounts of an observed body rather than a moving body.
>
> (2009b, p. 104)

Again, I strongly agree.

This is a fascinating exchange, and there is a lot more in it that I encourage interested readers to seek out. Shapiro is, bravely, very open about the traumatic element in her visceral response; and suggests, reasonably, that if she feels that way then many clients may feel the same—and that pressure to focus on embodiment may feel persecutory (paralleling Ferenczi's thinking as I explored it in Chapter Ten). Cornell tactfully picks up on Shapiro's acknowledged dissociation from her embodied experience (Shapiro, 2009, p. 94), and suggests, as I did earlier in this chapter, that this is exactly one of the things that body psycho-therapy addresses (Cornell, 2009b, p. 105). He is also very clear about the careful pacing and protection built into the work with Elizabeth, and the extent to which it was co-created with her (pp. 106–107).

I think that this exchange acts as an illustration of my argument in Chapter Ten that trauma *theory* itself represents traumatic *experience*. Shapiro is not really saying anything very different from the many psychoanalytic writers who have distanced themselves from engaging with embodiment; but she is able to be much more open about *the bodily nature of her disengagement*. She is able to explore her responses to the idea of this sort of bodywork right to the edge of trauma, and to explicitly connect her technical objections with her panicked visceral response.

It is clear, I think, that the idea of working with embodied relation-ship in ways beyond verbal discussion takes many therapists—not only psychoanalysts—into the territory of retraumatisation and dissociation. The most common response to this is to rule the idea off-limits. But I suggest that an alternative might be to realise that avoiding this work—symbolised by but not restricted to touch (Cornell doesn't actually talk about touching patients in his paper)—limits our capacity to respond to and work with our clients' material: that just as the clients are limited by their body-related trauma, so are therapists whose response to the idea is an immediate "No". This might lead practitioners to consider doing some therapeutic work on their issues around embodiment, for the benefit of both their clients and themselves.

Touch and embodied relating

In ERT we are fully open to and accepting of touch, as one of the chan-nels in which amplifying can take place, but also as a basic human need and sometimes a crucial form of comfort (Totton, 2003a, pp. 117–124; 2006). We are also of course aware that touch can sometimes feel retrau-matising for clients with certain kinds of experience. But if we our-selves are comfortable touching and being touched, then we can keep a balanced perspective, and remember that trauma can be experienced in almost *any* aspect of therapy, and that when this happens—so long as the therapist is ordinarily conscientious—it is generally because the trauma needs to come into the room.

Kym Maclaren writes very well from a phenomenological standpoint about the relationship between "enlivening" and "transgressive" touch:

> The enlivening touch, let me propose, is one for which a space has been prepared both in the development of the person being touched and in the history of relations between the toucher and touched. The touch felt as transgressive is one for which no such space has been prepared. Sexual abuse of a child involves a touch that calls for a bodily intentionality that the child cannot yet inhabit. An autistic child may likewise resist a hug because it solicits a form of bodily intentionality that the autistic child cannot comfortably shadow. The transgression of the sexually harassing touch solicits a coexistence that is unwarranted by the history of those two people.
>
> (2013, p. 7)

The process of preparation, as Cornell mentions, is as important as, and can take much longer, than the bodywork itself. And there are clients with whom I never do this sort of work; but if I ruled it out in advance, if I didn't hold it as a possibility, then I think a great deal would be lost (Totton, 2006, p. 161).

Conclusion

In discussing touch and normalising it as a part of therapy, I am conscious that I may be inviting many readers out of their comfort zones. As I have emphasised, though, there is no need to touch or be touched by clients in order to work with embodied relationship: it is entirely possible to do so "invisibly", with client and therapist continuing to stay in their respective chairs and to privilege verbal communication (it is of course impossible to eliminate non-verbal communication, though it can be bracketed out of awareness).

The more that a practitioner works with her embodied response, however, the harder I suspect it will be for her to avoid questioning the orthodox boundaries around bodies. This is because those boundaries have a large element of trauma to them: not so much the *clients'* trauma as that held by the *therapists* (often transmitting societal trauma), who have therefore been led to work in disembodied styles. The practice of tracking one's embodiment acts as a gentle form of self-therapy, so that phobic, anxiety-driven responses to the body are likely to be seen for what they are, challenging us to face them directly. So this is your health warning: you can work with embodied relationship without directly changing your normal practice, but—like the first toke that is supposed to put one on the slippery path to addiction—it may eventually lead you further than you expect or intend.

All of us, clients and therapists alike, have a right to choose where we want to go: what aspects of ourselves and of reality we want to explore, and what we want to leave well alone. As therapists, however, we also have a responsibility to work within our competence—that is, to know where, and how, we are able to accompany clients. One of the glorious side benefits of being a therapist is that we are constantly required to stretch ourselves, in order to meet our clients where they need to be: we have to exercise parts of ourselves that are sometimes deeply unfamiliar and awkward-feeling. And some clients, we have to accept, we are unable to accompany, because we can't or don't want to occupy the part of ourselves which would meet them.

There is, therefore, always a trade-off going on, between our courage to stretch ourselves and our courage to recognise our limitations (I am putting this in the most positive terms possible). Some of my most treasured memories of being a therapist are of moments when I felt deeply challenged in the room to come up with something that felt—almost—beyond my capacity, but which was vital for the work with a particular client. Some of my worst memories are of moments when, in retrospect, I failed the client by not rising to, not recognising, the challenge of the moment.

I say all this as context for what I want to say about working with embodied relationship. My whole argument in this book is that embodied relating is a crucial part of our work, of our lives, whether we know it or not—and, as Kamalamani reminds me (personal communication), whether we like it or not: that it is, in fact, the ground of psychotherapy. Therefore it is not an option to refuse to work with it. Our only option in that direction is to refuse to *admit* that we are working with it. Put like that, it surely doesn't sound very attractive; and that, I am claiming, is the realistic way to put it.

There are many clients who will happily join with us in our denial: clients whose chronic and acute trauma has forced them to deny their own embodiment. Verbally oriented forms of therapy can be useful to them in many ways—but can only, as it seems to me, shore up their disembodiment, their dissociation from corporeality: because these forms of therapy, despite their enormous strengths, *are themselves expressions of the same dissociation*. I think this is what Sue Shapiro is generously owning up to in the paper from which I quoted earlier in this chapter: she demonstrates her own phobic response to some aspects of embodiment, and then suggests that because many clients may feel the same way, concretely embodied work should be avoided. But is this an adequate response? Are we not obligated to try to find a safe way to work with what our clients are afraid of? The feebleness of Shapiro's attempts to meet this obligation are pretty obvious.

Bill Cornell's challenge to verbal psychotherapy feels much closer to my own position. As he suggests, psychoanalysis in particular has always been founded on embodiment, and paradoxically has always and with equal force shied away from it: I wrote a whole book (Totton, 1998) to explore this. Analysts who (re)discovered embodiment have been forced into marginal, untenable positions. Humanistic work has generally been far more body-friendly, but has had a strong tendency to underplay the difficulties and tensions it raises; and because it often doesn't work very deeply with relationship in general, by the same token it often doesn't work deeply with embodied relationship.

All of this is starting to change, however; and with this book I am aiming to support the change which is already happening—by bringing in what body psychotherapy has been exploring for the past eighty-plus years, but also by trying to help both body therapists and verbal therapists look more deeply, sense more deeply, into the foundations of our work, and draw on more of the resources that already exist to help us understand embodied relating.

CHAPTER TWELVE

Embodied connectedness

All bodies are in a state of continual flux like rivers, and the parts
are continually entering in and passing out.

—*Von Leibniz*, Monadology, *1980*

In this chapter I want to free myself a little from the constraints of
trying to convey information, and let my imagination flow. I am
going to explore some wider (wilder?) and more speculative ideas
about embodied relating, human history, birth, growing up, origins and
futures, telepathy, ecosystemic thinking, and the connectedness of all
things.

Embodied relating happens, of course, not only in the therapy room,
and not even only between human beings. There is a constant interplay
between our relationship with other people, our relationship with our
own bodymind experience, and our relationship with the world itself
and all the other-than-human and more-than-human entities which
exist there. Diminished contact with our own embodiment accompanies
and is accompanied by diminished delight in and love for the world we
inhabit, and diminished empathy for the suffering of other beings.

Conversely, being in and relating to the other-than-human world sustains in us the sort of embodied relaxation which I have been referring to throughout the book, which allows us to experience the arbitrariness of social demands:

> The natural things around me have no egos, no sense of themselves as socially defined selves. Therefore, they do not engage the part of my mind that is concerned with social norms, expectations, goals, and projects. In the midst of egoless nature, I am able to rest from the ongoing effort and tension of being an ego among other egos in the human, social world.
>
> (Schroeder, 2008, p. 65)

As an embodied-relational therapist, my endeavour in the therapy room and in life generally is for a free relationality in all three dimensions: contact with my body awareness (visceral, proprioceptive, and kinesthetic) and with my embodied emotions; contact with my environment and how it impacts on my bodily and mental experience and well-being; and contact with other people, using all the specialised sensitivities with which we have evolved and with which this book has been largely concerned.

Reich's case histories give marvellous descriptions of how these three dimensions cooperate to form a solid whole. More than once, he describes a client discovering through body psychotherapy a profound relationship with the cosmos:

> In the process of working through this connection, his personality underwent a conspicuous change. His superficiality disappeared; he became serious. The seriousness appeared very suddenly during one of the sessions. The patient said literally: "I don't understand; everything has become so deadly serious all of a sudden."
>
> (1942, p. 321)

As his body continues to surrender more deeply to energy flow, this patient recovers a memory from about the age of two:

> He was alone with his mother at a summer resort. It was a clear starry night. His mother was asleep and breathing deeply; outside

he could hear the steady pounding of the waves on the beach. The mood he had felt then was the same deeply serious, somewhat sad and melancholy mood which he experienced now.

(pp. 324–325)

In Embodied-Relational Therapy (ERT) we speak of "wild mind", and of the wild therapy which follows from recognising it (Totton, 2011): we can flexibly listen to and learn from body sensations, dreams, intuition, free association, the activity of clouds, birds and animals, alongside our powers of thinking and reasoning. To live in wild mind is to acknowledge the rich intelligence of the non-rational parts of myself and of the world around me. Surrendering to and trusting these messy, seemingly chaotic kinds of knowing brings a profound experience of support, and of release from having to hold it all together and have all the answers.

Being able to surrender and trust depends at least partially on our capacity for what is often called "secure attachment". I am thinking, though, of a very different kind of secure attachment from that available in contemporary Western society: one which is not a function of the isolated mother–child dyad, but is held within and inseparable from the wider social bond. To explain what I mean I am going to take a detour through hunter gatherer societies (summarising fuller discussions in Totton, 2011).

Embodied socialisation

Given a stable environmental context, hunter-gatherer cultures—the sorts of cultures which humans all lived in for many thousands of years—generally treat the world as "a benign spiritual home ... a giving environment" (Barker, 2006, p. 58). They relate to the world on the same basis of sharing that operates in their human community; frequently they don't distinguish in language between humans, animals, and plants as separate categories (pp. 58–59). The Native American ecopsychologist Jeanette Armstrong writes:

We survive within our skin inside the rest of our vast selves. ... Okanagans teach that our flesh, blood and bones are Earth-body; in all cycles in which the earth moves, so does our body. ... Our word for body literally means "the land-dreaming capacity".

(1995, pp. 320–321)

Forager culture includes the other-than-human within the same system of knowledge and relationship as the human, and models both these communities as essentially generous, essentially sharing. It can do this because it is not trying to *own* the world, but only to live within it, to pass through it. Humans belong to the land, not the land to humans. Hence they are both allowed and required to understand what happens where they live, and to find modes of encouragement and gratitude that lead the world to satisfy their needs.

Integral to this, probably a necessary condition for it, is that our embodied existence is fully accepted and integrated into culture. The anthropologist Richard Sorenson, who has written widely about "pre-conquest" cultures (i.e., those uninvaded by Western civilisation), describes their way of life as emerging "from a sensually empathetic tactile infant nurture common to its era but shunned in ours", which leads to:

> ... a coalescing of human affect in growing children ... this affect coalescence heightens spectacularly during adolescence to produce an expansive hypersensual rapport both with people and with nature ... preconquest people are, as a result, largely free of nega- tive emotions ... they are acutely vulnerable to negative emotions when in contact with them.

> (1997, p. 1)

Sorenson writes vividly and shockingly about the effective collapse of pre-conquest societies experiencing prolonged contact with Westerners (1998, pp. 97ff). Our attitudes and embodiment styles seem to resemble a contagious disease that almost instantly compromises the pre-conquest way of being-in-the-world. The undefended openness which is the greatest asset of such cultures becomes their greatest liability when they are confronted with people who do not share it. Just as the physical dis- eases brought by Westerners decimated populations with no acquired resistance (Totton, 2011, p. 67), pre-conquest cultures have no resistance to the psychological attitudes of their invaders, whether these are colo- nists armed with guns or, more recently, tourists armed with cameras.

The Neolithic shift in attachment

This leads me to revisit the question raised in Chapter Four: how are the attitudes of Western culture developed? Placing them in the context of other forms of human society, cultures which have not dissociated from their embodiment or their connection with the world, the question becomes more urgent and perhaps more puzzling. It's abundantly clear that a culture based on dominance as a central principle will readily come to dominate other humans, and other species. But how might the focus on dominance come about in the first place? Westerners have long tended to assume that such attitudes are self-evident, "natural" for human beings. But the evidence suggests a rather different story: it seems that the great majority of human cultures do *not* take this route, but are largely eradicated by the small number of mutated cultures which do, and which therefore spread, conquer, and multiply so enormously.

For foragers to survive, they must cooperate and share. For children to survive and reach adulthood, they must be constantly supported by grown-ups. Infants in forager cultures are held and carried at all times—not only by mothers, but by relatives and allies of many kinds (Hrdy, 2009, pp. 73–82; Sorenson, 1998, pp. 83–84). To grow up in this way—cherished and nurtured in an embodied way by all around you— is to directly experience the world as "a giving environment"; and this upbringing facilitates the development of an ecological self, an embodied wild mind.

Sarah Blaffer Hrdy (2009) highlights how the shift to sedentary agricultural society which marked the Neolithic era degraded childrearing. She identifies two aspects of forager society which, while not exactly fortunate in themselves, do lead to good nurturing. In most forager cultures, the relative shortage of high-grade nutrition means that the average age of menstruation is sixteen: mothers tend to be older, hence on average more capable. The same shortage of high-grade protein also means that mothers need to devote considerable time to their own survival needs, making it impossible for them to care for children by themselves: successful childrearing is *necessarily* a collective enterprise, involving at the very least grandmothers, and often a much wider range of group members. The harsh fact is that in this environment, poorly-parented children don't grow up at all.

By contrast, in agricultural society, because of a relative abundance of high-grade protein the age of puberty steeply declines, and also more infants survive, making the job of young mothers even more difficult. At the same time, though, the shift to patrilocal and patriarchal structures also means that younger mothers are living in their husbands' household and hence have less support from their own mothers and other kinswomen—as well as increasingly removing fathers from the "women's work" of childcare (Hrdy, 2009, pp. 287–288).

These factors, combined with the rise of competitive, dominance-based structures, set up a context for insecure and disorganised attachment, leading to potentially even worse childrearing in the next generation.

> Child survival became increasingly decoupled from the need to be in constant physical contact with another person, or surrounded by responsive, protective caretakers in order to pull through. ... Increasingly over the ensuing centuries, even young women still psychologically immature and woefully lacking in sympathy or social support could nevertheless be well-fed enough to ovulate and conceive while still in their early teens.
>
> (Hrdy, 2009, pp. 286–287)

Both infant attachment and the social bond were transformed by the social and economic changes that took place with the development of agriculture. The newly degraded status of women, together with the increased likelihood of survival for poorly reared children, gave rise to insecure and disorganised attachment patterns which must have been previously rare or unknown—as I have said, in Palaeolithic forager bands any infant who survived would necessarily be securely attached (Hrdy, 2009, p. 290). This in turn gave rise to disturbed and incompetent young mothers, and equally disturbed and dangerous young males, whose aggression and need for dependency were harnessed by the newly arising state—as has continued to happen in every army up to the present.

These social changes would make the world a much more dangerous place, full of insecure and traumatised people. Hunter-gatherer cultures were probably, as they are now, egalitarian and "flat" in their structure, based on sharing and cooperation. But the new kinds of people created by agrarianism would lack the capacity to cooperate freely. "Vertical", hierarchical social structures arose, offering protection in return for sub-mission: for many, in the circumstances, an irresistible bargain.

> How were healthy hunter-gatherers convinced to live in villages and cities where their health was measurably lower? The answer is that they were safer.
>
> (Steckel & Wallis, 2007, p. 31)

I believe it is fair to say that many of the problems we deal with every day in therapy have their origins in this Neolithic bargain. The social bond, partly influenced by these new attachment patterns, shifted from a free partnership of equals to a patriarchal hierarchy underwritten by theism, a state of affairs emotionally damaging to every man, woman, and child. These changes are the psychological equivalent of an asteroid strike; their effects are permanent, passed on to each new generation as chronic trauma (see Chapter Ten)—and also passed on dramatically as acute trauma to "pre-conquest" cultures, grounded in secure attachment, when they come into contact with societies like ours.

What would a therapist from a pre-conquest forager culture, if we can imagine such a person, make of us and our problems? Well, we know that shamans, the nearest equivalent figures, are not too impressed. Much of what we encounter in the therapy room is chronic or acute trauma created by the childrearing environment of the patriarchal nuclear family—an environment which therapy tends to treat as natural and innate. The sort of "secure attachment" which is the optimum outcome of such child rearing can arguably be seen as an obsessive and fragile dependence on a single, almost always female, carer; and the sort of "autonomous" adult ego which develops from this experience can be seen as one suited to and, with luck, equipped to survive in a society based on relationships of dominance and competition.

Moving from attachment to social bonding

The Polyvagal Theory developed by Stephen Porges (2011), which I introduced in Chapter Eight, is one piece of neuroscience which I feel does actively illuminate body psychotherapy. It is a recent theory which may or may not stand up scientifically over time, but as *imagery* I think it has enormous force and conviction and fits totally with the experience of body psychotherapy. It's a new interpretation of the autonomic nervous system (ANS), the aspect of our nervous system which operates involuntarily and outside our consciousness to control and balance our visceral organs, including heart, kidneys, digestion, etc. Porges's work focuses on one part of the parasympathetic side of the ANS. Very simply put, the function of the parasympathetic is basically to calm and smooth out and relax, whereas the sympathetic side is about activating and waking up (it's more complicated than that, but this picture is certainly not wrong, just simple).

Porges looks at one branch of a cranial nerve called the vagal nerve, a major part of the parasympathetic system. The branch on which he focuses works to calm and relax the heart (the other branch functions similarly with the guts). He shows that, although the vagal system is primarily about calming things down, this branch of it can actually be used as a flexible and controllable way to rapidly stimulate the heart and the metabolism in general, by lowering its effect: if the vagal nerve is *less* activated, the heart will be *more* active. This offers a much more flexible and less earth-shaking alternative to the sympathetic system's adrenalin-based way of activating the metabolism. The vagal system uses a process which can be easily ramped up and down without flooding us with adrenalin and leaving us exhausted.

So the vagal nerve offers a way of energising ourselves to act in the world without entering into survival mode, fight-flight-freeze ways of responding to events. In other words, it is a precise tool for social interaction. Instead of an on-off switch, it is continuously adjustable, like a tap: we can have precisely the level of activation appropriate to the situation, and alter this as the situation changes. Under normal circumstances, the sympathetic will only get activated if this vagal system is not working properly—like using a sledgehammer to crack a nut because the nutcrackers are broken.

As I explained in Chapter Eight, the social engagement system which Porges describes is a complex interactive network of cranial nerves and functional systems which enables us to interact socially in subtle, sensitive, and complex ways, while keeping our state of arousal calm through using the vagus nerve to lower our heart rate. And what is particularly pleasing for me as a body psychotherapist is that the whole system is focused on the *heart*, and on the ability of good, nourishing relating to calm and soften its activity. The theory, in other words, offers neuroscientific backing for the experience of *heart to heart contact*.

It also fleshes out and makes concrete the body psychotherapy concept of *facing* (Boadella, 1987), one of a triad which also includes *grounding* and *centring*. The prominent body psychotherapist David Boadella writes:

> Facing is concerned with recognition, with how we see people, with the qualities of lumination that develop when people really

face each other. Clear seeing between people ... encourages deeper being.

(1987, 113)

Boadella goes on immediately to discuss *sounding*, the role of speech and voice.

The social engagement system, then, is where many of our embodied-relational engrams are created and stored. Porges's theory is only one of several ways in which current neuroscience says that we are born ready to rock, socially speaking: that our social, relational energy is *bodily* energy—after all, what else could it be?—and that this energy needs to be plugged into a live relationship in order to develop. If this doesn't happen successfully—either for internal reasons, or because our carers fail to meet us in the dance of social engagement—then the body falls back on cruder, earlier, less subtly adjustable systems of activation. These are based either on the sympathetic nervous system's binary, fight-flight approach, flooding itself with adrenalin, or on the parasympathetic strategies of immobility and dissociation. An extreme response to things going wrong with the social engagement system, Porges suggests, is autism; less extreme responses might be shyness, boringness, shame, or aggression. And there will also be specific situational responses to specific stimuli—what I am calling relational engrams.

An important aspect of the social engagement system theory, though, is its focus on the biological conditions which allow and support human social bonding. As Porges says, drawing on the work of his partner Sue Carter (e.g., 2005):

> Social behaviors associated with nursing, reproduction, and the formation of strong pair bonds require a unique biobehavioral state characterized by immobilization without fear, and immobilization without fear is mediated by a co-opting of the neural circuit regulating defensive freezing behaviors through the involvement of oxytocin.

(Porges, 2005, p. 33)

Porges is discussing another process of "exaptation", like the one I mentioned in Chapter Eight. Here a parasympathetic system for defensive freezing has been developed into a way to relax and stay in contact even under strong stimulus—something of obvious relevance to psychotherapy. One of the things which attracts me about the social engagement system theory is that it represents a move from attachment theory, with its focus on mother–infant relationships, to a theory of *social bonding*, adult-adult relationship, which builds on infant attachment but transforms it by exaptation into a peer interaction.

Traditionally, psychotherapy has focused on the attachment dyad and the autonomous individual ego as the two sides of the therapy coin. I believe that it is time for us to consider other modes of subjectivity and relationality, especially modes which emphasise the collective and transpersonal. It will always be a crucial part of our job to elicit and explore infant relational engrams which impact on clients' capacity for here and now relating. But perhaps we need to move back a little towards Freud's original view of transference as an *obstacle* to therapy rather than its primary *modus operandi* (cf. Bollas, 2007).

Certainly I would like us to stop treating the therapeutic relationship as inherently one between child and parent, and to stop seeing this as the agent of cure rather than as what needs to be cured. Rather than "reparenting", I would like us to think more in terms of *de*parenting: progressing to a point where both client and therapist can recognise that there are no parents and no babies in the room. I know that I am being one-sided in this emphasis: my intention is to rebalance what is currently a highly unbalanced approach.

Connections and disconnections

We have been led round again from the general to the specific, the social to the personal; and I want now to take up another theme which I touched upon in Chapter Two, the "uncanny" connections between us which are often referred to as the "paranormal". As I pointed out in Chapter Two, there are many everyday aspects of therapy which we generally treat as normal, but which on examination fall far outside what is generally accepted as the boundary of normality. I want to explore this a bit further now, and to look at what leads most people to repress or to dissociate from what I believe to be a universal form of connection. What I am going to say links very directly with my discussion earlier in this chapter of the psychological openness that characterises pre-conquest societies, and its contrast with the closedness of most or all Westernised individuals.

Our bodies are not isolated one from another, or from the material and energetic world which gives birth to them. Information, in every sense, is the substance of our being; and information flows constantly through the world's networks, like the water that dowsers find beneath the ground. But much of this information, as psychotherapy knows very well, is intolerable to post-conquest individuals. "Intolerable information" is a possible definition of the repressed unconscious; and the "paranormal" is one form of almost intolerable information—intolerable because it informs us of the intimate presence of the other, which is understood as the equivalent of death by a self founded on separateness. To be transparent to the Other is to die as an ego: to die of shame.

Hence the fact, observed by Freud, that paranormal experiences in psychotherapy tend strongly to be associated with Oedipal issues and, in particular, with death. A part of the Oedipal transition, I suggest, is that we develop the need to protect ourselves from being open and visible to others, from having our "improper" feelings and impulses—jealous and murderous ones in particular—perceived and, as we expect, punished. To survive an Oedipal sense of guilt, we blind ourselves, psychically speaking: suppress most of the remnants of paranormal sensitivity which have survived thus far, since we cannot "see" without being "seen", just as we cannot touch without being touched. It is no coincidence at all that the strongest concentration of paranormal events in Western societies is around people described as "psychotic" or "borderline": survivors of Oedipal catastrophe. And no coincidence either that paranormal communication in therapy (e.g., Eisenbud, 1946, discussed in Totton, 2007; cf. Totton, 2003b) very often concerns issues of jealousy, competition, and Oedipal desire.

Like much of this chapter, this is speculative; but let me speculate a little further. Perhaps the Oedipal life-and-death struggle reproduces an earlier one, the struggle to be born. Imagine that we come into the world unshielded, open to the incomprehensible thoughts and feelings of the adults around us—the intaglio imprint of "enigmatic signifiers" (Laplanche, 1976) which we can neither process nor ignore. Unless we are made welcome to a quite exceptional degree, wrapped in calm and quiet until we can gradually be exposed to the world, our situation would be unbearable. The only way out would be through a fundamental dissociation or primal repression, separating in a single act not only our self from our self, but also self from other self, conscious from unconscious, and "mind" from "body".

This cutting of connection, synchronous with the cutting of the umbilical cord, also performs a primal cut upon our experience of self. In the extraordinary, free-associative words of Bion, spoken in a group supervision setting:

> Melanie Klein said—and I think it is borne out—at the very experience of birth itself, the full-term foetus feels castrated, mutilated, as if the mother's genitalia cut something off. Severed the umbilical cord? Severed the long-distance sense of smell? One would have to be this patient's analyst to guess, conjecture what the telephonic system is that has been cut off; what the messages are that she can't get.
>
> (2000, p. 180)

What are the messages that we can't get?—we, the clients, we, the therapists, we, the human beings. As with communities of plants and animals, we exist as points of concentrated meaning in a network; we swim in a swarm or soup of continuous, multidirectional communication, through which we both achieve and surrender our separate identities. For plants, the messages are primarily biochemical, transmitted partly through the air, but mainly through the subterranean web of mycelium which links plant communities (Buhner, 2002).

Our own subterranean web, the dream mycelium which Freud describes, is in one aspect largely composed of language; but in another aspect it is made up of embodiment. The messages we can't get are the messages that run between dreaming bodies. The castration of birth and the umbilectomy of the Oedipus complex are experiences of disconnection between dreaming bodies. What I have been calling the paranormal offers a reconnection with the community of being, which is both yearned for and resisted.

I suggest that the paranormal is aligned with what Lacan calls the Real. And the Real is bodily. The paranormal, the uncanny, the unrepresentable, the real—all relate to and derive from embodiment; all of them describe our confused perception of what Reich speaks of as:

> ... primary biophysical sensations, plasmatic streamings ... experiences which are almost completely blocked off in the so-called normal human being.
>
> (1945a, pp. 390–400)

In speaking of our confused perception, though, I am not meaning to imply that paranormal experiences are in any sense illusory or mistaken—although they quite plainly are influenced and distorted by passage through our own unconscious fantasies and desires, as many analytic writers have demonstrated.

To stay with Lacanian terminology for a moment: usually, in therapy and in everyday life, telepathy is not allowed to be either Real or real, but is forcibly aligned with the Symbolic or the Imaginary: in other words, it becomes either a transmission of meaning or a mirroring of selfhood (Totton, 2003b). The most fundamental distinction between telepathy and thought-reading is that the latter has an arrow of direction attached to it: one reads the thought of the other. That is the telepathy of the Symbolic. In the telepathy of the Imaginary, by contrast, both subjects enter into a trance of mutual reflection, which reinforces the self-possession of each. In true telepathy, there is no such direction, no such possession: both subjects are transparent to each other, under an open, intersubjective sky. A telepathy of the third, transitional space: of the Real.

Part of the project of psychotherapy is to help us tolerate the existence of the unconscious—not just as a theoretical entity, but as co-inhabiter, co-owner, of our bodies, our minds, our decisions and self-presentations. Body psychotherapy extends this project, aiming to establish the resources to endure our connectedness, through the bodily unconscious, with the rest of existence, including other people; to endure the reality that our experience is not under our control, and that exclusive ownership of our "selves" is not possible. We can then allow ourselves to be an *emergent* ego, a majority decision, a mutable and provisional summation of mind-body experience, rather than an *emergency* ego identified with muscular rigidity that resists experience in the interests of survival. I have tried to suggest how attention to the "paranormal" aspects of our work, and their entwinement with embodied relating, can help us in this project.

Embodied energy

It's very common for therapists in some traditions to talk about "the energy in the room", or "sensing the client's energy". If challenged, many would probably say that this is just a weak metaphor, a way of describing empathic resonance (whatever that may be). Many others would say: "No, there is an actual energy, or at any rate something that I can only experience as an energy." One stream of discourse which feeds into this is from body psychotherapy (Totton, 2003a, pp. 63–64), where Reich (e.g., 1942) spoke directly of "orgone energy" and its qualities of expansion, contraction and so on—and this, of course, was a development and concretisation of Freud's original theory of libidinal energy.

Someone influenced by Daniel Stern (1985, pp. 53–60), on the other hand, might suggest that all of this is a way of talking about "vitality affect". Vitality affects are a category of expressive qualities intended to be placed alongside the traditional affects like fear, rage, grief, joy, and so on. They are what Stern calls "amodal representations", patterns which can appear in any sensory or expressive channel and which are captured by dynamic, kinetic terms such as "surging", "fading away", "fleeting", "explosive", "crescendo", "bursting", and "drawn out". Many people have encountered examples of vitality affects in 5 Rhythms dance: "staccato", "lyrical", and so on. Stern argues that this sort of quality is primary in the infant's organisation of experience; it also clearly features in our adult perception and experience, and I think is often conceptualised by us as different kinds of "energy" we perceive in ourselves, in other people, and in relationships. Reich was clearly very sensitive to vitality affect, and this can be seen constantly in his writings.

So "energy" in psychotherapy is a complex word, in William Empson's (1951) sense: a nexus, a meeting point of several traditions and discourses in one term. One could probably write a book about it! But in doing so, it would be important to include the fact that a number of people, including some therapists, have a direct perceptual experience of seeing energy in, around, and between people, which for them is no less definite and actual than seeing the expression on someone's face or the colour of their eyes (Cameron, 2002). Often this perception is in fact visual, as I have implied; sometimes it flows through other sensory channels. One rough analogy would be an electromagnetic field around a dynamo, with the human being playing the role of the dynamo (Oschman, 2000).

What I want to avoid here is erecting a fence at any point along the spectrum from weak metaphor to strong metaphor to imagination to direct perception, and saying that on one side of this resides the normal and on the other side—the weird stuff, the mystical, the paranormal. The whole thrust of this book is that such a line can never be drawn, such a barrier can never be raised. As Susan Kozel suggests, there are many situations where embodied relating *feels like* a transmission of energy with profound effects:

> When a dance teacher or a choreographer ... conveys a movement or a movement quality by demonstrating with various degrees of proximity, or by actually laying hands on, she is patterning your physical and electromagnetic flow. When a yoga or Pilates teacher achieves a shift in your movement, simply by standing near to you and focusing on breathing—sometimes they don't even have to touch you, they'll just stand and breathe in a concentrated way next to you—you can feel your whole body realign, you can feel the texture of your muscles and your movement quality shift, that's a repatterning. When somatic techniques involving visualisation and shifts in channels of awareness are effective, a similar repatterning happens.

> (2004, n.p.)

I suggest that these sorts of experience should be treated seriously, while recognising that the whole spectrum must be taken into account and cannot be arbitrarily cut at any point.

In other writing I have used the example of dowsing (Bird, 1980): a piece of "paranormality" robust enough to be used by many engineering firms and other businesses concerned with underground pipes and cables. It is not really that hard to come up with a plausible normal-science explanation of how dowsing for underground water might work. It is known that a flow of water in the earth sets up an electromagnetic field and that although a dowser experiences the twig or rods or pendulum moving in her hands of their own accord, her hands are themselves moving, involuntarily and unconsciously. We can easily conceive in general terms of some mechanism by which the body picks up the electromagnetic field from the underground stream and reacts with a subliminal movement, an involuntary muscular contraction. A lot of theoretical and experimental work has actually been done on mechanisms whereby the human body might respond to fields of this kind, or to equivalent ones around other bodies, or around standing stones, for example (Graves, 2008).

No major problem so far; but then we discover (Bird, 1980) that the same dowser can also find water on *maps*, rather than in the (literal) field; that in fact she can find not only water, but any substance or object she is asked to, here or somewhere else on the planet, simply by altering her intention, through the same involuntary muscular contraction; or can discover what is happening in another person's body and what treatment is required (I am not claiming that this sort of information is always accurate!). Whatever simple line one might be trying to maintain between the normal and the paranormal has suddenly been crossed before our eyes: the body can not only know about what is beneath its feet, it can also know about what is happening elsewhere in the world or inside other bodies. It can know these things without knowing how it knows them.

This slide across lines is sometimes talked about in terms of the slogan "Energy follows thought, thought follows energy". Like all slogans, it oversimplifies, but it can help psychotherapists keep their bearings and remember the relevance of our ways of thinking about things. In the passage quoted above, for example, Kozel talks about various energy flows which are essentially one-way, *from* the practitioner (repatterning) *to* the client (repatterned). We need to think very carefully about this sort of model, and the power imbalance which it implies. Throughout this book I have been stressing the essential *reciprocity* of embodied relating.

Body psychotherapists reading this will probably have become alert at the mention above of "involuntary muscular contractions". These contractions are very important to our way of understanding: they constitute one of the strongest ways in which the unconscious affects consciousness. One involuntary contraction in particular, the orgasm, functions as the doorway to the unconscious of the body—it is most people's primary experience of relaxation and temporary dissolution other than actually losing consciousness. Beyond that is the whole world of what has been labelled "ideomotor action" (Spitz, 1997): a third category of nonconscious behaviour, alongside "excitomotor" activity (breathing and swallowing) and "sensorimotor" activity (startle reactions). Ideomotor actions can be complex and meaningful, but are always outside volition; they are also generally outside our conscious perception, in ourselves or in others. The dowser's response to water is an excellent example of an ideomotor action; and ideomotor activity is a good candidate for one of the "unfamiliar channels" of which Freud spoke (see Chapter Four), through which paranormal communication takes place.

No one is in control

Man [sic] can do what he wills but he cannot will what he wills.

(Schopenhauer, as summarised by Einstein, 1932, p. 201)

Both these entwined experiences, paranormality and embodiment, threaten our habitual dependence on a sense of being in control. Against all the evidence, we believe ourselves to be masters of our fate, conquering reality under the mystic banner of free will. But free will is one of the most incoherent of concepts: as Schopenhauer makes clear in the above quotation, the *sources* of my will are wholly beyond my control. If we interrogate free will too far, it becomes indistinguishable from randomness.

But is there really any need for us—in any sense of "us"—to be in control? If we can yield to the uncontrollability of life, the experience may be one of relief rather than panic: we discover that everything manages very well without our hands on the wheel. Our heart continues to beat, our guts to digest, our diaphragm and lungs to breathe, our brain to think ... The only thing missing from the picture is the frame. This opens the way for a deeper sort of "free will"—which I think is sometimes what people are referring to when they use the phrase: a sense of deep consent to and identification with what happens of its own accord. "Thy will be done".

I am restating more directly here what I implied in Chapter Eight: that coming into closer relationship with our own embodiment and that of others, and with the Flesh of the world, gives us the opportunity to distinguish between social rules and experienced reality. This introduces us to a profound relaxation and freedom from internalised demands, a little taste of wild mind, which is one of the greatest gifts of psychotherapy—and, of course, of many other liberation practices.

Appreciating the radical uncontrollability of the body is one way into an ecosystemic perspective. Both body and ecosystem are open non-linear systems, which balance themselves without external control—"orchestras without a conductor", as Wolf Singer (2005) characterises the brain. Self-regulation is carried out by a range of feedback systems, all functioning through circular causality as I described in Chapter One. The world is a set of nested ecosystems, of interdependent interdependences.

The Flesh of the world

When I reached this point in my writing, I knew that I was nearing the end of the book, but had no idea where it needed to go next. Then, thinking about Merleau-Ponty and connectedness, I noticed that one way in which he describes the Flesh is a highly bodily one: he writes of it as a kind of *connective tissue*—the "connective tissue of exterior and interior horizons" (1968, p. 131). He situates this connective tissue between sense data and the things in the world: "the tissue that lines them, sustains them, nourishes them, and which for its part is not a thing, but a possibility, a latency, and a flesh of things" (pp. 132–133). Hence David Abram's gloss which I have already quoted:

> The Flesh is the mysterious tissue or matrix that underlies and gives rise to both the perceiver and the perceived as interdependent aspects of its own spontaneous activity. It is the reciprocal presence of the sentient in the sensible and of the sensible in the sentient.
>
> (1997, p. 66)

Connective tissue, or fascia, is a very specific kind of bodily flesh: it is a web-work, partly organic and partly inorganic, which runs continuously throughout our whole body, surrounding and containing each of our organs and muscles, in a series of nested bundlings which both separate and connect, binding our bodies into a shape. In Chapter Three I quoted Jeffrey Maitland's statement that "Everything that is alive is a relationship" (1995, p. 154). He goes on to say:

> Your body is a relationship in which all relationships are related; fascia is the tissue of that relationship. It is the tissue within which all relationships are relating.
>
> (p. 154)

As I mentioned in Chapter Eight, connective tissue is partly composed of a colloidal "ground substance" which can move rapidly between two different phase states, warm fluid *sol* or cold thick *gel* (Juhan, 2003, Chapter Three; Oschman, 2000, pp. 168–171; Schultz & Feitis, 1996, p. 31). Deane Juhan writes: "Connective tissue in its various forms can be regarded as a fluid crystal" (2003, p. 66); and this allows it to be "watery, elastic, wiry or solid, depending on local functions or stresses" (Juhan, 2003, p. 115). Its crystalline nature also opens up the speculation that quantum coherence occurs in connective tissue and cytoplasm, and may constitute "the basis of living organization" (Mae-Wan Ho, quoted by Juhan, 2003, p. 394).

Excited by the web of associations—which I am treating primarily as a fertile metaphor—I started exploring for more uses of this image, and found a conference paper by a dance artist and philosopher, Suzan Kozel, who treats connective tissue as "a living metaphor with physical, social and philosophical relevance to the consideration of networks" (2004, n.p.). She explains:

> In addition to keeping everything connected and in place, the fascia also creates separation within our bodies. It creates space for nerves, blood vessels, fluids, and the rest. … We tend to think of networks mainly as ways to stay connected, but in fact networks preserve ways for us to stay separate. They actually enhance the gaps as well as the connections.
>
> (2004, n.p.)

Kozel goes on:

> Fascia … is enduring but it is also adaptive. It has maintained its general structure and its purposes over the millennia. Its functions are evident in the earliest stages of multicellular organisms, in which two or more cells are able to stay in contact, communicate and resist the forces of the environment. … Fibres run in various directions, so that they appear interwoven, without one direction dominating. Fascia is not linear. It has been called, in therapeutic journals, a potential space and an interstitial space.
>
> (2004, n.p.)

How much Merleau-Ponty was consciously thinking about all this when he used the image of connective tissue, I don't know; but it is certainly present in the background of his metaphor. And Kozel, in an immediately following passage, refers to the same book of Merleau-Ponty's from which I have been quoting, *The Visible and the Invisible* (1968):

> Merleau-Ponty has discussed the visible and the invisible, celebrating the function of the invisible. … Fascia is not actually seen or visually captured by medical devices. It does not show up on

X-Rays, it does not show up on electromyograms or computerised tomographic scans. The way we encounter fascia is by touch.

(2004, n.p.)

I think this is a good image with which to end: an interstitial tissue, invisible to technology, which connects and separates everything in the network; which is non-linear and multidirectional; and which is best encountered through touch. To be in touch with our own body brings us into contact with the bodies of others, and with the body of the world, the Flesh within whose spaces we all find our place. Through bodywork it is possible to shift the literal connective tissue of the body from its frozen phase state to a fluid one. And on the level of metaphor, working with embodied relating can also bring the dyadic system of client and therapist to the edge of chaos where a similar shift from frozen to fluid can occur. Might this contribute to a potential phase shift in the wider, planetary connective tissue?

We have come all the way back round to something I wrote in the Introduction:

> Like soil, embodied relating is a *medium*: "the Flesh" (Merleau-Ponty, 1968) as it manifests in human relationship. It is the medium through which we assimilate both nurturing and trauma as infants; the medium through which our patterns of creativity and defence are reproduced in the therapy room; and the medium through which, potentially, change can be generated and stuck patterns released. Equally, it is the medium through which stuck patterns can be created and maintained.

The image of connective tissue—"the common tissue of which we are all made" which, I am pleased to discover, Merleau-Ponty also called "the wild Being" (1968, p. 206)—seems to me a close match for what I said in this passage. Hopefully, the book as a whole extends, deepens, and enriches this fundamental perception.

CONCLUSION

The tragedy of writing is that it never turns out to be as good as it seemed before one started; the consolation is that it usually turns out much better than it seemed when it was nearly finished. Both of these things have certainly been true about this book, so that I approach writing this end piece with a not unpleasant mixture of wistfulness about what might have been, and satisfaction with what has actually emerged.

I started out with the primary intention of conveying one point: that everything in psychotherapy is founded on and grows out of embodied relating. I think I have managed to maintain this point of view throughout the book; but of course a lot of other themes have emerged out of that initial one—including several which were no part of my initial thinking, but which I am very grateful to have discovered in the process of writing: for example, the significance of play, and the connection between embodiment and complexity.

In my experience, this is how one knows that a book is going well: it comes alive, and seeks its own direction. Novelists often experience their characters saying and doing things that they weren't expecting, and I think something very similar happens in writing non-fiction—Robert Graves mentions somewhere that at a certain point in the process, every book one opens or conversation one has contributes exactly what is needed to take the next step.

I have certainly experienced this process while writing *Embodied Relating*—in particular, the cluster of meanings around connective tissue with which I ended the last chapter, and which almost made me want to start again and weave this metaphor into the whole structure of the book. Ultimately, though, it is there already: this omnipresent medium which can move readily between extreme strength and extreme delicacy, between hardness and softness, between connecting and separating, is in fact my subject, embodied relating.

One of Wilhelm Reich's ongoing concerns was what he called "mysticism", and how it can represent a dissociated version of embodied experience:

> Primary biophysical sensations, plasmatic streamings ... experiences which are almost completely blocked off in the so-called normal human being.
>
> (1945a, pp. 390–400)

He sees what he calls mysticism as representing the repressed traces of embodiment in armoured individuals:

> At the bottom of his nature, man [sic] still remains an animal creature. No matter how immobile his pelvis and back may be; no matter how rigid his neck and shoulders may be; or how tense his abdominal muscles may be; or how high he may hold his chest in pride and fear—at the innermost core of his sensations he feels that he is only a piece of living organized nature. But as he denies and suppresses every aspect of this nature, he cannot embrace it in a rational and living way. *Hence, he has to experience it in a mystical, other-worldly and supernatural way.*
>
> (1945b, p. 375; original italics)

One of my concerns in writing this book has been to find a middle way between what Reich opposes as "mechanism" and "mysticism": to establish a continuity between all the various ways in which we apprehend the other and the world, and to situate the "uncanny" as an aspect of our *response* rather than an aspect of the world itself. In this I have tried to follow the example of Maurice Merleau-Ponty, whose insights I have come to appreciate more and more.

My worry is that many body psychotherapists may find it difficult to see a lot of what I have written about as directly relevant to their practice. If so, I would respectfully suggest that they are mistaken. Once we accept that body psychotherapy is not simply a quasi-medical, "one-body" practice of straightening out twisted organisms, but that it necessarily requires and addresses embodied relating, then I think all the rest follows. Embodied relating doesn't just happen in the therapy room: like connective tissue, it runs through everything, connects and separates all of us and every aspect of life, very definitely including the social and the political. This means that our job is much more complex than we might like it to be; but no more so than Reich portrayed it in his original formulations. It is plain that Reich worked centrally with the embodied relationship, and that he saw it as embedded in a socio-political matrix. In a sense I have only been restating this in more contemporary language.

Having addressed body psychotherapists, I want to turn for a moment to the other side of the room, so to speak, and address practitioners whose work is—consciously—mainly with verbal interaction. I hope that this book has not stretched you beyond endurance. However, I do hope that it has stretched you a considerable distance! My endeavour has been to make clear *both* that you can work with embodied relationship without having to break your professional ties, *and* that making this shift will make a considerable difference to your understanding and your experience of what you are doing. I think this will be worthwhile.

I also think, though I may be mistaken, that this will be my final book directly about psychotherapy. It is the fifteenth that I have either written or edited; and that seems a reasonable contribution to the field. I think that with this book I have said most of what I know about therapy—of course I may learn more, and want to share it, but my intention now is to write books on other subjects, cultural, historical, and philosophical. Thanks to all the people I have interacted with over the years, and who have directly or indirectly contributed to my understanding and my writing.

St. Blazey, Cornwall
February 2015

REFERENCES

Abraham, K. (1921). Contributions to the theory of anal character. In: *Selected Papers on Psychoanalysis* (pp. 370–392). New York: Basic Books.

Abraham, K. (1924). The influence of oral erotism on character formation. In: *Selected Papers on Psychoanalysis* (pp. 393–406). New York: Basic Books.

Abram, D. (1997). *The Spell of the Sensuous*. New York: Vintage.

Adolphs, R., Baron-Cohen, S., & Tranel, D. (2002). Impaired recognition of social emotions following amygdala damage. *Journal of Cognitive Neuroscience, 14*(8): 1264–1274.

Allen-Collinson, J., & Owton, H. (2014). Intense embodiment: Senses of heat in women's running and boxing. *Body & Society*. Published online as doi:10.1177/1357034X14538849.

Armstrong, J. (1995). Keepers of the earth. In: T. Roszak, M. E. Gomes, & A. D. Kanner (Eds.), *Ecopsychology: Restoring the Earth, Healing the Mind* (pp. 316–324). San Francisco, CA: Sierra Club.

Aron, L. (1990). One person and two person psychologies and the method of psychoanalysis. *Psychoanalytic Psychology, 7*(4): 475–485.

Athanasiadou, C., & Halewood, A. (2011). A grounded theory exploration of therapists' experiences of somatic phenomena in the countertransference. *European Journal of Psychotherapy & Counselling, 13*(3): 247–262.

Aziz-Zadeh, L., Wilson, S. M., Rizzolatti, G., & Iacoboni, M. (2006). Congruent embodied representations for visually presented actions and linguistic phrases describing actions. *Current Biology, 16*: 1818–1823.

Baker, E. F. (1980). *Man in the Trap: The Causes of Blocked Sexual Energy*. New York: Collier.

Balint, M. (1950). Changing therapeutic aims and techniques in psychoanalysis. *International Journal of Psychoanalysis, 31*: 117–124.

Banda, J. (2014). Rapid home HIV testing: Risk and the moral imperatives of biological citizenship. *Body & Society*. Published online as doi:10.1177/1357034X14528391.

Barker, G. (2006). *The Agricultural Revolution in Prehistory: Why Did Foragers Become Farmers?* Oxford: Oxford University Press.

Bateson, G. (1955). A theory of play and fantasy. In: *Steps to an Ecology of Mind* (pp. 177–193). Chicago, IL: University of Chicago Press, 2000.

Bateson, G. (1971). The cybernetics of "self": A theory of alcoholism. In: *Steps to an Ecology of Mind* (pp. 309–337). Chicago, IL: University of Chicago Press, 2000.

Bateson, G. (1980). *Mind and Nature: A Necessary Unity*. London: Fontana.

Benthall, J., & Polhemus, T. (1975). *The Body as a Medium of Expression*. New York: Dutton.

Berman, M. (1990). *Coming to our Senses: Body and Spirit in the Hidden History of the West*. London: Unwin.

Bernstein, J. S. (2005). *Living in the Borderland: The Evolution of Consciousness and the Challenge of Healing Trauma*. London: Routledge.

Bichi, E. L. (2008). A case history: From traumatic repetition towards psychic representability. *International Journal of Psychoanalysis, 89*: 541–560.

Bion, W. R. (2000). *Clinical Seminars and Other Works*. London: Karnac.

Bird, R. (1980). *Divining*. London: MacDonald and Jane's.

Bloom, S. (2006). Societal trauma: Democracy in danger. In: N. Totton (Ed.), *The Politics of Psychotherapy: New Perspectives* (pp. 17–29). Maidenhead, UK: Open University Press.

Boadella, D. (1987). *Lifestreams: An Introduction to Biosynthesis*. London: Routledge & Kegan Paul.

Bollas, C. (1987). *The Shadow of the Object: Psychoanalysis of the Unthought Known*. London: Free Association.

Bollas, C. (1993). *Being a Character: Psychoanalysis and Self-Experience*. London: Routledge.

Bollas, C. (2007). *The Freudian Moment*. London: Karnac.

Bollas, C. (2008). *The Infinite Question*. London: Karnac.

Bondi, L. (2014). Understanding feelings: Engaging with unconscious communication and embodied knowledge. *Emotion, Space and Society, 10*: 44–54.

Booth, A., Trimble, T., & Egan, J. (2010). Body-centred counter-transference in a sample of Irish clinical psychologists. *Irish Psychologist, 36*(12): 284–289.

Borgogno, F. (2007). Ferenczi's clinical and theoretical conception of trauma: A brief introductory map. *American Journal of Psychoanalysis, 67*(2): 141–149.

Boston Change Process Study Group (2008). Forms of relational meaning: Issues in the relations between the implicit and reflective-verbal domains. *Psychoanalytic Dialogues, 18*: 125–148.

Bourdieu, P. (1977). *Outline of a Theory of Practice*. R. Nice (Trans.). Cambridge: Cambridge University Press.

Bourdieu, P. (1984). *Distinction: A Social Critique of the Judgement of Taste*. London: Routledge.

Bourdieu, P. (1990). *The Logic of Practice*. Cambridge: Polity Press.

Bowlby, J. (1988). *A Secure Base: Parent–Child Attachment and Healthy Human Development*. New York: Basic Books.

Bray, A., & Colebrook, C. (1998). The haunted flesh: Corporeal feminism and the politics of (dis)embodiment. *Signs, 24*: 35–67.

Breton, A. (1932). The communicating vessels (excerpts). In: F. Rosemont (Ed.), *Andre Breton: What Is Surrealism? Selected Writings*. London: Pluto Press.

Bromberg, P. (2011). *The Shadow of the Tsunami and the Growth of the Relational Mind*. London: Routledge.

Bruce, T. (2004). Play matters. In: L. Abbott & A. Langston (Eds.), *Birth to Three Matters* (pp. 130–139). Maidenhead, UK: Open University Press.

Bucci, W. (2005). The interplay of subsymbolic and symbolic processes in psychoanalytic treatment: Commentary on paper by Steven H. Knoblauch. *Psychoanalytic Dialogues, 15*(6): 855–873.

Budgeon, S. (2003). Identity as an embodied event. *Body and Society, 9*: 35–55.

Buhner, S. H. (2002). *The Lost Language of Plants: The Ecological Importance of Plant Medicines for Life on Earth*. White River Junction, VT: Chelsea Green Publishing.

Burghardt, G. M. (2005). *The Genesis of Animal Play: Testing the Limits*. Cambridge, MA: MIT Press.

Burkitt, I. (1999). *Bodies of Thought: Embodiment, Identity and Modernity*. London: Sage.

Burkitt, I. (2003). Psychology in the field of being: Merleau-Ponty, ontology and social constructionism. *Theory and Psychology, 13*: 319–338.

Burrows, A. M. (2008). The facial expression musculature in primates and its evolutionary significance. *Bioessays, 30*(3): 212–225.

Butler, J. (1989). Foucault and the paradox of bodily inscriptions. *Journal of Philosophy, 86*(11): 601–607.

Butler, J. (2006). *Gender Trouble: Feminism and the Subversion of Identity*. London: Routledge.

Caldwell, P. (2006). Speaking the other's language: Imitation as a gateway to relationship. *Infant and Child Development, 15*: 275–282.

Calhoun, C. (1993). Habitus, field, and capital: The question of historical specificity. In: C. Calhoun, E. LiPuma, & M. Postone (Eds.), *Bourdieu: Critical Perspectives* (pp. 61–88). Chicago, IL: University of Chicago Press.

Cameron, R. (2002). Subtle bodywork. In: T. Staunton (Ed.), *Body Psychotherapy* (pp. 148–171). London: Routledge.

Carroll, R. (2005). Neuroscience and "the law of the self": the autonomic nervous system updated, re-mapped and in relationship. In: N. Totton (Ed.), *New Dimensions in Body Psychotherapy* (pp. 13–29). Maidenhead, UK: Open University Press.

Carter, S. (2005). Biological perspectives on social attachment and bonding. In: C. S. Carter, L. Ahnert, K. E. Grossman, S. B. Hrdy, M. E. Lamb, S. W. Porges, & N. Sachser (Eds.), *Attachment and Bonding: A New Synthesis* (pp. 85–100). Cambridge, MA: MIT Press.

Cataldi, S. L., & Hamrick, W. S. (2007). *Merleau-Ponty and Environmental Philosophy: Dwelling on the Landscapes of Thought*. Albany, NY: SUNY Press.

Chemero, A. (2011). *Radical Embodied Cognitive Science*. Cambridge, MA: MIT Press.

Chiel, H. J., & Beer, R. D. (1997). The brain has a body: adaptive behavior emerges from interactions of nervous system, body and environment. *Trends in Neuroscience, 20*: 553–557.

Clark, A. (1998). *Being There: Putting Mind, Body, and World Together Again*. Cambridge, MA: MIT Press.

Clark, A., & Chalmers, D. (1998). The extended mind. *Analysis, 58*(1): 7–19.

Cornell, W. F. (2009a). Stranger to desire: Entering the erotic field. *Studies in Gender and Sexuality, 10*: 75–92.

Cornell, W. F. (2009b). Response to Shapiro's discussion. *Studies in Gender and Sexuality, 10*: 104–111.

Costall, A. (2000). James Gibson and the ecology of agency. *Communication and Cognition, 33*(1–2): 23–32.

Cox, R. (2007). The au pair body: Sex object, sister or student? *European Journal of Women's Studies, 14*: 281–296.

Cromby, J., & Nightingale, D. J. (1999). *Social Constructionist Psychology: A Critical Analysis of Theory and Practice*. Buckingham, UK: Open University Press.

Crossley, N. (1995). Merleau-Ponty, the elusive body and carnal sociology. *Body & Society, 1*: 43–63.

Csordas, T. J. (Ed.). (1994). *Embodiment and Experience: The Existential Ground of Culture and Self*. Cambridge: Cambridge University Press.

DeCasper, A. J., & Fifer, W. P. (1980). Of human bonding: newborns prefer their mothers' voices. *Science, 208*: 1174–1176.

DeCasper, A. J., & Spence, M. J. (1986). Prenatal maternal speech influences newborns' perception of speech sounds. *Infant Behavior and Development, 9*: 133–150.

Derrida, J. (1988). Telepathy. *Oxford Literary Review, 10*: 3–41.

Deutsch, F. (Ed.) (1959). *On the Mysterious Leap from the Mind to the Body.* New York: International Universities Press.

Dewey, J. (1925). Experience and nature. In: J. A. Boydston (Ed.), *John Dewey, The Later Works, 1925–1953, vol. 1: Experience and Nature.* Carbondale, IL: Southern Illinois University Press, 1981.

Dimen, M. (1998). Polyglot bodies: Thinking through the relational. In: L. Aron & F. S. Anderson (Eds.), *Relational Perspectives on the Body* (pp. 65–93). Hillsdale, NJ: The Analytic Press.

Dimen, M. (2004). At the crossroads: Feminism, psychoanalysis, politics. *Psychotherapy and Politics International, 2*(1): 32–49.

Dorak, T. (2002). Period living: Why do the menstrual cycles of women living together synchronise? *New Scientist, 2373*: 81.

Dosamantes-Beaudry, I. (1997). Revisioning dance/movement therapy. *American Journal of Dance Therapy, 19*(1): 16–23.

Douglas, M. (1973). *Natural Symbols.* New York: Vintage.

Duffell, N. (2000). *The Making of Them: The British Attitude to Children and the Boarding School System.* London: Lone Arrow Press.

Eagleton, T. (2013). Disappearing acts. *London Review of Books, 35*(23): 39–40.

Egan, J., & Carr, A. (2008). Body-centred countertransference in female trauma therapists. *Irish Association of Counselling and Psychotherapy Quarterly Journal, 8*: 24–27.

Ehrenwald, J. (1954). *New Dimensions of Deep Analysis; A Study of Telepathy in Interpersonal Relationships.* New York: Grune & Stratton.

Einstein, A. (1932). Conversation with James Murphy. In: M. Planck (Ed.), *Where is Science Going?* (pp. 201–221). London: Allen & Unwin.

Eisenbud, J. (1946). Telepathy and problems of psychoanalysis. *Psychoanalytic Quarterly, 15*: 32–87.

Eisman, J. (1985). Character typologies. In: R. Kurtz, *Hakomi Therapy* (pp. 19/1–19/14). Boulder, CO: Hakomi Institute.

Ekman, P. (2003). Darwin, deception, and facial expression. *Annals of the New York Academy of Sciences, 1000*(1): 205–221.

Empson, W. (1951). *The Structure of Complex Words.* London: Chatto & Windus.

Evans, M. (2002). Introduction. In: M. Evans & E. Lee (Eds.), *Real Bodies: A Sociological Introduction* (pp. 1–13). London: Palgrave.

Farnell, B. (1994). Ethno-graphics and the moving body. *Man, 29*: 929–974.

Farnell, B. (1995). *Do You See What I Mean: Plains Indian Sign Talk and the Embodiment of Action*. Austin, TX: University of Texas Press.

Ferenczi, S. (1988). *The Clinical Diary*. J. Dupont (Ed.). London: Harvard University Press.

Ferenczi, S. (1908). Psychoanalysis and education. In: J. Borossa (Ed.), *Ferenczi: Selected Writings* (pp. 25–30). London: Penguin, 1999.

Ferenczi, S. (1927). The problem of the termination of the analysis. In: J. Borossa (Ed.), *Ferenczi: Selected Writings* (pp. 245–254). London: Penguin, 1999.

Ferenczi, S. (1929a). The unwelcome child and his death drive. In: J. Borossa (Ed.), *Ferenczi: Selected Writings* (pp. 269–274). London: Penguin, 1999.

Ferenczi, S. (1929b). The principle of relaxation and neo-catharsis. In: J. Borossa (Ed.), *Ferenczi: Selected Writings* (pp. 275–292). London: Penguin, 1999.

Ferenczi, S. (1933). Confusion of tongues between adults and the child (the language of tenderness and of passion). In: J. Borossa (Ed.), *Ferenczi: Selected Writings* (pp. 293–303). London: Penguin, 1999.

Ferenczi, S., & Rank, O. (1925). *The Development of Psychoanalysis*. Chicago, IL: Institute for Psychoanalysis, 1986.

Field, N. (1989). Listening with the body: An exploration in the counter-transference. *British Journal of Psychotherapy, 5*(40): 512–522.

Fink, B. (1995). *The Lacanian Subject: Between Language and Jouissance*. Princeton, NJ: Princeton University Press.

Fodor, J. A. (1981). *Representations*. Cambridge, MA: MIT Press.

Fogassi, L., & Gallese, V. (2004). Action as a binding key to multisensory integration. In: G. Calvert, C. Spence, & B. E. Stein (Eds.), *Handbook of Multisensory Processes* (pp. 425–442). Cambridge, MA: MIT Press.

Fogel, A. (2009). *Body Sense: The Science and Practice of Embodied Self-Awareness*. New York: W. W. Norton.

Foucault, M. (1973). *The Birth of the Clinic*. London: Tavistock.

Foucault, M. (1976). *The History of Sexuality (Vol. I)*. New York: Vintage.

Foucault, M. (1977a). *Discipline and Punish: The Birth of the Prison*. London: Penguin.

Foucault, M. (1977b). *Language, Counter-Memory, Practice: Selected Essays and Interviews*. Oxford: Blackwell.

Foucault, M. (1984a). *The History of Sexuality (Vol. II)*. New York: Vintage.

Foucault, M. (1984b). *The History of Sexuality (Vol. III)*. New York: Vintage.

Foucault, M. (1997). The ethics of the concern of the self as a practice of freedom. In: P. Rabinow (Ed.), *Ethics* (pp. 281–301). London: Penguin.

Fournier, V. (2002). Fleshing out gender: Crafting gender identity on women's bodies. *Body and Society, 8*: 55–77.

Fraser, M., & Greco, M. (Eds.) (2005). *The Body: A Reader*. New York: Routledge.

Freud, S. (1905e). Fragment of an analysis of a case of hysteria. *S. E., 7*. London: Hogarth.

Freud, S. (1908b). Character and anal erotism. *S. E., 9*: 167–176. London: Hogarth.

Freud, S. (1908e). Creative writers and day-dreaming. *S. E., 9*: 143–153. London: Hogarth.

Freud, S. (1909a). Some general remarks on hysterical attacks. *S. E., 9*: 227–234. London: Hogarth.

Freud, S. (1912b). The dynamics of transference. *S. E., 12*: 97–108. London: Hogarth.

Freud, S. (1912e). Recommendations to physicians practising psycho-analysis. *S. E., 12*: 109–120. London: Hogarth.

Freud, S. (1919h). The uncanny. *S. E., 17*: 222–223. London: Hogarth.

Freud, S. (1921c). *Group Psychology and the Analysis of the Ego. S. E., 18*: 65–144. London: Hogarth.

Freud, S. (1930a). *Civilization and Its Discontents. S. E., 21*: 57–145. London: Hogarth.

Freud, S. (1933a). *New Introductory Lectures on Psycho-Analysis. S. E., 22*: 3–182. London: Hogarth.

Freud, S., & Breuer, J. (1895d). *Studies on Hysteria. S. E., 2*. London: Hogarth.

Galatzer-Levy, R. M. (1978). Qualitative change from quantitative change: Mathematical catastrophe theory in relation to psychoanalysis. *Journal of the American Psychoanalytic Association, 26*: 921–935.

Galatzer-Levy, R. M. (2004). Chaotic possibilities: Toward a new model of development. *International Journal of Psychoanalysis, 85*(2): 419–441.

Gallagher, S. (2005). *How the Body Shapes the Mind*. Oxford: Clarendon Press, 2006.

Gallagher, S. (2012). *Phenomenology*. London: Palgrave.

Gallagher, S. (2013). The socially extended mind. *Cognitive Systems Research, 25*(6): 4–12.

Gallese, V., & Goldman, A. (1998). Mirror neurons and the simulation theory of mind-reading. *Trends in Cognitive Sciences, 12*: 493–501.

Gallese, V., & Lakoff, G. (2005). The brain's concepts: The role of the sensory-motor system in conceptual knowledge. *Cognitive Neuropsychology, 22*(3/4): 455–479.

Gallese, V., & Sinigaglia, C. (2010). The bodily self as power for action. *Neuropsychologia, 48*: 746–755.

Gallop, J. A. (1988). *Thinking Through the Body*. New York: Columbia University Press.

Geertz, C. (1973). Thick description: toward an interpretive theory of culture. In: *The Interpretation of Cultures: Selected Essays* (pp. 3–30). New York: Basic Books.

Gendlin, E. T. (1998). *Focusing-Oriented Psychotherapy: A Manual of the Experiential Method*. New York: Guilford Press.

Gergen, K. (1999). *An Invitation to Social Construction*. London: Sage.

Gergen, K. (2001). *Social Construction in Context*. London: Sage.

Gerhardt, S. (2004). *Why Love Matters: How Affection Shapes a Baby's Brain*. London: Routledge.

Gibson, E. J. (1992). How to think about perceptual learning: Twenty-five years later. In: H. L. Pick, P. W. van den Broek, & D. C. Knill (Eds.), *Cognition: Conceptual and Methodological Issues* (pp. 215–237). Washington, DC: American Psychological Association.

Gibson, E. J., & Pick, A. D. (2000). *An Ecological Approach to Perceptual Learning and Development*. Oxford: Oxford University Press.

Gibson, J. J. (1979). *The Ecological Approach to Visual Perception*. Boston, MA: Houghton-Mifflin.

Gibson, J. J. (1982). *Reasons for Realism: Selected Essays of James J. Gibson*. Hillsdale, NJ: Lawrence Erlbaum.

Gislén, A., Warrant, E. J., Dacke, M., & Kröger, R. H. H. (2006). Visual training improves underwater vision in children. *Vision Research, 46*: 3443–3450.

Goldstein, H. (1980). *Classical Mechanics (2nd ed.)*. New York: Addison-Wesley.

Grammer, K., Fink, B., & Neave, N. (2005). Human pheromones and sexual attraction. *European Journal of Obstetrics & Gynecology and Reproductive Biology, 118*(2): 135–142.

Graves, T. (2008). *Needles of Stone*. Lancaster, UK: Grey House in the Wood.

Grossinger, R. (1986). *Embryogenesis*. Berkeley, CA: North Atlantic Books.

Grossinger, R. (1995). *Planet Medicine: Origins*. Berkeley, CA: North Atlantic.

Grossinger, R. (1998). Why somatic therapies deserve as much attention as psychoanalysis in the New York Review of Books, and why bodyworkers treating neuroses should study psychoanalysis. In: D. H. Johnson & I. J. Grand (Eds.), *The Body in Psychotherapy: Inquiries in Somatic Psychology* (pp. 85–106). Berkeley, CA: North Atlantic Books.

Grosz, E. (1994). *Volatile Bodies: Towards a Corporeal Feminism*. Bloomington, IN: Indiana University Press.

Guastello, S. J., Pincus, D., & Gunderson, P. R. (2006). Electrodermal arousal between participants in a conversation: Nonlinear dynamics and linkage effects. *Nonlinear Dynamics, Psychology, and Life Sciences, 10*(3): 365–399.

Haan, S. de, Jaegher, H. de, Fuchs, T., & Mayer, A. (2011). Expanding perspectives: The interactive development of perspective-taking in early childhood. In: W. Tschacher & C. Bergomi (Eds.), *The Implications of Embodiment: Cognition and Communication* (pp. 129–150). Exeter, UK: Imprint Academic.

Hamilton, V. (1982). *Narcissus and Oedipus: The Children of Psychoanalysis.* London: Karnac.

Hancock, P., Hughes, P., Jagger, E., Paterson, K., Russell, R., & Tulle-Winton, E. (2000). *The Body, Culture and Society: An Introduction.* Buckingham, UK: Open University Press.

Haraway, D. (1991). *Simians, Cyborgs and Women: The Reinvention of Nature.* London: Routledge.

Harlow, H. F. (1972). *Learning to Love.* San Francisco, CA: Albion.

Harney, M. (2007). Merleau-Ponty, ecology, and biosemiotics. In: S. L Cataldi & W. S. Hamrick (Eds.), *Merleau-Ponty and Environmental Philosophy: Dwelling on the Landscapes of Thought* (pp. 133–146). New York: SUNY Press.

Harris, A., & Kuchuk, S. (Eds.) (2015). *The Legacy of Sandor Ferenczi: From Ghost to Ancestor.* London: Routledge.

Hart, S. (2011). *The Impact of Attachment.* New York: W. W. Norton.

Hayles, N. K. (1993). The materiality of informatics. *Configurations, 1*(1): 147–170.

Hayles, N. K. (1999). *How We Became Posthuman: Virtual Bodies in Cybernetics, Literature and Informatics.* Chicago, IL: University of Chicago Press.

Heitzler, M. (2013). Broken boundaries, invaded territories: The challenges of containment in trauma work. *International Body Psychotherapy Journal, 12*(1): 28–41.

Heron, J. (1992). *Feeling and Personhood: Psychology in Another Key.* London: Sage.

Hickok, G. (2014). *The Myth of Mirror Neurons: The Real Neuroscience of Communication and Cognition.* New York: W. W. Norton.

Hickock, G., Bellugi, U., & Klima, E. S. (1996). The neurobiology of sign language and its implications for the neural basis of language. *Nature, 381:* 699–702.

Hillman, J. (1979). *The Dream and the Underworld.* New York: Harper & Row.

Hinshelwood, R. D. (1994). *Clinical Klein.* London: Free Association.

Horst, F. C. P. van der, LeRoy, H. A., & Veer, R. van der (2008). "When strangers meet": John Bowlby and Harry Harlow on attachment behavior. *Integrative Psychological and Behavioral Science, 42*(4): 370–388.

House, R., & Totton, N. (2011). *Implausible Professions: Arguments for Pluralism and Autonomy in Psychotherapy and Counselling.* Ross-on-Wye, UK: PCCS Books.

Hrdy, S. B. (2009). *Mothers and Others: The Evolutionary Origins of Mutual Understanding.* London: Belknap.

Hubbard, L. R. (1988). *Dianetics: The Modern Science of Mental Health*. East Grinstead, UK: New Era Publications.

Iacono, A. M. (2002). Francisco Varela and the concept of autonomy. *European Journal of Psychoanalysis*, *15*. Retrieved from http://www.psychomedia.it/jep/number15/iacono.htm.

Ikemi, A. (2005). Carl Rogers and Eugene Gendlin on the bodily felt sense: What they share and where they differ. *Person-Centered and Experiential Psychotherapies*, *4*(1): 277–288.

Ikemi, A. (2013). You can inspire me to live further: Explicating pre-reflexive bridges to the other. In: J. H. D. Cornelius-White, R. Motschnig-Pitrik, & M. Lux (Eds.), *Interdisciplinary Handbook of the Person Centered Approach: Research and Theory* (pp. 131–140). New York: Springer.

Jacoby, R. (1975). *Social Amnesia: A Critique of Conformist Psychology from Adler to Laing*. Boston, MA: Beacon Press.

Johnson, D. H. (1995). *Bone, Breath and Gesture: Practices of Embodiment*. Berkeley, CA: North Atlantic.

Johnson, M., & Rohrer, T. (2007). We are live creatures: Embodiment, American pragmatism, and the cognitive organism. In: J. Zlatev, T. Ziemke, R. Frank, & R. Dirven (Eds.), *Body, Language and Mind, Vol 1: Embodiment* (pp. 17–54). Berlin: Mouton de Gruyter.

Juhan, D. (2003). *Job's Body. 3rd Edition*. Barrytown, NY: Station Hill Press.

Kafka, F. (1995). *Metamorphosis, In the Penal Colony and Other Stories*. New York: Schocken.

Kamalamani (2102). *Meditating with Character*. Winchester, UK: O Books.

Kauffman, S. (1995). *At Home in the Universe: The Search for Laws of Self-Organization and Complexity*. Oxford: Oxford University Press.

Keleman, S. (1989). *Emotional Anatomy*. Berkeley, CA: Center Press.

Kepner, J. (2003). The embodied field. *British Gestalt Journal*, *12*(1): 6–14.

Keysers, C. (2011). *The Empathic Brain*. Groningen, Netherlands: Social Brain Press.

Kim, H. (2014). The biopolitics of transnational adoption in South Korea: Preemption and the governance of single birthmothers. *Body & Society*. Published online as doi:10.1177/1357034X14533596.

Kinman, C. J. (2001). *A Language of Gifts*. Abbotsford, BC, Canada: C. Kinsman & Associates.

Kirshner, L. A. (1994). Trauma, the good object, and the symbolic: A theoretical integration. *International Journal of Psychoanalysis*, *75*(2): 235–242.

Klein, M. (1936). Weaning. In: *Love, Guilt and Reparation and Other Works, 1921–1945* (pp. 290–305). New York: Vintage.

Klein, M. (1952). Notes on some schizoid mechanisms. In: E. Spillius & E. O'Shaughnessy (Eds.), *Projective Identification: The Fate of a Concept* (pp. 19–45). London: Routledge, 2013.

Knight, C. (2000). Play as precursor of phonology and syntax. In: C. Knight, M. Studdert-Kennedy, & J. R. Hurford (Eds.), *The Evolutionary Emergence of Language: Social Function and the Origins of Linguistic Form* (pp. 99–122). Cambridge: Cambridge University Press.

Koch, S. C., Fuchs, T., Summa, M., & Muller, C. (Eds.) (2012). *Body Memory, Metaphor and Movement*. Amsterdam: John Benjamins.

Kolk, B. van der (1994). The body keeps the score: memory and the evolving psychobiology of post traumatic stress. *Harvard Review of Psychiatry, 1*(5): 253–265.

Kolk, B. van der (2014). *The Body Keeps the Score: Mind, Brain and Body in the Transformation of Trauma*. New York: Viking.

Kolodny, N. (1996). The ethics of cryptonormativism: A defense of Foucault's evasions. *Philosophy & Social Criticism, 22*: 63–84.

Kozel, S. (2004). Connective tissue: the flesh of the network. In: K. Vince (Ed.), *Dance Rebooted: Initializing the Grid*. Online at http://ausdance.org.au/publications/details/dance-rebooted-conference-papers.

Kristeva, J. (1984). *Revolution in Poetic Language*. New York: Columbia University Press.

Kristeva, J. (1995). *New Maladies of the Soul*. New York: Columbia University Press.

Kristeva, J. (1996). *Interviews*. R. M. Guberman (Ed.). New York: Columbia University Press.

Kurtz, R. (1985). *Hakomi Therapy*. Boulder, CO: Hakomi Institute.

Lacan, J. (1950). Presentation on transference. In: B. Fink (Trans.), *Ecrits* (pp. 176–185). New York: W. W. Norton, 2006.

Lacan, J. (1953). The function and field of speech and language in psychoanalysis. In: A. Sheridan (Trans.), *Ecrits: A Selection*. London: Routledge, 1977.

Lacan, J. (1966). *Écrits*. Paris: Seuil.

Lacan, J. (1977). *Écrits: A Selection*. A. Sheridan (Trans.). London: Routledge.

Lacan, L. (1988). *The Seminar. Book I. Freud's Papers on Technique, 1953–54*. J. Forrester (Trans.). Cambridge: Cambridge University Press.

Lakoff, G. (1987). *Women, Fire and Dangerous Things: What Categories Reveal About the Mind*. Chicago, IL: University of Chicago Press.

Lakoff, G., & Johnson, M. (1981). *Metaphors We Live By*. Chicago, IL: University of Chicago Press.

Lakoff, G., & Johnson, M. (1999). *Philosophy in the Flesh: The Embodied Mind and its Challenge to Western Thought*. New York: Basic Books.

Lane, M. (Ed.) (2007). *Plato: The Republic*. London: Penguin Classics.

Laplanche, J. (1976). *Life and Death in Psychoanalysis*. Baltimore, MD: Johns Hopkins University Press.

Laplanche, J. (1992). *Seduction, Translation, Drives*. J. Fletcher & M. Stanton (Eds.). London: ICA.

Lashley, K. (1950). In search of the engram. *Society of Experimental Biology*, Symposium 4: 454–482.

Laub, D., & Auerhahn, N. C. (1993). Knowing and not knowing massive psychic trauma: Forms of traumatic memory. *International Journal of Psychoanalysis, 74*: 287–302.

Laub, D., & Lee, S. (2003). Thanatos and massive psychic trauma: the impact of the death instinct on knowing, remembering, and forgetting. *Journal of the American Psychoanalytic Association, 51*(2): 433–464.

Lawler, S. (2004). Rules of engagement: Habitus, power and resistance. *Sociological Review, 52*(s2): 110–128.

Lax, R. F. (Ed.) (1989). *Essential Papers on Character Neurosis and Treatment.* New York: New York University Press.

Le Breton, D. (2014). From disfigurement to facial transplant: Identity insights. *Body and Society.* Published online as doi:10.1177/1357034X 14536448.

Le Guin, U. (1972). *The Lathe of Heaven.* St. Albans, UK: Panther.

Leder, D. (1990). *The Absent Body.* Chicago, IL: University of Chicago Press.

Legrand, D. (2006). The bodily self: The sensori-motor roots of pre-reflective self-consciousness. *Phenomenology and the Cognitive Sciences, 5*: 89–118.

Leibniz, G. F. W. von (1980). *Discourse on Metaphysics, Correspondence with Arnauld, Monadology.* La Salle, IL: Open Court.

Lester, R. J. (2004). Material bodies and the transformation of the social. *Theory and Psychology, 14*: 409–419.

Levine, P. A. (1997). *Waking the Tiger: Healing Trauma.* Berkeley, CA: North Atlantic.

Lieberman, P. (1975). On the evolution of language: A unified view. In: R. H. Tuttle (Ed.), *Primate Functional Morphology and Evolution* (pp. 501–540). The Hague, Netherlands: Mouton Publishers.

Lindblom, J. (2007). *Minding the Body: Interacting Socially through Embodied Action.* Linköping Studies in Science and Technology Dissertation No. 1112. Linköping, Sweden: Department of Computer and Information Science, Linköpings Universitet. Retrieved from http://liu.diva-portal. org/smash/get/diva2:23965/FULLTEXT01.

Lyon, M. J., & Barbalet, J. M. (1994). Society's body. In: T. J. Csordas (Ed.), *Embodiment and Experience: The Existential Ground of Culture and Self* (pp. 48–66). Cambridge: Cambridge University Press.

Lyons-Ruth, K. (1998). Implicit relational knowing: Its role in development and psychoanalytic treatment. *Infant Mental Health Journal, 19*(3): 282–289.

Mace, W. (1977). James Gibson's strategy for perceiving: Ask not what's inside your head but what your head's inside of. In: R. Shaw & J. Bransford (Eds.), *Perceiving, Acting and Knowing* (pp. 43–65). Hillsdale, NJ: Erlsbaum.

Maclaren, K. (2013). Touching matters: Embodiments of intimacy. *Emotion, Space and Society.* http://dx.doi.org/10.1016/j.emospa.2013.12.004.

Macy, J. (1991a). *Mutual Causality in Buddhism and General Systems Theory: The Dharma of Natural Systems.* New York: SUNY Press.

Macy, J. (1991b). *World as Lover, World as Self.* Berkeley, CA: Parallax Press.

Maitland, K. J. (1995). *Spacious Body: Explorations in Somatic Ontology.* Berkeley, CA: North Atlantic.

Marcus, S. (2013). *Freud and the Culture of Psychoanalysis: Studies in the Transition from Victorian Humanism to Modernity.* London: Routledge.

Marks-Tarlow, T. (2011). Merging and emerging: A nonlinear portrait of intersubjectivity during psychotherapy. *Psychoanalytic Dialogues, 21*(1): 110–127.

Marks-Tarlow, T. (2012a). *Clinical Intuition in Psychotherapy: The Neurobiology of Embodied Response.* New York: W. W. Norton.

Marks-Tarlow, T. (2012b). The play of psychotherapy. *American Journal of Play, 4*(3): 352–377.

Marks-Tarlow, T. (2014). Play and the art of psychotherapy: An interview with Terry Marks-Tarlow. *American Journal of Play, 6*(3): 299–320.

Maroda, K. (2002). *Seduction, Surrender, and Transformation: Emotional Engagement in the Analytic Process.* London: Psychology Press.

Masson, J. (Ed.). (1985). *The Complete Letters of Sigmund Freud to Wilhelm Fliess.* London: Belknap Press.

Massumi, B. (2014). *What Animals Teach Us About Politics.* London: Duke University Press.

May, T. (2005). To change the world, to celebrate life: Merleau-Ponty and Foucault on the body. *Philosophy & Social Criticism, 31*(5–6): 517–531.

McNay, L. (1999). Gender, habitus and the field. *Theory, Culture & Society, 16*: 95–117.

Meltzoff, A. N., & Moore, M. K. (1995). Infants' understanding of people and things: From body imitation to folk psychology. In: J. L. Bermudez, A. Marcel, & N. Eilan (Eds.), *The Body and the Self* (pp. 43–69). Cambridge, MA: MIT Press.

Merleau-Ponty, M. (1962). *ThePhenomenology of Perception.* London: Routledge & Kegan Paul.

Merleau-Ponty, M. (1964). *Sense and Non-sense.* Evanston, IL: Northwestern University Press.

Merleau-Ponty, M. (1968). *The Visible and the Invisible.* C. Lefort (Ed.). Evanston, IL: Northwestern University Press.

Meyer, K., & Damasio, A. (2009). Convergence and divergence in a neural architecture for recognition and memory. *Trends in Neuroscience, 32*(7): 376–382.

Mindell, A. (1985a). *Working with the Dreaming Body*. London: Routledge & Kegan Paul.

Mindell, A. (1985b). *River's Way: The Process Science of the Dreambody*. London: Routledge & Kegan Paul.

Mitchell, R. W. (1991). Bateson's concept of "metacommunication" in play. *New Ideas in Psychology, 9*(1): 73–87.

Mitchell, S. A. (2000). *Relationality: From Attachment to Intersubjectivity*. London: The Analytic Press.

Morris, M., & Patton, P. (Eds.) (1979). *Michel Foucault: Power, Truth, Strategy*. Sydney: Feral Publications.

Murray, L., & Trevarthen, C. (1985). Emotional regulation of interactions between two-month-olds and their mothers. In: T. Field & N. Fox (Eds.), *Social Perception in Infants* (pp. 177–197). Norwood, NJ: Ablex.

Oberman, L. M., & Ramachandran, V. S. (2007). The simulating social mind: The role of the mirror neuron system and simulation in the social and communicative deficits of autism spectrum disorders. *Psychological Bulletin, 133*(2): 310–327.

Ogden, P., Minton, K., & Paine, C. (2006). *Trauma and the Body: A Sensorimotor Approach to Psychotherapy*. New York: W. W. Norton.

Oliver, K. (1993). *Reading Kristeva: Unraveling the Double-bind*. Bloomington, IN: Indiana University Press.

Orbach, S. (2003). There is no such thing as a body. The John Bowlby Memorial Lecture 2003, Part 1. *British Journal of Psychotherapy, 20*(1): 3–14.

Oschman, J. (2000). *Energy Medicine: The Scientific Basis*. Edinburgh, UK: Churchill Livingstone.

Pally, R. (2001). A primary role for nonverbal communication in psychoanalysis. *Psychoanalytic Inquiry, 21*(1): 71–93.

Palombo, S. R. (1999). *The Emergent Ego: Complexity and Coevolution in the Psychoanalytic Process*. Madison, CT: International Universities Press.

Palombo, S. R. (2007). Complexity theory as the parent science of psychoanalysis. In: C. Piers, J. P. Muller, & J. Brent (Eds.), *Self-Organizing Complexity in Psychological Systems* (pp. 1–13). Plymouth, NH: Jason Aronson.

Panksepp, J. (2004). *Affective Neuroscience: The Foundations of Human and Animal Emotions*. Oxford: Oxford University Press.

Panksepp, J. (2006). The core emotional systems of the mammalian brain: The fundamental substrates of human emotions. In: J. Corrigal, H. Payne, & H. Wilkinson (Eds.) *About a Body: Working with the Embodied Mind in Psychotherapy* (pp. 14–32). Hove, UK: Routledge.

Pateman, T. (2006). Children's play and adults' play from the standpoint of Gregory Bateson and Donald Winnicott. Retrieved from http://www.selectedworks.co.uk/play.html on April 24, 2015.

Pellis, S. M., & Pellis, V. C. (1996). On knowing it's only play: The role of play signals in play fighting. *Aggression and Violent Behavior, 1*(3): 249–268.

Pellis, S. M., & Pellis, V. C. (1997). Targets, tactics, and the open mouth face during play fighting in three species of primates. *Aggressive Behavior, 23*: 41–57.

Perry, B. D. (1997). Memories of fear: How the brain stores and retrieves physiologic states, feelings, behaviors and thoughts from traumatic events. In: J. Goodwin & R. Attias (Eds.), *Images of the Body in Trauma* (pp. 9–38). New York: Basic Books.

Perry, B. D., Pollard, R. A., Blakley, T. L., Baker, W. L., & Vigilante, D. (1995). Childhood trauma, the neurobiology of adaptation, and "use-dependent" development of the brain: How "states" become "traits". *Infant Mental Health Journal, 16*(4): 271–291.

Pfister, T., Li, X., Zhao, G., & Pietikäinen, M. (2011). Recognising spontaneous facial micro-expressions. In: *Computer Vision (ICCV), 2011 IEEE International Conference*: 1449–1456.

Phillips, A. (1995). *Terrors and Experts*. London: Faber & Faber.

Piers, C. (1998). Contemporary trauma theory and its relation to character. *Psychoanalytic Psychology, 15*(1): 14–33.

Piers, C. (2000). Character as self-organizing complexity. *Psychoanalysis and Contemporary Thought, 23*(1): 3–34.

Piers, C., Muller, J. P., & Brent, J. (2007). *Self-Organizing Complexity in Psychological Systems*. Plymouth, NH: Jason Aronson.

Pineda, J. A. (Ed.) (2010). *Mirror Neuron Systems*. Valley Stream, NY: Humana Press.

Porges, S. W. (2005). The role of social engagement in attachment and bonding: a phylogenetic perspective. In: C. S. Carter, L. Ahnert, K. E. Grossman, S. B. Hrdy, M. E. Lamb, S. W. Porges, & N. Sachser (Eds.), *Attachment and Bonding: A New Synthesis* (pp. 33–54). Cambridge, MA: MIT Press.

Porges, S. W. (2011). *The Polyvagal Theory: Neurophysiological Foundations of Emotions, Attachment, Communication, and Self-Regulation*. New York: W. W. Norton.

Postle, D. (2007). *Regulating the Psychological Therapies: From Taxonomy to Taxidermy*. Ross-on-Wye, UK: PCCS Books.

Rattasepp, S. (2010). The idea of extended organism in 20th century thought. *Hortus Semioticus, 6*: 31–39.

Reich, W. (1942). *The Function of the Orgasm*. New York: Farrar, Straus & Giroux, 1973.

Reich, W. (1945a). *Character Analysis*. New York: Farrar, Straus & Giroux, 1972.

Reich, W. (1945b). *The Mass Psychology of Fascism*. London: Penguin, 1975.

Ridley, C. (2006). *Stillness: Biodynamic Cranial Practice and the Evolution of Consciousness*. Berkeley, CA: North Atlantic.

Rizzolatti, G., & Craighero, L. (2004). The mirror-neuron system. *Annual Review of Neuroscience, 27*: 169–192.

Rose, N., & Abi-Rached, J. M. (2013). *Neuro: the New Brain Sciences and the Management of the Mind*. Princeton, NJ: Princeton University Press.

Ross, M. (2000). Body talk: somatic countertransference. *Psychodynamic Counselling, 6*(4): 451–467.

Rothschild, B. (1994). Transference & countertransference: a common sense perspective. *Energy and Character, 25*(2): 8–12.

Royle, N. (1991). *Telepathy and Literature: Essays on the Reading Mind*. Oxford: Blackwell.

Rudnytsky, P., Bokay, A., & Gampieri-Deutsch, P. (Eds.) (2000). *Ferenczi's Turn in Psychoanalysis*. New York: New York University Press.

Ruesch, J., & Bateson, G. (1951). *Communication: The Social Matrix of Psychiatry*. Piscataway, NJ: Transaction Publishers, 2008.

Rust, M. -J. (2008). Climate on the couch. *Psychotherapy and Politics International, 6*(3): 157–170.

Sacks, O. (2011). *Seeing Voices: A Journey into the World of the Deaf*. London: Picador.

Sampson, E. E. (1998). Establishing embodiment in society. In: H. J. Stam (Ed.), *The Body and Psychology*. London: Sage.

Samuels, A. (1993). *The Political Psyche*. London: Routledge.

Sapir, E. (1949). *Selected Writings of Edward Sapir in Language, Culture and Personality*. D. G. Mandelbaum (Ed.). Berkeley, CA: University of California Press.

Scheiermacher, F. D. E. (1977). *Hermeneutik und Kritik*. Frankfurt, Germany: Suhrkamp.

Schlessinger, N. (1966). Supervision of psychotherapy. *Archives of General Psychiatry, 15*: 129–134.

Schore, A. (2005). A neuropsychoanalytic viewpoint. Commentary on a paper by Steven H. Knoblauch. *Psychoanalytic Dialogues, 15*(6): 829–854.

Schore, A. N. (2000a). The effects of a secure attachment relationship on right brain development, affect regulation, and infant mental health. *Infant Mental Health Journal, 22*(1–2): 7–66.

Schore, A. N. (2000b). The effects of early relational trauma on right brain development, affect regulation, and infant mental health. *Infant Mental Health Journal, 22*(1–2): 201–269.

Schroeder, H. W. (2008). A felt sense of the natural environment. *The Folio, 21*: 63–72.

Schultz, R. L., & Feitis, R. (1996). *The Endless Web: Fascial Anatomy and Physical Reality*. Berkeley, CA: North Atlantic.

Schütz-Bosbach, S., Mancini, B., Aglioti, S. M., & Haggard, P. (2006). Self and other in the human motor system. *Current Biology, 16*(18): 1830–1834.

Senghas, A., Kita, A., & Ozyurek, A. (2004). Children creating core properties of language: Evidence from an emerging Sign Language in Nicaragua. *Science, 305*: 1779–1782.

Sewall, L. (1999). *Sight and Sensibility: The Ecopsychology of Perception.* New York: Tarcher Putnam.

Shapiro, S. A. (1996). The embodied analyst in the Victorian consulting room. *Gender and Psychoanalysis, 1*(3): 297–322.

Shapiro, S. A. (2009). A rush to action: Embodiment, the analyst's subjectivity, and the interpersonal experience. *Studies in Gender and Sexuality, 10*: 93–103.

Sharpe, E. F. (1940). Psycho-physical problems revealed in language: An examination of metaphor. *International Journal of Psychoanalysis, 21*: 201–213.

Shaw, R., Turvey, M., & Mace, W. (1982). Ecological psychology: The consequence of a commitment to realism. In: W. B. Weimar & D. S. Palermo (Eds.), *Cognition and the Symbolic Processes II* (pp. 159–226). Hillsdale, NJ: Lawrence Erlbaum.

Sheets-Johnstone, M. (1990). *The Roots of Thinking.* Philadelphia, PA: Temple University Press.

Sidney, Sir P. (1595). An apology for poetry. In: T. Pollard (Ed.), *Shakespeare's Theatre: A Sourcebook* (pp. 146–165). Oxford: Blackwell, 2004.

Siegel, D. J. (1995). Memory, trauma and psychotherapy: A cognitive science view. *Journal of Psychotherapy Practice and Research, 4*: 93–122.

Singer, W. (2005). The brain—an orchestra without a conductor. *Max Planck Research, 3*: 15–18.

Sorenson, E. R. (1997). Sensuality and consciousness V: The emergence of the "savage savage". The study of child behavior and human development in cultural isolates. *Anthropology of Consciousness, 8*(1): 1–9.

Sorenson, E. R. (1998). Preconquest consciousness. In: H. Wautischer (Ed.), *Tribal Epistemologies: Essays in the Philosophy of Anthropology* (pp. 79–113). Aldershot, UK: Ashgate Publishing.

Soth, M. (2005). Embodied countertransference. In: N. Totton (Ed.), *New Dimensions in Body Psychotherapy* (pp. 40–55). Maidenhead, UK: Open University Press.

Spitz, H. (1997). *Nonconscious movements: From mystical messages to facilitated communication.* Manwah, NJ: Lawrence Erlbaum.

Spruiell, V. (1993). Deterministic chaos and the sciences of complexity: Psychoanalysis in the midst of a general scientific revolution. *Journal of the American Psychoanalytic Association, 41*(1): 3–44.

Stanton, M. (1991). *Sandor Ferenczi: Reconsidering Active Intervention.* Plymouth, NH: Jason Aronson.

Stanton, M. (1997). *Out of Order: Clinical Work & Unconscious Process.* London: Rebus Press.

Steckel, R. H., & Wallis, J. (2007). Stones, bones and states: A new approach to the Neolithic revolution. Online at http://www.nber.org/confer/2007/daes07/steckel.pdf.

Stephens, L., Ruddick, S., & McKeever, P. (2014). Disability and Deleuze: An exploration of becoming and embodiment in children's everyday environments. *Body & Society.* Published online as doi:10.1177/1357034X14541155. Last viewed April 24, 2015.

Stern, D. N. (1985). *The Interpersonal World of the Infant.* New York: Basic Books.

Stern, D. N. (2010). *Forms of Vitality: Exploring Dynamic Experience in Psychology, the Arts, Psychotherapy, and Development.* Oxford: Oxford University Press.

Stone, M. (2006). The analyst's body as tuning fork: embodied resonance in countertransference. *Journal of Analytical Psychology, 51*(1): 109–124.

Straub, W. F., & Williams, J. M. (Eds.) (1984). *Cognitive Sport Psychology.* Lansing, MI: Sport Science Associates.

Strean, H. S., & Nelson, M. C. (1961). A further clinical illustration of the paranormal triangle hypothesis. *Psychoanalysis and the Psychoanalytic Review, 49*: 61–76.

Sutton, J. (2008). Material agency, skills and history: Distributed cognition and the archaeology of memory. In: C. Knappett & L. Malafouris (Eds.), *Material Agency: Towards a Non-Anthropocentric Approach* (pp. 37–55). New York: Springer. Retrieved April 24, 2015 from http://www.johnsutton.net/SuttonMaterialAgency.pdf.

Sweetman, P. (1999). Anchoring the (postmodern) self? Body modification, fashion and identity. *Body and Society, 5*: 51–76.

Taylor, C. (1995). *Philosophical Arguments.* Cambridge, MA: Harvard University Press.

Thelen, E., & Smith, L. B. (1994). *A Dynamic Systems Approach to the Development of Cognition and Action.* Cambridge, MA: MIT Press.

Thera, N., & Bodhi, B. (Eds. & Trans.) (1970). *A guttara Nik ya. Discourses of the Buddha: An Anthology, Part I.* Kandy, Sri Lanka: Buddhist Publication Society. Online at http://www.bps.lk/olib/wh/wh155-p.html#S8. Retrieved April 24, 2015.

Thompson, E. (2007). *Mind in Life.* Cambridge, MA: Harvard University Press.

Thompson, E. (2009). Life and mind: From autopoiesis to neurophenomenology. In: B. Clarke & M. B. N. Hansen (Eds.), *Emergence and Embodiment:*

New Essays on Second-Order Systems Theory (pp. 77–93). London: Duke University Press.

Thompson, E., & Stapleton, M. (2008). Making sense of sense-making: Reflections on enactive and extended mind theories. *Topoi, 28*: 23–30.

Thrift, N., & Dewsbury, J.-D. (2000). Dead geographies—and how to make them live. *Environment and Planning D: Society and Space, 18*: 411–432.

Totton, N. (1998). *The Water in the Glass: Body and Mind in Psychoanalysis*. London: Rebus/Karnac.

Totton, N. (2002). Foreign bodies: Recovering the history of body psychotherapy. In: T. Staunton (Ed.), *Body Psychotherapy* (pp. 7–26). London: Brunner Routledge.

Totton, N. (2003a). *Body Psychotherapy: An Introduction*. Maidenhead, UK: Open University Press.

Totton, N. (2003b). "Each single ego": Telepathy and psychoanalysis. In: N. Totton (Ed.), *Psychoanalysis and the Paranormal: Lands of Darkness* (pp. 187–208). London: Karnac.

Totton, N. (2005a). Do bodies tell the truth? *Association of Chiron Psychotherapists Newsletter, 30*: 8–14, 20–26.

Totton, N. (2005b). Embodied-Relational Therapy. In: N. Totton (Ed.), *New Dimensions in Body Psychotherapy* (pp. 168–181). Maidenhead, UK: Open University Press.

Totton, N. (2006). A body psychotherapist's approach to touch. In: G. Galton (Ed.), *Touch Papers: Dialogues on Touch in the Psychoanalytic Space* (pp. 145–161). London: Karnac.

Totton, N. (2007). Funny you should say that: Paranormality, at the margins and the centre of psychotherapy. *European Journal of Psychotherapy & Counselling, 9*(4): 389–401.

Totton, N. (2008). Body psychotherapy and social theory. *Body, Movement and Dance in Psychotherapy, 4*(3): 187–200.

Totton, N. (2010). Being, having and becoming bodies. *Body, Movement and Dance in Psychotherapy, 5*(1): 21–30.

Totton, N. (2011). *Wild Therapy: Undomesticating Our Inner and Outer Worlds*. Ross-on-Wye, UK: PCCS Books.

Totton, N. (2012). "Nothing's out of order": Towards an ecological therapy. In: M. -J. Rust & N. Totton (Eds.), *Vital Signs: Psychological Responses to Ecological Crisis* (pp. 253–264). London: Karnac.

Totton, N. (2015, forthcoming). The risk-taking practitioner: implementing freedom in clinical practice. In: J. Lees (Ed.), *Counselling, Psychotherapy and the Future of Healthcare: Fantasy, Reality and Transformation*. London: Routledge.

Totton, N., & Edmondson, E. (2009). *Reichian Growth Work: Melting the Blocks to Life and Love. 2nd Edition*. Ross-on-Wye, UK: PCCS Books.

Totton, N., & Jacobs, M. (2001). *Character and Personality Types*. Maidenhead, UK: Open University Press.

Totton, N., & Priestman, A. (2012). Embodiment and relationship: Two halves of one whole. In: C. Young (Ed.), *About Relational Body Psychotherapy* (pp. 35–68). Stow, Galashiels, UK: Body Psychotherapy Publications.

Trevarthen, C., & Aitken, K. J. (2001). Infant intersubjectivity: Research, theory and clinical applications. *Journal of Child Psychology and Psychiatry*, 42(1): 3–48.

Turner, B. (1996). *The Body and Society (2nd edition)*. London: Sage.

Turner, J. S. (2000). *The Extended Organism: The Physiology of Animal-Built Structures*. Cambridge, MA: Harvard University Press.

Uexkull, J. von (1934). A stroll through the worlds of animals and men. In: C. Schiller (Ed.), *Instinctive Behavior: The Development of a Modern Concept* (pp. 8–80). New York: International Universities Press.

Varela, C. R. (2005). Harré and Merleau-Ponty: Beyond the absent moving body in embodied social theory. *Journal for the Anthropological Study of Human Movement*, 13: 67–86.

Varela, F. J., Thompson, E., & Rosch, E. (1991). *The Embodied Mind: Cognitive Science and Human Experience*. Cambridge, MA: MIT Press.

Vulcan, M. (2009). Is there any body out there?: A survey of literature on somatic countertransference and its significance for DMT. *The Arts in Psychotherapy*, 36: 275–281.

Wacquant, L. (2005). Habitus. In: J. Beckert & M. Zafirovski (Eds.), *International Encyclopedia of Economic Sociology* (pp. 315–319). London: Routledge,

Wallin, D. (2007). *Attachment in Psychotherapy*. New York: Guilford Press.

Warin, M. (2014). Material feminism, obesity science and the limits of discursive critique. *Body & Society*. Published online as doi:10.1177/1357034X14537320.

Watts, A. (1969). *The Book on the Taboo Against Knowing Who You Are*. London: Jonathan Cape.

Wetherell, M. (2014). Trends in the turn to affect: A social psychological critique. *Body & Society*. Published online as doi:10.1177/1357034X14539020.

Wilden, A. (1987a). *The Rules Are No Game: The Strategy of Communication*. London: Routledge & Kegan Paul.

Wilden, A. (1987b). *Man and Woman, War and Peace: The Strategist's Companion*. London: Routledge & Kegan Paul.

Wilkinson, M. (2010). *Changing Minds in Therapy: Emotion, Attachment, Trauma, and Neurobiology*. New York: W. W. Norton.

Williams, S. J. (1998). Bodily dys-order: Desire, excess and the transgression of corporeal boundaries. *Body and Society*, 4: 59–82.

Williams, S. J., & Bendelow, G. (1998). *The Lived Body: Sociological Themes, Embodied Issues*. London: Routledge.

Wilson, R. A., & Foglia, L. (2011). Embodied cognition. In: E. N. Zalta (Ed.), *The Stanford Encyclopedia of Philosophy* (Fall 2011 Edition). Retrieved from http://plato.stanford.edu/archives/fall2011/entries/embodied-cognition/.

Winnicott, D. W. (1947a). Further thoughts on babies as persons. In: *The Child, the Family, and the Outside World* (pp. 85–92). London: Penguin, 1964.

Winnicott, D. W. (1947b). Hate in the countertransference. In: *Through Paediatrics to Psychoanalysis: Collected Papers* (pp. 194–203). London: Karnac and the Institute of Psychoanalysis, 1992.

Winnicott, D. W. (1953). Transitional objects and transitional phenomena. In: *Through Paediatrics to Psychoanalysis: Collected Papers* (pp. 229–242). London: Karnac and the Institute of Psychoanalysis, 1992.

Winnicott, D. W. (1971). *Playing and Reality*. London: Routledge.

Winston, J. S., Strange, B. A., O'Doherty, J., & Dolan, R. J. (2002). Automatic and intentional brain responses during evaluation of trustworthiness of faces. *Nature Neuroscience, 5*(3): 277–283.

Witherington, D. C. (2011). Taking emergence seriously: The centrality of circular causality for dynamic systems approaches to development. *Human Development, 54*: 66–92.

Wittgenstein, L. (1922). Tractatus Logico-Philosophicus. London: Routledge & Kegan Paul.

Wrye, H. K. (1996). Bodily states of mind: Dialectics of psyche and soma in psychoanalysis. *Gender and Psychoanalysis, 1*(3): 283–296.

Yang, J. (2014). Informal surrogacy in China: Embodiment and biopower. *Body & Society*. Published online as doi:10.1177/1357034X14539357.

Young, I. (1990). *Throwing Like a Girl and Other Essays in Feminist Philosophy and Social Theory*. Bloomington, IN: Indiana University Press.

Young, K. (2002). The memory of the flesh: The family body in somatic psychology. *Body & Society, 8*(3): 25–47.

Young, R. M. (1994). *Mental Space*. London: Free Association.

Zanardi, C. (1995). The maternal in psychoanalysis: From mind/body to body/mind. *Psychoanalysis and Contemporary Thought, 18*(3): 419–454.

INDEX

and nonlinear dynamic systems
162
and semiotic language 140
as -esqueness 119–120
as symptom 91–92
limitation sequence 93
matrix for ensembles of engrams
96, 104, 110
opportunity sequence 93
socially produced via the family
68, 85–86, 89–90, 106–107
see also boundary, oral, control,
holding, crisis and thrusting
characters; creative, denying
and yearning character
versions
Chemero, A 14, 24
Clark, Andy and Chalmers, Dave
16, 60
co-creation 27, 56, 172, 176, 182
cognition 12–17, 19–21, 32, 35, 41–42,
60–62, 122, 152
as internal modelling 13–14, 60
see also enaction, mental
representation
embodied 12–14, 32, 35, 41–42,
60–62
radical 14
colour, perception of 22
complexity theory 40, 154, 161–164,
207
see also non-linearity
connective tissue 81, 123–124,
204–206, 208–209
see also fascia
contact, intersubjective 25, 34,
36, 43, 45, 47, 50, 52, 58,
97–98, 104–105, 112, 187–188,
194–196, 206.
eye 25, 36, 98, 112
contact, physical 33, 160, 179–180, 192
see also touch
control character 99–101

Cornell, William (Bill) xiv, 178–183, 185
corporeality 9–11, 57, 62, 75, 80, 106,
179, 185
see also intercorporeality
countertransference 30–33, 37–40,
50, 76–81, 116, 152, 161, 165,
171, 181
communicative 50
embodied xvii–xviii, xx, 30–31,
33, 37, 171
see also cross-transference,
reciprocal transference/
countertransference,
transference
coupling, structural 14, 22, 27, 58,
164–166
in therapy 164–166
craniosacral therapy 124
creative character version 92–93, 96
see also individual characters
crisis character 104–105, 120, 158
Crossley, Nick 33, 62, 71–72
cross-transference xviii, xx, 30, 40
culture 3–12, 22, 35, 54, 56, 59, 62–63,
65–68, 70, 72, 74–85, 87, 91,
102, 106, 116, 119, 122, 132,
145, 151, 153, 155, 160, 174,
189–193, 209
co-constructed with embodiment
6, 8
dominance-based 191
family 56
forager (hunter-gatherer,
preconquest) 189–193
impact on therapy 76–81
Neolithic 191–193
over nature 3
see also society
cybernetics 7–8, 23, 120

dance 11, 83, 101, 156, 195, 200–201,
205
5 Rhythms 200

For Product Safety Concerns and Information please contact our EU
representative GPSR@taylorandfrancis.com
Taylor & Francis Verlag GmbH, Kaufingerstraße 24, 80331 München, Germany

www.ingramcontent.com/pod-product-compliance
Lightning Source LLC
Chambersburg PA
CBHW070354270326
41926CB00014B/2543

9 781782 202936